Praise for

(Not that You Asked)

"Taunting, revealing, irreverent and earnest." —*The New York Times*

"Pleasure-obsessed, self-deprecating, horny, hilarious."—*The Forward*

"Refreshingly irreverent . . . absurdly funny." —*The Boston Globe*

"[Almond] scores big in every chapter of this must-have collection. Biting humor, honesty, smarts and heart: Vonnegut himself would have been proud." —*Kirkus Reviews* (starred review)

"Rich, fearless [and] cutting." —*The Los Angeles Times*

"Gleefully unrepentant." —*Vanity Fair*

"Steve Almond has a big mouth. A smart mouth. A dirty mouth. A mouth that roars. Spectacularly." —*The Hartford Courant*

"If truth is beauty, as posited by Keats, then Almond's first collection of essays is the smokin'est hottie on the block." —*South Florida Sun-Sentinel*

"Brutally honest . . . The wicked humor of "Dear Oprah" features an in-your-face attack on "the Savior of Publishing" and her book club. But best of all is a beautiful and angry essay on "The Failed Prophecy of Kurt Vonnegut." —*Publishers Weekly*

"Chock full of profanity and sex . . . [*(Not That You Asked)* is also] about those things which Almond feels strongly about: the integrity of literature; the emptiness of popular media; the responsibility of mankind." —*The Buffalo News*

By Steve Almond

God Bless America: Stories
Rock and Roll Will Save Your Life
(Not That You Asked) Rants, Exploits and Obsessions
Which Brings Me to You: A Novel in Confessions
    (with Julianna Baggott)
The Evil B.B. Chow and Other Stories
Candyfreak: A Journey Through the Chocolate Underbelly of America
My Life in Heavy Metal

(Not that You Asked)

Steve Almond

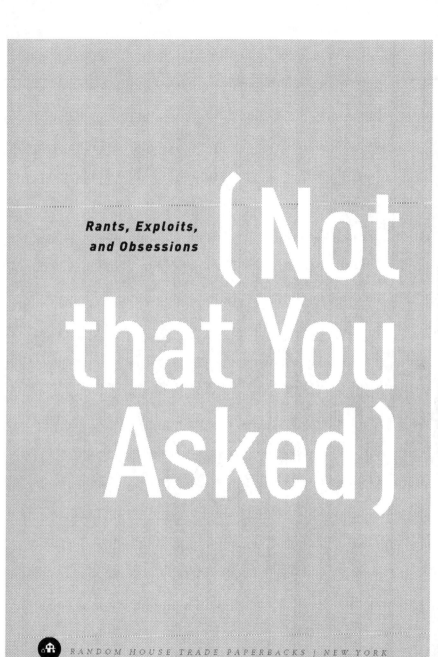

**Rants, Exploits,
and Obsessions**

(Not
that You
Asked)

RANDOM HOUSE TRADE PAPERBACKS | NEW YORK

Published in the United States by Random House Trade Paperbacks, an imprint of
The Random House Publishing Group, a division of Random House, Inc., New York.

RANDOM HOUSE TRADE PAPERBACKS and colophon are trademarks of Random House, Inc.

Originally published in hardcover in the United States by Random House, an
imprint of The Random House Publishing Group, a division of Random House, Inc.,
in 2007.

Some of the essays in this work were previously published:

"Heart Radical" originally published in *Bat City Review,* Spring 2006; "How to Write Sex Scenes"
originally published in *The Boston Phoenix*, May 2003; "Cash Cowed" originally published in *The
Boston Phoenix*, March 2005; "Death by Lobster Pad Thai" originally published in *Death by Pad
Thai,* edited by Douglas Bauer (New York: Crown Publishers, 2006); "You're *What?*" originally
published in *Blindsided by a Diaper*, edited by Dana Hilmer (New York: Crown Publishers, 2007),
as "Blindsided by a Sonogram"; "Chestfro Agoniste" originally appeared at www.Nerve.com,
September 2005; "My First Fake Tits" originally appeared at www.Nerve.com, May 2006, as
"Plastic Not So Fantastic"; "How Reality TV Ate My Life" originally published by *Ninth Letter,*
Spring/Summer 2005; "Blog Love" originally appeared at www.Salon.com, October 2005, as
"Me and My Blog Bitch"; "Tesla Matters (Dude)" originally published in *Virginia Quarterly Review*,
Summer 2005, as "Heavy Metal Will Save Your Life"; "Pretty Authors Make Graves" originally
published in *Virginia Quarterly Review*, Winter 2005.

LIBRARY OF CONGRESS CATALOGING-IN-PUBLICATION DATA

Almond, Steve.
    Not that you asked: rants, exploits, and obsessions / by Steve Almond.
        p. cm.
    ISBN 978-0-8129-7759-2
1. Almond, Steve.   2. Authors, American—21st century—Biography.
3. United States—Social life and customs—20th century—Humor.
4. UnitedStates—Social life and customs—21st century—Humor.
I. Title.
    PS3601.L58Z46 2007
    813'.6—dc22
    [B]   2007005616

www.atrandom.com

Designer credit: Barbara M. Bachman

146122990

To Erin and Josephine

And Lot's wife, of course, was told not to look back where all those people and their homes had been. But she did look back, and I love her for that, because it was so human.

—KV

CONTENTS

(Not that You Asked)

{

How This
Book Became
an Official
Oprah's Book
Club™ Pick

(Not that You Asked)

DEAR OPRAH

Dear Oprah Winfrey,

I am writing to inform you that I cannot accept your kind offer to name this book as your October 2007 selection for Oprah's Book Club™. I realize this letter may come as something of a shock, given my reputation for shameless self-promotion, which I hope precedes me. I also realize that authors who cross you tend to wind up with an awful lot of egg on their faces. Fortunately, I walk around most days with a four-cheese omelette hanging from my chin, so no problem there.

The truth is, I don't give a shit how many books you sell. I don't care how much dough you give away, or how many famous people you make cry. At the end of the day, you're a TV star. You show up on a tiny screen and give lonely people a place to park their emotions for an hour. You're the world's leading retailer of inspiration. You're the Wal-Mart of Hope.

Literature, though, isn't supposed to be a convenient shopping experience. It's a solitary imaginative endeavor aimed at arousing the anguish hidden inside us, the bad news of our hearts. There's no celebrity shrink on hand to dispense hankies, no empathic host to buzz-manage our tears. There's no assurance that our frail human experiment will end in triumph by the final commercial break. You tell me, Oprah: Should the Savior of Publishing be available with your basic cable package?

I can already hear your fans howling for my head. But from where I'm sitting, you're just another zillionaire narcissist for whom fame (the illusion of unconditional love) has become the true goal and your public acts of good merely the means. Whatever noble cause you're pimping this week, in the end you're pimping yourself. Because if you really gave a shit about all us little people, you'd hoist your fluctuating ass out of the luxury self-help suite and express some outrage over the state of this nation: the young Americans snuffed over in Iraq, the poor ones economically sodomized by your pal Dubya, a realpolitik that dependably rewards bigotry over policy.

But outrage isn't your thing, Oprah. To express such a vulgar emotion would violate the dictates of the brand. All we have to do to solve the crisis of empathy in this country is buy your lousy magazine, right? The one with you on the cover every single fucking month. *Forget confronting evil. Just keep dreaming and hoping and snuffling with Oprah, keep gulping down the aspirational sugar pills. What a crock.*

The answer is no.

> *Until we meet again,*
> *Phil Donahue*

P.S. Kidding! My real name is Steve Almond.

Dear Ms. Winfrey,

I'm not sure if you got the last letter I sent. I hope not. I don't want to make excuses, so I'm not going to mention that I suffer from depression, or that my infant daughter was ill, or that I'd just finished a truly disappointing blackened grouper sandwich that left me queasy and out of sorts.

The point is contrition. I'd like to apologize for the things I wrote. I talked this over with some of the folks at my publishing house yesterday—there were twelve in all, I guess—and they felt that I had done both of us a disservice by refusing your gracious (potential) offer to select my book for Oprah's Book Club™. Their contention was that insulting you may have gratified my own righteous indignation, but did little to promote the greater cause we share. That crack about your ass, for instance. I didn't mean that it literally fluctuates.

A lot of this boils down to insecurity. There's a part of me that worries you won't really choose my book for Oprah's Book Club™. The letter was my way of rejecting you before you could reject me. Pretty third-grade on my part.

I have deep respect for the work you do, not just as a media figure, but as a literary philanthropist. You could easily have hitched your wagon to the Freakshow Express, like Springer. Instead, you've spent your cultural capital encouraging people to read writers like Toni Morrison and William Faulkner. That I failed to acknowledge this reflects nothing beyond my own chronic bitterness.

This is all by way of saying that, on the off chance that you have read my previous letter, I hope you will file it under Unintended Satire, or perhaps Temporary Dementia. Rest assured, I have no plans to pull a Franzen. It would be an honor to appear on your show. And I promise not to jump on your couch! (Unless you'd like me to.)

Yours in apology & admiration,
Steve Almond

Dear Oprah,

This is going to seem a little crazy, but I'm enclosing another copy of the letter I sent along earlier this week. I know how much mail you must get. Better safe than sorry.

Great show yesterday, by the way! I have to admit that I had not given a great deal of thought to the challenges of menopause, but I appreciated how you handled the jerk who referred to his wife as Señora Hot Flasha. My wife and I had a long talk after the show and I came away with a whole new perspective. It's like you say, "Menopause isn't a process, people, it's a journey.*"*

> *Let's talk soon,*
> *Steve*

P.S. I've enclosed a photo of our little angel. That's her peeking out from an official Oprah 4 Prez *tote bag. What can I tell you—she's a fan!*

Oprah,

One thought I had, in terms of planning—one of the essays in my book is about Condoleezza Rice. Long story short, I slam her pretty hard. I'm thinking it might be cool to do a show that's about "healing" the rift between Condoleezza and myself. She could (for instance) apologize for the lies that got us into the Iraq war, and I could apologize for referring to her as "the President's office wife." Then we might hug. Or do some music together. Or both.

> *Think about it.*
> *Steve*

Oprah!

Just a silly note to tell you that my wife and I rented The Color Purple. *Again. What can I tell you? You got jobbed at the Oscars. Your performance made Anjelica Huston's look like dinner theater. Also:*

my publicist was wondering when I might hear back from you. (I explained about your schedule, but you know how these people get.)

Also also: Would it be too forward of me to refer to you, in future correspondences, as my homegirl?

> Oprah in '08!
> Steve

Dearest O,

Last night I was looking through The Uncommon Wisdom of Oprah Winfrey: A Portrait in Her Own Words and I came across this quote:

"I don't do anything unless it feels good. I don't move on logic. I move on my gut. And I have a good gut!"

You were talking about your business philosophy. But it got me thinking about your actual gut, and the way the tabloids cover it so obsessively. It's like, in a way, your body has become public property, up there on display for everybody to gawk at and poke and prod. I'm sure this thought has occurred to you a few million times, but here you are, the most influential black woman in human history, and somehow you're still the white man's slave.

That's fucked up.

> Steve

Oprahlove,

I hope you won't take this the wrong way, but I get a bad feeling about Stedman. Every time I see a photo of him, I think: Snidely

Whiplash. Lord knows you've waited long enough to find a man who will treat you right. But I can't help feeling he's sponging off you. It's like when TomKat snubbed you for their wedding. I know you rose above that, but when I think about that ungrateful little Scientology hobbit and the way he frog-marches his stick-figure wifey around—I don't know, it just gnaws at me.

I guess I feel kind of protective of you is what I'm saying.

I hope that's all right.

Steve

Special Ops!

Given the hours you keep, I'm not upset you haven't yet responded to my letters. I will say that certain folks at my publishing house have begun to express some concern. But I'm not even writing about that.

I'm writing because I had this strange dream last night. I was back in California (where I grew up) wandering through a desert; it must have been the Mojave. I was very weak and my tongue had swollen into a giant cigarette filter and I could feel this immense grinding weight on my shoulders. Every few steps the sun struck like a whip. The only thing I could think to do is what you advise in A Journal of Daily Renewal. *I closed my eyes and burrowed into my* spirit place *and even though I was technically in the midst of a dream, I could see what the dream meant: I was experiencing the hardships my ancestors had as slaves in Egypt. I was still carrying around all that negative energy. So I stopped dead in my tracks and took ten cleansing breaths. When I opened my eyes the weight was gone and I was standing before the gates of the Promised Land. Only the Promised Land wasn't in Palestine, it was in Montecito. It was your 42-acre mountain view estate! I opened my right fist and there was a slip of paper with the security code for the gate. So up the winding path I flew, past the Lake of Serenity and the Rejuvenation Redwoods and the blinding lawns. It all looked exactly like it does in the* Special Collector's Edition DVD of Oprah's Legends Weekend. *Then I came to a huge house, which, it turned out, belonged to the caretaker, who was Rosie O'Donnell, only she was thin so I didn't recognize her at first. She pointed to a speck in the distance. "You want the Main House, spanks." It took a long time to reach the main house, even without the stone block on my shoulders. There were little golf carts around, but I knew that would be cheating. I was on a walkabout, not a golfcartabout. Finally, I reached your home and I rang the doorbell and banged on all the doors and windows. But you didn't answer. No one answered.*

    Bottom-line me here: Should I be worried?

Steve

Dear Oprah:

It's been a few months now since we began this correspondence, and I have to be honest. I'm not sure you're holding up your end of the bargain. I realize we got off on the wrong foot. It's also true that one or more of my previous letters may have been written under the influence of mild psychotropics. But that's not the issue. The issue is business. You've got 20 million readers to satisfy and I've got a book so hot it's burning a hole in my publisher's panties. I'm trying to tell you that, from my end, all is forgiven.

    Also: I'm not going to stop writing until we make this happen. To quote a certain someone, "I don't believe in failure!"

Still at the same address,
Steve Almond

Dear Oprah,

You're going to think wow *when you open the enclosed gift.*

You recognize that little face, no?

Need a hint?

It's my daughter! Josephine.

She's a lot bigger than the photo I sent along four months ago, right? Try 21 pounds (minus whatever she lost in transit). That's almost as big as the turkey you and Stedman served to those autistic orphans last Thanksgiving!

Anyway, it occurred to me last night, in the midst of re-reading The Gospel According to Oprah, *that a gesture of trust was needed to seal the bond between us. So here she is, the little gal I call "our practice baby." She's been pretty good, overall. A bit flatulent after certain meals, but who isn't? Both my wife and I feel that you'll make an amazing mother to our (former) daughter.*

I know what you're thinking: Hey Steve, won't adopting your child complicate my plan to select your book for Oprah's Book Club™? Won't people cry nepotism and/or bribery? *Of course they will! And you know what the sponsors will be crying? Ratings! Especially after your special double episode featuring a tearful author/daughter reunion, with special guest babysitter . . . Condi Rice!*

Seriously, homegirl: I've got goose bumps on my scalp.

Steve

P.S. The baby isn't eating solid food just yet, so the missus expressed some milk for her. Please refrigerate immediately.

Why I Crush
on Vonnegut

(Not that You Asked)

EVERYTHING WAS BEAUTIFUL AND NOTHING HURT

THE FAILED PROPHECY OF KURT VONNEGUT
(and How It Saved My Life)

Part One

You are writing for strangers.
Face the audience of strangers.

t would be fair to call me one of the Kurt Vonnegut cult, though a member in poor standing. I read all of his books in high school and college, most of them six times, and I'm sure I walked around for a good number of years spouting little Vonnuggets of wisdom, as his followers so incessantly do.

I devoted most of my senior year in college to a detailed study of his work, writing a thesis titled "Authorial Presence in the Works of Kurt Vonnegut," a copy of which I recently asked my mother to send me, in her capacity as Chief Curator of the Steve Almond Archives, a capacity, I should add, that she views as the necessary burden of having raised an itinerant narcissist. The Archives have fallen on hard times in the past few years, the result being that the original bound copy of the document—which I feel compelled to note was *dedicated* to the Chief Curator—no longer exists. It was apparently lent out to my uncle Peter, a man whose own literary archive resides in the backseat of his car.

The Chief Curator was able to find, after what she described as "many hours of excavation," a draft of the thesis, which included the proofreading marks of my college pal James Shiffer, who, perhaps not coincidentally, no longer speaks to me. The last page bore a circular stamp at the bottom right. I initially took this to be some sort of academic notarization before coming to recognize it as a large, oddly filigreed coffee stain.

I WAS REVISITING my thesis because I had been asked to write an appreciation of Vonnegut, a request I initially refused. I was at work on a dying novel, after all, and I hate to be distracted in the midst of such satisfying masochism. But the request lingered. It activated certain deeply rooted fanboy tendencies. I started thinking about how much Vonnegut had meant to me, and why, and whether writing about him might lead to a rendezvous. That was what I wanted. I wanted to interview him. I wanted to sit around on his porch smoking Pall Malls with him, or at least breathing in his secondhand smoke.

Note: This is the fantasy of every single Vonnegut fan.

EIGHTEEN YEARS AGO, upon my successful expulsion from college, I was invited to stay with a friend of my girlfriend, out in Sagaponeck, Long Island. I was on the brink of breaking up with this particular girlfriend. But it was also true that these friends of hers were neighbors of Vonnegut. Friends, actually. (They called him Kurt!) So I took a bus out there and hung around for a few days, feeling poor and unsophisticated and properly caddish. In my backpack was a bound copy of my thesis.

All weekend, I fantasized about dropping it off in his mailbox, with a note explaining that I was staying just down the road. He was a busy guy, and a notorious grouch, so he wouldn't read my thesis immediately. But eventually he'd crack the thing and read a few pages and realize, with a discernable jolt, that, by God, this young Almond fellow knew a few things, that I alone among his legion of literary investigators had divined his essence, understood his crusade, could be trusted with his secrets. This would lead to an invite for cocktails, a long wistful discussion, many Pall Malls, and his eventual decision to adopt me.

But I chickened out.

CLUCK CLUCK.

FAST-FORWARD TO EARLY 2006. I had agreed to write about Vonnegut. But the word on the street was that *no one* got to Vonnegut. The best I could hope for was to get a note to his attorney, one Donald Farber. I imagined this Farber as a dead ringer for Bela Lugosi, with a massive desk upon which sat a single small rubber stamp. From time to time, a small, possibly deformed assistant would place a document before him, allowing Farber the solemn pleasure of whacking a bright red "No" on each request.

Around this time, I traveled down to Hartford, Connecticut,[1] for a reading and by chance started thumbing through a local paper and suddenly saw Kurt Vonnegut staring at me. He was slated to appear at something called the Connecticut Forum, along with authors Joyce Carol Oates and Jennifer Weiner. This was obviously kismet, but I managed not to notice, and immediately filed this information away in the precise part of my brain that has been eroded by pot smoke. The newspaper got tossed into my own backseat archive.

A month later, while uncharacteristically cleaning my car, I came upon the ad for the Connecticut Forum, which was taking place the very next evening. I was no longer suffering under the delusion that I would be able to contact Vonnegut directly. And thus, a notion now took root inside my pointy little head: I had to go see Kurt Vonnegut. I had to drive down to Hartford and ask him for an interview. I became convinced this would be my one and only shot at a face-to-face. The man was eighty-three years old. He had

---

1. Hartford, I was recently informed, is "the world capital of closeted insurance executives." Sweet.

been smoking those Pall Malls (unfiltered) for longer than my parents have been alive. To put it indelicately: He would soon be dead.

THE CONNECTICUT FORUM event was sold out, naturally. But my friend Catherine, who appears to know every person of consequence in Hartford, managed to finagle me a ticket. And not just to the panel, but to the cocktail reception and dinner beforehand, at which *the authors would be appearing.*

I spent all that Friday composing a brief letter of introduction[2] and rehearsing what I would say to Vonnegut. I bought a special envelope, one that would fit into his pocket. I got a haircut. For the first time in years, I had a pair of pants dry-cleaned.

ABOUT THE HAIRCUT: It was the worst of my adult life. I had asked my stylist Linda to make sure the bangs weren't too long, as I didn't like the idea of looking shaggy for Vonnegut. I wanted him to be able to see my eyes, and specifically the nobility shining forth from them. But Linda left the bangs about a half-inch short and boxy at the corners. I looked like a Beatle, if you can imagine the Beatles reuniting for a tour at age forty and returning (ill-advisedly) to the moptop look.

---

2. An excerpt of the letter follows. Note: In a misguided effort to endear myself to Vonnegut, I addressed him as Mr. Rosewater, a reference to the benevolent protagonist of his novel *God Bless You, Mr. Rosewater.*

Dear Mr. Rosewater,

As fate would have it, I've just been asked to write an appreciation of your work. I wondered if you would be willing to be interviewed. I have read most everything you've ever written. I became a writer, in large part, because of my admiration for you. My own books (three fiction and one nonfiction) all express the essential notion that our species will perish if we do not awaken our mercy.

You must be good and tired of people asking you for things aside from your work. I am sorry to trouble you. I wouldn't ask if I thought my proposed book, or the world, could do without you.

With Deep Respect,
Steve Almond

———

ANOTHER IRRELEVANT DETAIL: On the way down to Hartford I was pulled over by a cop for eating a ham sandwich.

It is illegal to eat pork on Connecticut byways.

I ARRIVED IN Hartford in an addled state. It did not help that I was attending what I would call a corporate event. Honestly, I had no idea what the Connecticut Forum was. But it was immediately apparent *they have a lot of money.* As soon as Catherine and I arrived at the venue we started to encounter people who had that unmistakable sheen of prosperity: tailored suits, jewelry, the subtle dermal cross-hatchings of a ski tan.

We got talking to one such couple in the elevator.

"Are you all Vonnegut fans?" I asked.

"Not really," the man said. He was probably in his midfifties. "I've never read any of his books."

"None of them? Not even *Slaughterhouse-Five?*"

He shook his head.

"What about Joyce Carol Oates?"

"What has *she* written?" he asked pleasantly.

AND THIS IS WHAT I mean by a corporate event. Most of the people at this cocktail/dinner thingee were there not because they were fans of the authors, but because it was a way of supporting the arts, being a good corporate citizen.

Being a good corporate citizen means shaving an infinitesimal portion from your profits—profits that have skyrocketed as the government has dedicated itself to the financial aggrandizement of the private sector while virtually eliminating public funding for the arts (forget the poor)—and politely tossing it at programs like the Connecticut Forum, where lots of well-heeled patrons can experience the joys of literature or, at least, a literary dog and pony show, along with noshing on some truly excellent hors d'oeuvres.

I'm sounding angry here. What I felt in talking with these folks in the elevator was something closer to despair.

———

THE COCKTAIL RECEPTION was in a massive lobby. I staked out a spot near the table with the *Kurt Vonnegut* sign and gulped a glass of wine and said hello to my official hosts, the good people of Bank of America. They were all incredibly nice. This is one of the characteristics of the rich: If you are dressed properly, and don't appear to want their money, they are incredibly nice.

After a while, one of the guys in our circle said, "Isn't that him?" We all turned and there was Kurt Vonnegut, shuffling toward his little table. I had never seen Vonnegut in any form other than his author photo. I expected a towering figure with a froth of brown curls. But gravity had tamped him down; his famous curls were ashy and shorn.

We forget what the truly old look like in this culture, because we tuck them away in group homes when they start to look too scary.[3] Vonnegut was terribly frail. The flesh had shrunk away from his eyes and gathered in folds above his collar. He stared out at the room full of strangers and sighed.

"That's so sad!" Catherine said. "He's going to sit there and nobody is going to go up and talk to him."

It was sad. For about thirty seconds, none of us could work up the nerve to approach Kurt Vonnegut. He was such a legend, so much larger than life in the minds of his fans, and here he was, revealed as a mere mortal, closer to tortoise than god.

This was my big chance. I needed to *move*. But I couldn't do it. My whole plan felt suddenly absurd. Pushy. Or worse than pushy— grabby. I didn't want to be just one more person grabbing at the guy. This would dishonor my status as a true fan. By the time I'd decided I was being a ninny (twenty-four seconds later) a young couple had walked up to him, and this set off a kind of Brownian surge. He was immediately enveloped by people, all of whom wanted to speak with him at the same time.

---

3. It should be noted, as well, that the median age of our current celebrities is roughly nineteen.

A bald fellow at the back of the scrum shouted out, "Hey Kurt! I was in your house in Cape Cod back in 1969! Your nephew invited me to a party."

"Is that so?" Vonnegut's voice was faint and wheezy.

Someone asked about his kids and he ticked off their names. "Mark went crazy," he said, referring to his eldest son. "But he's okay now. He wrote a fine book."

"*Eden Express!*" said a woman with a camera. "I almost brought my copy."

Vonnegut coughed delicately. He looked pleased.

An eager-looking blond woman asked him what he thought of George W. Bush.

"He makes me wish Nixon were still president," Vonnegut muttered.

"Who do you think was the greatest president in your lifetime?"

"I was fortunate to have lived during the reign of a man named Franklin Delano Roosevelt." He added, to no one in particular, "It was the polio that made him compassionate, you know. Being sick like that."

"You look great," someone else said.

"Nonsense," he said.

A pretty girl with auburn hair stepped shyly into Vonnegut's view.

"This girl came all the way from California to see you!" the blond woman exclaimed.

"Why would you do that, my dear? It's sunny in California!"

The girl was trembling a little. She wore a white blouse that framed her breasts. There was a moment of suspense while she stood, flushed, struggling to speak. "I wanted to thank you," she stammered. "Reading your work was what made me start to think for myself."

Vonnegut gazed at her. There was nothing lascivious in his eyes. He was merely sipping at her beauty. She radiated transference. It was as if Vonnegut were her father, some idealized version, which, of course, he was.

—

BY THE TIME I worked up the nerve to approach him, Vonnegut looked wiped, so I didn't waste any time.

"I've been asked to write a biography of you," I said.

"By whom?" he said.

It was a fair question, and I did what any self-respecting young fiction writer would do in this situation: I fictionalized. "Giroux & Schuster."

Vonnegut sighed. "I've heard nothing about it. My papers are collected at the Indiana University library. You are welcome to go look at them."

And that, as far as he was concerned, was that. He wasn't defensive, exactly. But he declined to look at me. I felt like a traveling salesman being shown the door.

"What I was hoping is that you might want to be interviewed."

Vonnegut gazed mournfully at his knuckles, as if hoping to discover a lit cigarette between two of them.

I handed him my letter. He inspected the envelope briefly—such a lovely envelope!—and slipped it into his coat pocket.

The end.

WAS I BUMMED? I was bummed as hell. My one chance to meet Vonnegut had been such a bust, such a nothing.

Then again, the guy was eighty-three years old. He was in Hartford, Connecticut. He had five hundred people coming at him. I wasn't going to get much. So we moved on to dinner, which consisted of large hunks of cow and a wedge of chocolate cake.

I was seated at the table with Jennifer Weiner. I didn't know her work, only that she was regarded as a popular chick lit author. She made a great point of proclaiming how honored and humbled and *baffled* she was to be part of a panel with Oates and Vonnegut. Little old her! It wasn't that hard to figure out, really: She was the fizzy pop culture component.

—

THE PANEL ITSELF was deeply strange, in the way that only a literary panel can be strange, which is to say the logical result of foisting together three socially maladroit loners before a large crowd of gawkers. The authors made no mention of each other's work. They didn't respond to one another's ideas. They weren't very nice to each other, actually. The most stunning example of this antagonism came less than half an hour in. Vonnegut was lamenting the destructive capacities of humankind, listing specific atrocities (the Holocaust, Nagasaki, the Roman Games) when Oates cut him off.

"What sex—excuse me, Kurt—what sex is doing all this bad stuff?"

Vonnegut looked confused. He hadn't expected to be interrupted, nor had he quite heard Oates.

"What?"

"Which *sex* is doing all this stuff?" Oates asked again, in a chiding tone.

It was an astounding moment.

Here was Kurt Vonnegut, who had fought in the Second World War, who had been a POW during the firebombing of Dresden, who had converted that experience into one of the most powerful antiwar novels ever published, who had spent his entire life as an artist decrying the horror of war, who, as a citizen, had protested against Vietnam (and all the foul wars that would follow it), who has been, in short, the most celebrated and influential literary pacifist of the twentieth century.[4] And rather than let him speak to a group of 2,700 well-heeled Hartfordians, Oates was trying to paint him as a warmongering hypocrite because he . . . had a penis. She

---

4. From *Slaughterhouse-Five:*

> Wherever you went there were women who would do anything for food or protection for themselves and their children and the old people . . . the whole point of war is to put women everywhere in that condition. It's always the men against the women, with the men only pretending to fight among themselves . . . the ones who pretend the hardest get their pictures in the papers and medals afterwards.

sounded like a freshman-year feminist, drunk on her own sanctimony.

Vonnegut offered a joke in response, something about how
men made war because they were better at science. Harvard had
done a study. He was trying to lighten the mood. Oates was not
amused.

If Vonnegut were less a gentleman, he might have suggested to
Oates that aggression is a compulsion that transcends gender. As
evidence, he might have pointed out to the crowd that Oates had
just released a collection, *Female of the Species,* in which the protagonist of every single story is a female killer.

I DON'T MEAN to play Vonnegut as the helpless victim here. He
looked irritable throughout. And he seemed too tired to mask his
feelings. He reminded me of my grandfather Irving in his final
years. The word often used is "crotchety," which boils down to im-
patience with the bullshit that passes for social nicety.

At one point, for instance, the moderator asked him about
Bush's State of the Union speech, specifically his notion that America is addicted to oil.

"That certainly isn't a thought he could have by himself," Vonnegut responded. The audience exploded into laughter. But Vonnegut wasn't joking. "Everything that distinguishes our era from
the dark ages—since we still have plagues and torture chambers—
is what we've been able to do with petroleum, and that is going to
end very soon." He stared out into the audience. "I think the world
is ending," he said softly. "Our own intelligence tells us we're perfectly awful animals, that we're tearing the place apart and should
get the hell out of here."

A thudding silence ensued.

The moderator turned to Jen Weiner and asked if she had a
more hopeful message to offer the audience.

Weiner looked a bit panicked. "Wow," she said. "I wasn't expecting to have to deliver a message about humanity tonight."

"Well, *leave,*" Vonnegut murmured.

I DON'T THINK Vonnegut meant to be cruel. He was simply taken aback that any author would sit before a packed house of fellow citizens and have nothing to say on the subject. More so, that she would act offended at the notion that she *should* have something to say.

Nonetheless, the damage was done. Weiner spent the rest of the panel sniping at Vonnegut. Unfortunately, Weiner is one of those people deeply invested in the idea that her body contains no mean bones. So her attacks were of the throw-a-rock-but-hide-your-hand variety. She made a joke about Vonnegut wanting to kick her off the stage. She asked him why he would offer advice to high school kids if he felt the world was ending. She expressed shock that Vonnegut had any children.[5]

So he was getting it from both sides now.

AS IT TURNED OUT, Vonnegut needn't have bothered chiding Weiner. She did a bang-up job of revealing herself to the crowd. Her most emphatic statement of the night was about how great it was to hang out on the set of *In Her Shoes,* the movie they made from one of her books. And how she actually *got to meet Cameron Diaz.* And how super excited she was to be meeting Cameron, but all she could think to say is, "Where's Justin?" which is *totally funny* if you happen to know that Cameron Diaz is totally dating the singer Justin Timberlake!

I REALIZE THAT I'm being harsh toward Oates and Weiner, and I realize that my motives may be questioned. I feel protective of Vonnegut. He alone seemed to grasp that the panel was a rare chance for writers to speak about what they actually do, and why it might matter. He was compulsively honest with the crowd—about his fears, his doubts, even his own motives. This is why I found the

---

5. For the record, Vonnegut has seven kids, three of whom he adopted after his sister died of cancer and his brother-in-law died in a train wreck.

conduct of his colleagues so odious. They weren't just petty or vain. They were disingenuous.

Oates, for instance, insisted her famous infatuation with violence had nothing to do with her own internal life. Instead, she offered a wistful account of her upbringing on a farm with lots of animals and a river flowing past. She sounded like Laura Ingalls Wilder, not a woman who has made her nut channeling serial killers.[6]

VONNEGUT WAS ALSO the only author who seemed burdened by the state of the human race, and the American empire in particular. He kept making these big, clanging statements. The crowd had no idea what to do. Our citizens aren't used to having their fantasies punctured. We don't mind watching guys like Jon Stewart josh around about that silly war in Iraq, or global warming. But when someone actually points out that our species is goose-stepping toward extinction—*without* a comforting laugh line at the end— things get uncomfortable.

Far from offering support, his co-panelists played him as a cranky doomseeker.[7] Neither one had much to say about the moral crises facing this country. Oates spoke of her stories as if they were

---

6. Asked about her interest in boxing, Oates insisted she was drawn to subjects "very different" from herself. I immediately pictured her in silk shorts and a mouthpiece, working the speedbag. I recognize that this image is both gratuitous and erotically disturbing. It should be taken as a measure of my frustration with her comments on the panel, and not (I should emphasize) a dismissal of her fiction, which I admire precisely because it exposes our shared lust for mayhem.

7. Weiner later posted a summary of the evening on her blog, here excerpted:

Mr. Vonnegut didn't appear to have much use for authors who hadn't figured out a cogent philosophy of life, on par with his "just get off the planet" line—and I would have paid good money for a snapshot of the high school students' faces when he informed them that human beings are a disease on the face of the planet and the best thing they can do is not reproduce and leave as quickly as possible. . . .

merely problems of language to be solved, an oddly bloodless attitude given her preoccupation with, well, blood. Weiner seemed
most interested in meeting really cool celebs. These were the two
authorial personas on display: the geeky genius whose art is her-
metically sealed off from the vulgarities of the real world, and the
crowd-pleaser slavish after shiny morsels of fame.[8] Vonnegut, in
his belief that artists should serve as instruments of destiny, was utterly alone.

As the first half of the evening drew to a close, Weiner and Oates
made a beeline for the wings. Vonnegut rose to his feet with great
deliberation. He took a cautious first step, to avoid tripping over his
microphone wire. Then he began a long, shuffling trip across the
empty stage. "Oh, no," the woman next to me said tenderly. "He's
all by himself!"

AFTER INTERMISSION came questions from the audience.

Someone asked, "What is the political responsibility of a
writer?"

Vonnegut responded, "We need to say what political responsibility does an *American* have."

Someone asked, "What's the single most beautiful thing you've
ever seen?"

Vonnegut said, "My Lord, that's a tough question, because
there's so much beauty, really; it's what keeps me going in life, is

---

Note how incredibly classy Weiner is—not at all bitter or defensive, as you
might expect from someone who got punked in front of 2,700 people.

8. I would be remiss if I failed to mention this quintessential Weiner moment: Oates had named Emily Dickinson as her favorite writer, and was in
the midst of discussing Dickinson's work, when Weiner piped up with the
following question: "Did you know that you can set 'Because I Would Not
Stop for Death' to the tune of 'Yellow Rose of Texas'? Have you ever done
that?" Weiner then began chanting the words of the poem in a frantic,
square-dancey cadence.

Regrettably, I am not making this up.

just glimpsing beauty all the time. I suppose the most beautiful thing, though you can't see it exactly, is music."

Someone asked what his essential topic was.

Vonnegut said, "I write again and again about my family."

Toward the end, a girl named Mary asked Vonnegut, "Can you sum up your philosophy of life in two sentences? And will you go to the prom with me? It is my senior year."

It was the kind of setup Vonnegut should have knocked out of the ballpark. But he looked exhausted. More than that, he looked heartbroken. This is what Weiner and Oates seemed unable to grasp: The man was heartbroken.

Not sexist. Not cranky. Heartbroken.

He had spent his entire life writing stories and essays and novels in the naked hope that he might redeem his readers. As grim and dystopic as some of those books were, every one was written under the assumption that human beings are capable of a greater decency. And not because of God's will, that tired old crutch. But because of their simple duty to others of their kind.

Now, in the shadow of his own death, he was facing the incontrovertible evidence that his life's work had been for naught. Right before his eyes, Americans had regressed to a state of infantile omnipotence. They drove SUVs and cheered for wars on TV and worshipped the beautiful and ignorant and despised the poor and brushed aside the science of their own doom. They had lost interest in their own consciences, and declined to make the sacrifices that might spare their very own grandchildren.

"My philosophy of life?" Vonnegut said. "I haven't a clue."

"What about the prom?" the moderator said, hopefully.

Vonnegut made a crack about the girl being jailbait.

IT WAS A LAUGH LINE, and some people did laugh. But there was a terrible disappointment in the moment: Vonnegut, for all his gifts of compassion, was failing in a simple act of generosity.

He knew that this girl, Mary, wanted only a taste of his wisdom, his famous wit. She had read his books and, like all his fans, she had come to love him as a father, someone who had seen the worst of human conduct and refused to lie about the sort of trouble we were in, but who had not allowed his doubt to curdle into cynicism, who, for all his dark prognostication, was a figure of tremendous hope. The evidence was in his books, which performed the greatest feat of alchemy known to man: the conversion of grief into laughter by means of courageous imagination. Like any decent parent, he had made the astonishing sorrow of the examined life bearable.

And this was what Mary wanted from him now: a little of his old magic. So did the rest of the folks sitting in the Bushnell Theater in downtown Hartford, not just the ones who stood and applauded when he was introduced, all us drooling acolytes, but the ones who regarded him merely as an eloquent grump, a fading prophet, an old man shouting the world off his porch.

And Vonnegut seemed to know it, too. He gazed out at the audience, not like his hero Twain, with his inexhaustible charms, his dazzling knack for the mot juste, but in the silent burden of our present condition. His image was magnified, eerily, on the video screen overhead. The camera shook for a moment. He looked stricken. I thought of that passage in *Breakfast of Champions* where, in exhaustion, he drops the fictional disguise altogether:

> "This is a very bad book you're writing," I said to myself.
> "I know," I said.
> "You're afraid you'll kill yourself the way your mother did," I said.
> "I know," I said.

I thought of Vonnegut, a twenty-one-year-old private, returning to Indianapolis to bury his mother after she took her own life. And his imprisonment in Dresden, just a few months later, all that ashen death, the passing of his sister, the madness of his son, his own suicide attempt in the haunted year of 1984. The camera was still fixed on Vonnegut's face, and it occurred to me, with great clarity, that he was going to die before he could say another word. He would simply and quietly sit back in his chair and perish. He was all done with the rescuing racket.

Instead, he gathered himself and smiled at all the nice strangers before him and said, with an almost girlish lilt, "Of course I'll go to the prom with you, Mary. And I love to dance." And though nobody quite realized it, including Vonnegut himself, he had, with those two fine sentences, answered both her questions.

THE CROWD RESPONSE to the panel was about what you'd expect. People thought it had been a good show. They liked the fighting. They liked gossiping afterward about the fighting. Simply put: They were Americans.

Catherine wanted me to come have a drink with a bunch of the money folks, but I had a long drive back to Boston. It was pouring, too, and neither of us had an umbrella, so we lingered in the lobby. The girl with the auburn hair was lingering, too. Her name was Susan. She was talking with the blonde who had utzed her to talk to Vonnegut. The blonde was indignant. She told us that she and Susan had paid a thousand dollars to attend the cocktail party and dinner. They had been promised a meeting with Vonnegut.

"They just did a group photo, but I wasn't anywhere close to Kurt," she said.

"I made sure to get myself right next to him," Susan said. "I could see that's all we were going to get."

A thousand bucks for a few minutes of jittery small talk? It sounded like a Bush fundraiser.

But then Susan told a little story, in her soft Texan accent, that took a little of the edge off my gloom.

"I followed him, you know. Every time he went to have a cigarette. I just followed him and bummed a cigarette and we sat there talking. He was totally cool, too. Totally on top of it. They wouldn't let us smoke inside and it was too cold outside, so you know what we did? We got in one of those things, those doors that spin around—"

"A revolving door?"

"Yeah. We got in one of the compartments and he pushed it around till there was just a crack. It was pretty warm in there and we could just blow the smoke outside."

IT WAS A MISERABLE night for driving. The rain had dissolved into fog, which draped the bare winter trees; my head was still spinning. Focusing on that image—Vonnegut and pretty young Susan puffing away like a couple of truants—helped me feel a little less hopeless. This made no sense. Vonnegut has been killing himself for years, or trying to, with those unfiltered Pall Malls.

But something occurred to me as I sped through that dirty shroud of fog, something Vonnegut has been trying to explain to the rest of us for most of his life. And that is this: Despair is a form of hope. It is an acknowledgment of the distance between ourselves and our appointed happiness.

At certain moments, it is reason enough to live.

Part Two

If you really want to hurt your parents and you don't have enough nerve to be homosexual, the least you can do is go into the arts.

It is an odd and disquieting experience to read the undergraduate thesis you wrote eighteen years ago, not unlike finding photographs of yourself dressed up as a member of Flock of Seagulls. (I am not suggesting here that I ever dressed up like a member of Flock of Seagulls; I am merely using what we in the lit business call an *analogy*.)

Nonetheless, I cannot proceed any further without some mention of the document. I have read it twice in the past week and am therefore ready to enumerate its major intellectual conclusions:

1. Kurt Vonnegut *rules*.
2. You should totally read his books.
3. I will never be an academic.

———

I WOULD ALSO LIKE to reassure those of you concerned that I may not have used the verb *adumbrate* frequently enough in my thesis. In fact, I found occasion to use the verb three times in the first thirty pages alone: "More fundamentally, I hope through this investigation to adumbrate Vonnegut's unorthodox conception of author/text/reader relations." My thesis is full of sentences like this.

ONE OF THE FUNNEST things about rereading the thesis is tallying up all the critics and authors I pretended to have read, but hadn't. A partial list would include James Joyce, Stendhal, Cervantes, Twain, Leslie Fiedler, Ortega y Gasset,[1] Northrop Frye, Rubin,[2] and Wayne Booth.[3]

Whom, then, *did* I read?

I read Vonnegut. I read his novels. I read his stories. I read his essays. I read his interviews. I read his commencement speeches. Had his shopping lists been made available, I would have read those. I also quoted him at length. Approximately one-third of the thesis word count is Vonnegut. I did this mostly because I was, and remain, stupendously lazy. But it is also true (as I shrewdly noted back then) that Vonnegut has not attracted much formal criticism. The foremost commentator on Vonnegut is Vonnegut himself.

MY THESIS WAS not a total wash. It was merely a partial wash. But it also had what I believe the Chief Curator has referred to as "a certain plucky undergraduate charm."

I was interested in the ways Vonnegut makes himself known in his fiction—writing prefaces to his novels, introducing himself as a

1. No idea who he is, or what his first name might be.

2. Ditto.

3. Actually, I did read the first hundred pages of Booth's very thick and impressive-looking volume *The Rhetoric of Fiction,* and I derived a great deal of pleasure from carrying it around with me, on the off chance that some New Critical thug wanted to *throw down.* (None did.)

character—and how these interventions affected what I called, rather grandly, "the fictional contract."

My best crack at a summary of the thesis ran like so:

> Many novelists and critics take as their credo the following sentence from James Joyce's *A Portrait of the Artist as a Young Man:*
>
> "The artist, like the God of Creation, remains within or behind or beyond or above his handiwork, invisible, refined out of existence, indifferent, paring his fingernails."
>
> My thesis might be thought of as an attempt to explore what happens when a writer steps forward and, in full view of the audience, bites his nails frantically.

I do not remember having read *A Portrait of the Artist as a Young Man,* and have grave doubts as to whether I ever did, but I do remember taking extraordinary pride in having come up with this last bit.

The thesis also included a term of my very own invention: *realismo.*[4] Realismo, as I defined it, entailed "both the reality claims made by the author *and* their acceptance by the reader." I am sorry to inform you that this quite obviously brilliant formulation has not, as yet, found its place within the parlance of the lit crit crowd.

As if I even care.

AND WHILE WE'RE bashing those dweebs, let me mention, as a significant furthermore, that people read mostly for emotional reasons, not ideas. They seek a chance to experience the feelings inside themselves—lust, shame, agony—for which daily life offers no outlet. The more openly obsessed our narrator is, the better. (Consider Humbert and the thousand eyes wide open in his eyed blood.)

---

4. I believe the Chief Curator had this neologism in mind when she used the adjective *plucky,* though perhaps she realized—as I did not, obviously—that *realismo* is an actual word in Spanish.

From this perspective, my thesis turns out to be perfectly fascinating, not for its facile notions about authorial presence, but for the moony allegiance it expresses toward Vonnegut. It was a love letter, for God's sake![5] A chance for me to pronounce my adoration for Vonnegut, to defend his style, to advocate for him in what I took to be the court of academic opinion.

TWO DECADES LATER, I can see the thesis as something even more excruciatingly personal: an artistic prospectus. I was explaining to myself, often explicitly, the sort of writer I wished to become.

The main thing was that Vonnegut made an *impact* on readers. He wasn't one of those recluses who hid behind coy fictional guises. Every sentence he wrote, every character, was stamped in his image. He came clean on the page as a guy losing his shit. Like in that famous opening chapter of *Slaughterhouse-Five,* the image of Vonnegut lying in bed, sleepless, drunk-dialing his old war buddies and stinking of mustard gas and roses.

He was honest about why he wrote, too. He copped to that central (if rarely mentioned) impulse of the writing life: He wanted attention. He spoke bluntly, courageously, about prevailing injustices, not just on the page, but in public. He was funny, self-deprecating, easy to read, a (gasp) populist. He wanted to speak to everyone and he wanted everyone to shape the hell up. He hated rich people and warmongers and fanatics. He didn't pretend not to care.

AND THAT'S NOT ALL.

> Vonnegut was an atheist.
> *(So was I!)*
> Vonnegut was a Scorpio.
> *(So was I!)*
> Vonnegut was a youngest child.
> *(So was I!)*

---

5. I fantasize on *page one* of the thesis about the prospect of meeting Vonnegut, though I stop short of cataloguing what I might wear.

Vonnegut viewed film and television as enemies of human progress.

(So did I!)

Vonnegut hated literary critics.

(So did I!)

Vonnegut even seemed to intuit the emotional crises in my life: that I felt exiled by my family, simultaneously disgusted and humiliated by the world of men, desperate for human comfort. He spoke of loneliness constantly. He characterized writers as people "who feel somehow marginal, somehow slightly off-balance all the time."

He was, to summarize, not just my role model, but my shrink.

I AM NOT SUGGESTING that I recognized my own motives in writing about Vonnegut. Of course I didn't—I was a college student.

But it was more than that. I wasn't a writer. I had no concept (aside from Vonnegut) of what a writer might be. I didn't take a single creative writing class at Wesleyan. Instead, I became what one of my classmates called, not unkindly, a "campus cartoon character." I undertook a variety of extracurricular activities. I edited the newspaper (so did Vonnegut!). I was a sports broadcaster for the college radio station.[6] I was a resident adviser. I sang in a gospel choir. I raced around our lovely campus asking, with my every gesture and deed, the same question: *What will the story of my life be?*

I DON'T ESPECIALLY like thinking about my college years. They were a bleak era for me, and a bleak era for the country. Ronald Rea-

6. I cannot begin to describe how pathetic it was to serve in this capacity for a Division Three liberal arts college. I would compare it to carrying a spittoon for one of the minor dwarves, such as Sneezy. The memory that leaps to mind is of an away game against our archrival, Amherst. The halftime score was, if memory serves, 51–0. I am talking about football, though we broadcast other sports, too, such as women's field hockey. I was privileged to be one of the broadcast team who worked the famous Wesleyan-Colby bloodbath of 1987, a match that took place in a persistent drizzle and which was, inexplicably, a home game.

gan had just won his second term in a landslide, and the staggering cruelties advocated by what has come to be known as the conservative movement were very much in vogue. Greed was good, facts were stupid things, Jesus was in, personal sacrifice was out, the nation was beginning a long, slow decline into moral disassociation.

The details were straight out of a B movie. Astrologers were setting the agenda upstairs at the White House, while a gang of nutty neocons trashed the basement, running guns to Iran and funneling the cash to the death squads (the term "terrorists" was not yet in vogue) who opposed a legally elected government in Nicaragua.

I had no idea what to do about any of this. I felt guilty and pissed off all the time. I listened to "I Will Dare" by the Replacements 12,000 times. I took a class called Nuclear War. My final project was a newspaper report that detailed the destruction of my hometown by a hydrogen bomb.

BOOM.

THE VONNEGUT PASSAGE that haunted me throughout my college years is one of the few not quoted in my thesis. It comes from a curious little essay called "Biafra: A People Betrayed," in his 1974 collection *Wampeters, Foma & Granfalloons.* Vonnegut is reporting from the small African nation of Biafra, whose beleaguered citizens are bracing for a genocidal invasion by the Nigerian army.

He writes,

> What did we eat in Biafra? As guests of the government, we had meat and yams and soups and fruit. It was embarrassing. Whenever we told a cadaverous beggar, "No chop," it wasn't really true. We had plenty of chop, but it was all in our bellies.

I had never read so ruthless and candid a summary of the relationship between the fed and starving of this world. Vonnegut was writing not only about injustice, but the peculiar American talent

for self-deception (his own included), for espousing laudable beliefs just so long as you don't have to live up to them.

TO UNDERSTAND WHY this passage hit me so hard will require
some family background. My mother was born and raised in the
Bronx. Her mother, Annie Rosenthal, was an elementary school
teacher in Harlem. Her father, Irving, was an actuary. Both were
members of the Communist Party. My grandmother was eventually
asked to testify about her activities before the New York Board of
Education. She took an early retirement instead. Secrecy and fear
pervaded their apartment.

My own parents came of age during the 1960s. Both were early,
vocal opponents of the war in Vietnam. My father helped under-
graduates organize antiwar protests at Stanford, where he had taken
a job on the faculty of the medical school. He was later arrested
himself for taking part in a protest at a nearby air force base. His
teaching contract was not renewed. What I am trying to convey here
is that I am descended from people who suffered for their beliefs.
I arrived at college eager to do the same thing.

BUT WESLEYAN WASN'T exactly what I was expecting. It was, to be
ruthless and candid, the world capital of Entitled Sanctimony, the
kind of place where students staged protests to demand divestment
from South Africa, then headed over to the dining hall to stuff
themselves full of ice cream, where the lower-class toughs who
played hockey and joined frats were considered dangerous misogy-
nists, where kids in carefully torn polo sweaters gathered to chant
grave, humanist slogans, then dispersed to drop acid on Foss Hill,
where noblesse oblige had mutated into a kind of desperate narcissistic accessory.

I did my best to fit in, to obey, for instance, the elaborate protocols surrounding gender and race nomenclature.[7] But it was impos-

---

7. I dutifully referred to members of the opposite sex as *womyn*, this being lin-
guistically preferable to the suffixally oppressive wo*men*.

sible to ignore certain facts, such as that most black students wanted nothing to do with white students, and that the residents of Middletown regarded the lot of us as spoiled brats. I spent a few winter afternoons camped on the corners of Main Street, handing out pamphlets on nuclear disarmament, which the locals accepted politely, then deposited in the nearest trash can.

It was also impossible to ignore the affluence of my classmates. They had new cars and elaborate stereo systems and Park Avenue apartments stuffed with high art. They spent vacations at beach houses and in tennis clubs, and their ease in these exotic precincts struck me hard; these were people born on the banks of what Vonnegut called the Money River.

I don't mean to make my classmates sound like dolts. They were trying to care about the world, however indulgently. My scorn for them was an expression of my own guilt. I couldn't shake the benighted notion that the best way to honor the family legacy was to suffer for my beliefs.

SO I WASHED DISHES in the cafeteria. I volunteered at a mental health facility. I endured the routine miseries of the unpaid internship. And I read Vonnegut voraciously, through the long, muggy summer evenings, dripping sweat onto the pages of my yellowed paperbacks.

He was the one guy who cut through the bullshit. He understood that our essential crisis was not one of policy but morality, individual greed, inconsideration, suicidal self-regard. He was mad as hell, but—unlike my classmates—he found the absurd comedy within his fury. He didn't write quiet little novels about bourgeois plight. He wrote about what we college students called, always with that frisson of knowing dread, *the real world.* In Vonnegut, I found a path back to the political ideals of my family.

But my Vonnegut mania was about more than politics. His books filled me with a terrible personal longing. I had grown up in a family beset by sorrow and had come to believe, unconsciously, that the world was a broader reflection of this sorrow, that it was my job to save the place, that only by banishing pain would my own joy become permissible. Vonnegut operated on the same absurd, sentimental assumptions. He regarded civilization as a failed family, curable only by the reestablishment of clans in which members felt duty-bound to love one another. Happy families. He wrote about them over and over. They became his utopia, then mine as well.

NOW COMES a difficult confession.

To this point, I have made myself sound every bit the loyal Vonnegut disciple. But by the middle of my senior year, I felt vaguely ashamed of my thesis, and specifically that it was about Vonnegut.

I had discovered Bellow by then; *Henderson the Rain King* had ripped my head off. In my upper-level classes, we were studying *The Iliad* and *The Inferno* and *Lear*. My classmates were using phrases like "transcendental signifier"—and they meant it. My pal Steve Metcalf was writing his thesis about *Ulysses*, which struck me as perhaps the most sophisticated thing one could do on earth, aside from being James Joyce himself.

I began telling people that my thesis was about *authorial presence in the modern text*, that it was about John Barth and Milan Kundera, though, in the end, I devoted five pages to these authors. I renounced Vonnegut. He became another childish pleasure I would now have to hide from the world. (Others included candy consumption, a weakness for prog rock, and a tendency to conduct imaginary discussions with my twin brother.)

THE VONNEGUT APOSTASY.

It happens to thousands of readers every year. They reach a point in their lives where they turn away from Vonnegut, toward authors who offer a greater complexity of prose, a more nuanced version of the world, whose authorial mission entails an examination of individual consciousness rather than collective fate. I would wager that Vonnegut is the least acknowledged influence in modern letters.

In my case, I should admit that vanity, not boredom, was the culprit. I felt that my worship of Vonnegut marked me as somehow lacking in depth, which, as an English major at an elite liberal arts college, was the one thing I wanted to project. Copping to Vonnegut made me feel like a dork.

The feeling has lasted a long time.

I am *still* embarrassed to admit how much Vonnegut meant to me. When I am asked to name favorite books or authors, I gravitate toward the ones that look the most respectable on paper, and leave Vonnegut off the list.

But it's more than embarrassment, I think. It has something to do with the way artists absorb influence. They tend to focus on those figures whom they discover later in life, when they have some coherent self-concept and the vocabulary to articulate the conscious facets of their admiration. It was easy enough for me to identify Bellow as an inspiration because I read him thinking: *This man is my inspiration!* Vonnegut got into the groundwater before my ambition took root.

In this sense, as I've suggested, he was more like a parent. And what was the reward for all his hard work? He got taken for granted.

VONNEGUT'S BOOKS remain critically underappreciated. But I don't really give a shit about critical appreciation. As a measure of cultural influence, it turns out to matter a lot less than an expensive hairstyle. The real issue here isn't his role as an author, but as a prophet.

I'm in no position to lecture anyone on biblical matters, as I find the Holy Books to be wishful poetry for the most part. But I do know the basic plot of the prophetic books: *Prophet warns people to shape up. People don't listen. Prophet winds up howling in hole.* This is the plot of Vonnegut's life.

People may regard him as a literary legend and all the rest of that glitzy stuff, but nobody with any sort of power has heeded his call.

One wonders now where our leaders got the idea that mass torture would work to our advantage in Indochina. It never worked anywhere else. They got the idea from childish fiction, I think, and from a childish awe of terror.

Vonnegut wrote this thirty-five years ago.

LET ME OFFER one more Vonnugget before I move on to the literary excavation that closes this wobbly triptych:

I now believe that the only way in which Americans can rise above their ordinariness, can mature sufficiently to rescue themselves and to help rescue their planet, is through enthusiastic intimacy with works of their own imaginations.

This is Vonnegut in a wildly optimistic mood.

In darker moments, he has expressed an equally convincing belief that our greatest works of literature will amount to nothing more than toilet paper. This has been, as far as I can tell, the central existential struggle of his life: Does what I do *matter*?

I CAN'T BLAME him for his doubts. Vonnegut has now been writing for nearly half a century. He has been preaching the same line as Jesus on the Mount: humility, pacifism, intolerance for all forms of human suffering.

During the late sixties, he might even have believed that America was going to right itself. Instead, he has watched the country fall under the spell of leaders who demand nothing from us but the indulgence of our darkest impulses. He has watched his fellow citizens shrink before his eyes, become idolaters of convenience, screen addicts, brutes who cheer for death and call themselves patriots. He has watched the popular press, and the so-called opposition, cower before their moral duties.

And so we come (at last) to the point. Why, after twenty years, am I taking up with Vonnegut again? The cynical answer would be because he will soon be gone. That is getting it all exactly backwards. I am writing about Vonnegut now not because he is leaving us, but because we have left him.

Part Three

> *He may have been a genius,*
> *as mutants sometimes are*

don't imagine you've ever tried to gain access to the Reading Room at Indiana University's Lilly Library, but I am here to tell you that security there stops just short of the cavity search. No food or drink allowed. No writing instruments. No cameras. You are given a locker for your possessions and instructed to walk over to a padded door. There is a click. You now have 1.5 seconds to open the door. If you fail to open the door you are led outside and shot in the head.

WHY WAS I at the Lilly Library? I was there because Kurt Vonnegut had asked me to go see his papers, during our heart-stopping encounter in Hartford. Or okay, maybe it wasn't really a request. Maybe it was more like a brushoff. Fine.

The fact remained: I did need to drive my wife from Southern California to Boston. And Indiana was, more or less, *on the way*. And thus, I had forced her to rise at 5:30 A.M.[1] and to drive with me from the lush suburbs of St. Louis, where the lots are the size of

---

1. Why 5:30 A.M.? This will be hard to answer without calling into question my competence as a planner/husband. Briefly: I figured I'd need at least two days to look over Vonnegut's papers, but I was also psychopathically in the thrall of the World Cup and needed, or felt I needed, to reach Boston by Saturday afternoon, when France played Brazil, which would only happen, based on my calculations (again, questionable) if I squeezed in Day One of the excavation after driving from St. Louis.

football fields, through the corn prairies of downstate Illinois as they came greenly awake at dawn, and onto Route 46 with its quiet procession of church and farm, its gleaming brown soil, and finally into Bloomington.

It was high summer, broiling, and the campus was swarming with incoming freshmen, their faces illuminated by the coming liberation into that kingdom of sports and pizza and cheap beer and— right, sorry!—higher education. They moved about in nervous eager packs, well-fed American youths, the boys dribbling invisible basketballs, the girls heavily deodorized and whispering, That is so, like, *whatever.*

KURT VONNEGUT, JR., was born on November 11, Armistice Day, 1922, in Indianapolis, Indiana, the youngest child of a prominent local architect. His mother, Edith, would later kill herself. Her maiden name was Lieber, which means *love* in German.

According to an exhaustive family history prepared by an anonymous relative, all eight of Vonnegut's great-grandparents were part of the vast migration of Germans to the Midwest between 1820 and 1870. The name Vonnegut derives from a distant paternal relation who had an estate—*ein gut*—on the river Funne, in Westphalia. The name was changed upon immigration, because Funnegut sounded too much like "funny gut."

You can trust me when I tell you that Vonnegut's forebears were not comic forces. Here is a direct quote from his great-great-grandfather Jacom Schramm:

> It appears human weakness makes it impossible to sustain a republic on this earth for any length of time, and the majority of people need, necessarily, a driving leader without whom they will inevitably wind up in chaos. Nevertheless, the Americans are still very proud of their freedom, even though they are the worst of slaves, and there is sure to be a bloody revolution before a monarchic government can gain a foothold here.

———

I WILL NOW RESIST the urge to make a disparaging remark about the Bush administration.

HOW THE SCION of such hardass German stock became so soft-hearted is not entirely clear. Vonnegut has often blamed the Indianapolis public school system, ironically, given his spotty academic record. A sampling of his years at Shortridge High, for instance, reveals that despite earning an A+ in chemistry his senior year, despite a verified IQ of 137, he ranked 240th in a class of 760.

Of central interest is a newspaper clipping about Vonnegut and two schoolmates, who plan to drive down to New Mexico over the summer to dig up Indian skulls. The boys are pictured demonstrating how to light a campfire. Vonnegut is a foot taller than the others and the approximate width of a beanpole. He wears a fedora. His face is narrow, unlined, absurdly young, with an expression of improvised gravity that doesn't quite conceal his chronic embarrassment.

I HAD HOPED to make photocopies of this odd little document, but when I asked the Reading Room Monitor about this she cocked her head.

"Do you have permission from the author to make copies?"

"Of course," I said, "Mr. Vonnegut, Kurt, actually asked me to come out."

"You have a letter on file, then?"

"On file," I said, thoughtfully.

There now ensued a rather lengthy drama involving a hushed appeal up the chain of command, tense colloquies, trips to the computer to check "the database," and a culminating interview with one Saundra Taylor, Curator of Manuscripts. I had, in fact, called Ms. Taylor several weeks earlier, on the assumption I would need a reservation to see the Vonnegut papers because they were so wildly popular.[2]

———

2. Taylor told me that the Sylvia Plath collection actually got a lot more requests. I was devastated.

"There shouldn't be a problem," Taylor said. "Just have Mr. Vonnegut or his legal representative fax us a letter."

"That's the thing," I said. "Mr. Vonnegut was the one who asked me to inspect his papers. It was more of a personal request, based on when I met with him. I've come all the way out from Boston and I only have two days. My wife is with me." The rest of the reading room staff was now staring. "She's *six months pregnant*," I added, pathetically.

Ms. Taylor looked pained. It was this sort of moment, I imagined, that separated the minor Special Collection librarians from the big leaguers. Here was a thin, anguished scholar,[3] clearly desperate, perhaps prepared to make a scene. What I wanted was simple enough, even reasonable, but in direct contravention to her role as guardian of the collection and the protocols thereof. She paused a moment and smoothed down the corner of a file folder with her thumbnail.

I felt I should say something; perhaps suggest that my wife, in addition to her pregnancy, had lupus.

"It would be best," Ms. Taylor said, with soft finality, "if you took notes."

THIS WAS NOT GOOD. It had been my intention to use my two days at Lilly to Xerox the documents that struck me as most revelatory, so I could study them later. I did some quick math. The Vonnegut archive contained 4,000 documents. Assuming I worked uninterrupted for the next two days, I would have fourteen hours to inspect the whole shebang, or 840 minutes. This came out to 12.5 seconds per document.

The problem was my reading skills, which are poor, as a result of my having been raised on a steady diet of *What's Happening* reruns and not, as I may have implied in certain settings, the col-

---

3. You can stop laughing now. I am merely suggesting that—so far as Ms. Taylor was concerned—I might very well have *been* a scholar (i.e. I was wearing chinos, my shirt was tucked in, etc.).

lected works of Balzac. It takes me 12.5 seconds to read a standard photo caption.

I AM ALSO PRONE to distraction, which gives me another bad habit in common with Vonnegut. This comment is based partly on the fact that he dropped out of Butler University, and ditched Cornell after two piss-poor years to join the army, but even more on the fascinating doodles that he left scattered on virtually all of the schoolwork in his archive. I'm thinking in particular of an assignment for Anthropology 220, the back of which bears the following in pencil:

> I Sherwood like to have everything baked with Robinhood flour. Nottingham like it. . . . Many's the time I've Maid Marion in the kitching, baking.

I spent considerably longer than 12.5 seconds (best estimate 17 minutes) studying this inscription. I was most intrigued by the word *kitching*. Was the misspelling intentional, a veiled pun referring to Maid Marion's nether regions? It had such a ribald ring to it. The old *kitching*. Get a load of that *kitching*. That is so, like, *kitching*.

I felt flushed with a strange joy. Vonnegut was a fellow punster! A fellow horndog! I'd gained official access to the sick little kingdom of his mind.

NEAR AS I CAN FIGURE, this doodle dates from his years at the University of Chicago, where he came to get a master's in anthropology. He was just back from the war then, freshly married to his high school sweetheart, twenty-three years old and clearly bored out of his skull by grad school.

What can I tell you about his thesis, "On the Fluctuations Between Good and Evil in Simple Tales"? I can tell you that it sucks almost as badly as my own. His essential argument is against what he calls "the passionate, partisan, rococo argle-bargle of contemporary literary criticism" that unnecessarily complicates the meaning and purpose of stories. The thesis includes hand-drawn graphs tracing the fortunes of characters in various folktales, and devotes twenty pages—nearly half its length—to reprinting a short story by D. H. Lawrence.

What does all this have to do with anthropology?

Not much.

Vonnegut is merely explaining to himself, as I later would, the sort of writer he hopes to become. "Let it be understood," he writes, "that a contemporary master story teller cares deeply about the form of his tales because he is obsessed with being entertaining, with not being a bore, with leaving his audience satisfied." (Translation: *Screw the critics.*) The attributes of his later work are all manifest here—the sharp command of plot, the brutal wit, the contempt for authority.

In 1946, the anthropology faculty unanimously rejected Vonnegut's thesis.[4]

THE NEXT YEAR, Vonnegut moved to Schenectady to work as a public relations writer at General Electric, where his older brother Bernard was a research scientist. He was, to put it mildly, adrift. And here, as a hack on behalf of whizbang technology, with a wife and an infant son to support, Vonnegut made the most foolhardy decision of his brief lifetime: He would become a writer. Worse yet, a short story writer.

His early record was not promising:

"We are sorry to report that this manuscript did not find an opening here" (*The Atlantic,* 1948).

"There is a brisk style to this [*sic*] stories but I'd feel rather dubious that they would take with editors" (Russell & Volkening Literary Agency, 1949).

"Centralized, as it is, around an older character, and placed in a rural setting, it hasn't sufficient plot and pace to go over with the

4. I should mention that I was, to this point, reading as fast as I could and tapping out notes on my computer while also fretting over how little time I had, an activity to which I devoted nearly as much time as the actual note taking. This, if I may be frank, is called Judaism.

younger readers we are trying to attract to the magazine" (*Redbook*, 1949).

The Vonnegut archive contains reams of these rejections. Reading over them sent me into a kind of rapture of indignation. *You fuckers!* I wanted to shout. *Do you know who you're fucking with? Kurt Fucking Vonnegut! Do you realize how fucking stupid you're going to look someday?*

I don't imagine it will come as a surprise that I spent most of the nineties receiving rejections of this sort, sitting around in one or another shithole shouting these same imprecations. Such is the fate of short story writers everywhere. We are captains of a dying industry, drama queens, very poor planners.

I DON'T MEAN TO compare myself with Vonnegut. Or actually, that's bullshit. Of course I mean to compare myself with Vonnegut. (The entire point of my visit to Bloomington was to compare myself with Vonnegut.) What I mean is that my decision to write short stories was a cinch compared to his. I was single. I had supportive parents, savings socked away, a miserable little MFA program where I could spin my training wheels. Vonnegut, on the other hand, had a wife and children and no dough. He was a child of the Depression. He had watched his parents tumble from wealth into hard times, insanity, and self-annihilation. The guy tried to go the straight route, dutifully tromped off to Dad's alma mater and majored in biochemistry, took the office job. Why, then, did he fall off the wagon, into something as disreputable and unreliable as storytelling?

IT WOULD BE EASY enough to say that he was a born writer, which plays to all our romantic notions about talent and destiny, that heroic claptrap we've been peddling to ourselves since *The Iliad*. But I suspect Vonnegut was drawn to writing by something more subversive than his abundant self-regard, something closer to mourning, that dark cloud he kept belching in Hartford. He wouldn't get to the heart of it for another twenty years, but even in his early stories, he seems woefully out of synch with the era.

The fifties were dawning, after all. America was booming! The scientists at GE—as scripted by Vonnegut himself—were promising a brave new world for all those bouncing babies. But he wasn't buying. He could see that technology would do nothing to correct (and might even exacerbate) the essential design flaw, which was human, which resided in our failure to love one another properly, our loyalty to greed and hatred, the gradual hammering of our hearts into swords.

His first published story, "Report on the Barnhouse Effect," stars a scientist who learns to control objects with his mind. He gets recruited by the government as a secret weapon.

AS AN INVETERATE thief of office supplies, I will now note a fact that amuses me beyond all reason: Vonnegut stored his early stories in GE News Bureau folders. On the folder for "The Euphio Question," someone—his wife, Jane, I suspect—has written the following in giant red letters: "Sold to Collier's on February 23, 1951 for $1250!"

And buried in the early drafts of this very story, on the back of a manuscript page, is what ranks as my all-time favorite Vonnegut doodle, a bit of short division:

$$\frac{16}{5000\overline{)80000}}$$

Under this, he has written "16 shorts," and a list of titles. Here was Kurt Vonnegut doing what all ambitious young story writers do—taking inventory, figuring the math, pining after a book. And why not? This was (at least in my imagining of things) an exhilarating era for Vonnegut. After years as the family ne'er-do-well, he could sense that he might actually triumph.

AND CAN I ALSO SAY, while we're not on the subject, what a joy it was to see the handiwork of Vonnegut's own hand, the impatient whir of his mind scattered across all those oniony pages, his letters, his outlines, his plays (Vonnegut wrote plays, dozens of them, who *knew?*) and above all his drafts, corrected, amended, slashed at, his rewrites spilling sideways into the margins, all his *decisions*. Nobody tells you this when you become a writer: that you'll spend 99 percent of your time making decisions.

Thanks to computers, I've been able to flush all *my* bad decisions into cyber oblivion, where, with any luck, they will remain, while my collected works are gathered on a disk the size of a cereal flake.

VONNEGUT'S WRITING schedule for the first two months of 1950 begins like so:

1. Between Timid and Timbuktu (Jan. 6–Jan. 9)
2. The Ants (Jan. 8–Jan. 10)
3. Ice-9 (Jan. 27–Feb. 10)

He lists half a dozen other stories, most written in the space of a few days. The page also includes his schedule for the composition of his first novel, *Player Piano*. He wrote the second chapter in two days, and the whole manuscript in a few months.

Anyone who has struggled with stories, and especially a first novel, will recognize how revoltingly fast Vonnegut was writing, particularly given that he was still working full-time for GE, and that he had two young children at home. The man was a machine.

THIS IS NOT to suggest that he was a flawless machine, or even a particularly profitable one. Most of the three hundred stories gathered in his archive remain unpublished, for good reason. I now find it necessary to quote from "God's Gift to Women," the account of a would-be Lothario nicknamed Gine:

> "Fresh meat for Gine," said Leora, and she smiled like a pirate who had just captured a fresh young beauty, and she looked poor Amy up and down . . .
> "He isn't married."
> "He isn't?" said Amy pipingly.

Yes, *pipingly.*

Most astounding is the number of different ways Vonnegut finds to screw up. His drafts are at once tepid and moralizing, crammed with feckless heroes and labored metaphors. Reading over them was like being trapped in an elevator with my own early stories.

VONNEGUT IS ON record as saying that the reason he writes is so he can edit himself into something approaching charm.[5] I realize that it may come off as a bit of dirty pool to go mucking through his initial efforts, particularly because it gave me an almost obscene pleasure to see Kurt Vonnegut writing so badly.

Or maybe I mean it gave me a twisted sort of faith.

I mentioned above that I don't believe in talent, and what I meant by this is that a knack for the language, the stuff identified early on by well-meaning high school teachers, is about as useful a predictor of literary success as shoe size. When students march into one of my undergrad workshops with *talent,* I regard them as doomed. They are likely to suffer the illusion that writing is about applause rather than humiliation.

But we all come to the keyboard as pitiful supplicants. We all pull the same insecure stunts. We all have our own drawer of horrors. Those who succeed, in the end, are the ones with the biggest drawers.

Which brings us to the file for "The Commandant's Desk." It begins with a 1951 letter addressed to Knox Burger, the editor at *Collier's* who urged Vonnegut to quit his PR job and write full-time.

Dear Knox:

Here, for operation Brandy Alexander, is THE COMMANDANT'S DESK.

I think it's pretty good, and, since I am representing myself in this particular deal, let me say my boy deserves a <u>fat bonus.</u>

5. As far as I can tell, this is the raison d'être of all writers.

I'm selling my house and moving somewhere on the Atlantic Coast, probably Massachusetts. We're renting a place in Provincetown for July, August, and September, and hope you'll pay us a call. . . .[6]

Signed [in pencil]
Kurt Vonnegut

Burger responds with two single-spaced pages of edits. The rest of the file consists of subsequent drafts, six of them by my count. Vonnegut spends two years trying out different narrators, tones, endings. There are notes for further revisions, outlines, more than two hundred pages in all. "The Commandant's Desk" was never published.

VONNEGUT WROTE HIS pal Burger a second fascinating note, but before I could finish transcribing it, I got a tap on the shoulder. "Your wife is outside," the attendant said.

This was good. I had left Erin at the main library, working on her novel. Now I could explain about the no-copying situation, that we might need to stay an extra day. The moment I saw Erin I could tell that was not going to happen.

"Is everything okay?"

She shook her head.

We went outside to talk.

"I'm exhausted," she said. "I can't work here. I need to lie down. I need rest."

"Sure," I said. "Take the day off."

She shook her head and turned away for a moment. When she turned back she was silently weeping.

"I'm sick of this."

---

6. How familiar this all seems to me! The strutting tone, the inside jokes, the desperate whiff of personal ingratiation. How many letters like this have I written to editors over the years?

"Sick of what?" I said.

But I knew what she meant.

I've neglected to mention this, because I've been so hooked on the Vonnegunutia, but upon our arrival in Bloomington, we'd been on the road for three weeks. Erin had spent one of these patiently absorbing the complex distress of my family. She'd slept in Lovelock, Nevada, and Salt Lake City, and York, Nebraska. She'd driven thirty-three hundred miles in a tiny Honda packed to the roof with her worldly possessions. And she had done all this while six months pregnant with our first child. The sun beat down on her pale face.

"I want to go home," she said.

I was torn. I knew I needed to accommodate her needs. I needed not to be a self-absorbed writer jerkoff. At the same time . . . we were in Bloomington. It was all *right here*. Vonnegut had something to tell me, I was convinced of it.

I hugged her for a long time and told her we could leave immediately if she wanted, head straight back to Boston, but that she could also, if it was okay, if she didn't mind, I felt it might be good for her, just for right now, for today, to get a hotel room—a nice one, a *fancy* one—and give herself the day off. Then we'd get dinner and see where things stood.

IT'S WHAT WRITERS DO, this shuck and jive, this nervous dance to balance the emotional needs of those you love against your own need for glory. To quote that other letter to Burger:

Jesus—wouldn't it be nice to write just one play a year, or just one anything?

I've pretty well pooped out as a hack. The old Moxie is gone. As for the book: I like it, I believe in it. But it's disloyal. . . .

Everything's going to be just grand, though. Jane says so. She says she knows it in her bones. And I no kidding believe her. I'd better, with two houses and $20,000 in mortgages.

Vonnegut wrote this in 1955. He was thirty-two years old. His first novel had come and gone. *Sirens of Titan* wouldn't come out for another four years. He was still pumping out the stories, still dreaming about a collection. He had three kids now.

I can't fathom how Vonnegut did it. To think of myself at that age—sitting alone in a rented room, writing my lameass stories, hurling my body at the nearest soft disaster. I was such a punk. And here I was pushing forty, with a tolerant wife and a single baby on the way, a few books under my belt—and *I* felt besieged?

Vonnegut has said in the past that he was lucky, that he began his career during the golden age of magazines, when you could make a living as a story writer. But that's nonsense. The record indicates that the guy was running one continuous hustle. He worked as an English teacher for troubled kids. He ran a Saab dealership. He even tried inventing a board game.[7]

WHEN I TOLD my wife about Vonnegut's scattered endeavors, she said, "He sounds like you." It was evening. We had picked up a pizza and now we were wandering the aisles of a dazzling midwestern supermarket. They had everything: seven kinds of lettuce, im-

---

7. Vonnegut's 1956 letter to Karl Saalfield (president of Saalfield Games) is a classic. It includes twenty pages of specs for "General Headquarters," a troop warfare game best described as a cross between chess, Stratego, and quantum mechanics. On the other side of one particularly baroque diagram I found this oddity, jotted down in Vonnegut's elegant chicken scratch:

In 1925, Hal Irwin had a contractor build him a French Chateau out at 57th and North Meridian Street in Indianapolis.
   There's still old Metzger pear trees out through there, and a lot of em would still bear, if somebody'd think to spray em—hard little pears, taste like rock candy and lemon juice. . . . Hal had had Ella the cook out there, on her days off, rehearsing it

The story stops right here. Vonnegut must have been struck by the idea in the midst of his diagramming. That's the scenario I like best, that his imagination dragged him away from matters of money and war, back to the tawdry precincts of human desire.

ported cheeses, vanilla chai smoothies, the glittering bounty of the cheap oil era, toward which I felt a sudden strange sympathy. A light rain fell outside, streaking the high windows, beading the bright cars beyond. We were so lucky to be living in this time, in this place. We had no idea, really.

It was the same feeling I got out on the road, as we sped across America,[8] through all those little retail environments, with their brightly lit gas stations and calorific convenience stores. They would be dead soon, petroleum ghost towns, like the abandoned farmhouses slowly collapsing off in the distance. So maybe it was nostalgia I was feeling, a kind of pre-nostalgia. These *were* the good old days. Why hadn't I noticed?

I SHOULD RETURN to the Lilly Reading Room, but before I do I want to mention something that goes unmentioned (so far as I could tell) in the Vonnegut archive. In 1958, his older sister Alice succumbed to cancer, two days after her husband's death in a train wreck. Vonnegut adopted three of the couple's four children. His greatest period of artistic growth occurred at a time that he had no fewer than six children in his home.

WHEN WE LAST LEFT our hero, though, he was a young writer bursting with ideas, who spent his days writing short stories, fretting over dough, doodling, and inventing board games. How in the hell did this schlub become Kurt Vonnegut?

8. Ten years ago, when I was applying to grad school, I very nearly decided to attend the University of Alaska at Fairbanks, because I became hopelessly enamored with the idea of driving from my home in Miami Beach to Fairbanks, the northernmost hub of America if you don't count Barrow, which (my apologies to the brave residents of that city) I don't. The route ran 5,021 miles. It was a great plan, very cinematic, its central flaw being that it would oblige me to actually *live* in Fairbanks, which is a hundred miles south of the Arctic Circle and dark up to eighteen hours a day and where—according to a newspaper clipping sent to me by the Chief Curator at the inception of the plan—perfectly innocent citizens are occasionally killed by moose.

I fully intend to answer this question, but to do so, I'll need to share with you a letter the novelist John Irving wrote to Vonnegut, his former teacher, in 1982:

I think you are (and have been for as long as I've known your work) the best writer in this country. Period. I'm afraid I have an almond macaroon for a heart, when it comes to your writing.

I know we are all insecure about what we truly mean. But your books always create the perfect illusion that you know exactly all those parts of the story as you are telling us just one of the parts, and that simply makes everything sound true—makes you the absolute authority. You have to be a writer to feel that.

Günter Grass can give me this impression, too. No one else living gives it. Dickens gave it. Hardy gave it. Well, it's a short list.

This strikes me as an apt description of Vonnegut. His trademark as a writer, the key to his magnetism, resides in the awesome assurance of his voice. His narrators all sound like the same plain-spoken God. I am now ready to reveal the source of Kurt Vonnegut's divine voice: *a shitload of failure.*

I'm not being cute here. To a greater extent than anyone likes to admit, writers evolve simply because they tire of their own mistakes. The best example I can offer happens to be the best book Vonnegut ever wrote, *Slaughterhouse-Five.*

SLAUGHTERHOUSE-FIVE is impossible to describe to anyone who has not read it. It is a mix of science fiction, farce, autobiography, war reportage, and meta-fiction. It is somehow all of these things at once, in the service of a single theme: the chaos of war, which is to say, young men sent to foreign countries to kill strangers. The event at the heart of the novel is the firebombing of Dresden, which burned to death more than 25,000 Germans, nearly all of them civilians, and which Vonnegut survived as a twenty-two-year-old POW. He spent the next two decades trying to write about the experience. And he failed at it, over and over. "Guns Before Butter" begins like so:

> The three American soldiers remained seated within the roofless shell of a building amid the smashed masonry and timbers of Dresden, Germany. The time was early March, 1944. Kniptash, Donnini, and Coleman were prisoners of war.

All his initial war stories are like this: hard-bitten and stagy. The characters are thin as dimes. What matters in them are the episodes that keep cropping up—a man is shot for stealing a teapot, another almost dies on a boxcar—memories that would haunt Vonnegut until he exorcised them in *Slaughterhouse-Five.*

BY THE TIME Vonnegut took up Dresden again, in the late sixties, he was riding an unbelievable hot streak. He had published four novels in the space of six years, including the masterpiece *Cat's Cradle,* for which the University of Chicago would award him a belated master's degree. He was a bestselling author. You might assume that he tore through *Slaughterhouse-Five.*

He did not.

His initial draft—at least the initial draft that made its way to Bloomington—is a standard-issue war story, starring a scarred veteran named Weary. "Three in our labor unit in Dresden died," it begins, wearily.

By his second draft, Vonnegut has come to recognize the necessity of personal confession. But he has lost the struggle against his own nihilism:

> I used to pretend, even to myself, that I was deeply sorry about Dresden, tinkered with the idea of writing a book about the massacre with neatly underplayed indignation. But these things happen and there is no stopping them, so the hell with them. . . . The American conscience is dead.

The human conscience is dead. It has almost certainly always been dead.

Elsewhere, no doubt as a compensatory measure, he comes off as glib.

That is why the name of this book is "Slaughterhouse-Five."
Zowie.
Whiz-bang.
Mother, pin a rose on me.
Wow.
Some title for a war book. And how.

Vonnegut actually crossed out this passage. He knew he was playing to the balconies. And that's what I'm getting at here. Vonnegut needed to make all these mistakes. He needed to work through his anger, his evasions, his boredom with conventional approaches. By the third draft, he has found an outlet for his exuberance, in a campy science fiction subplot. He has also found the humility that precedes absolution. There is an air of surrender to the narrative, which begins, "I would hate to tell you what this lousy little book cost me in money and anxiety and time." He is done lying to the reader, done posing, done pretending his own depression and failure are not part of the story.

I fucking love that about Vonnegut.

ANOTHER WAY TO put it would be this:

He himself was the most enchanting American at the heart of each of his tales. We can forgive this easily, for he managed to imply that the reader was enough like him to be his brother.

Vonnegut said this about his hero Twain, though he was speaking about himself too, as we always do. That is the great game writers play: pretending what we do is a matter of superior imagination, or empathy, when, in fact, our defining impulse is a desire to be noticed.

OF VONNEGUT'S MANY speeches, most notable is his 1981 tribute to the labor leader Eugene Debs, a fellow Hoosier. He quotes the words Debs uttered before being sentenced to twenty years in prison for speaking out against World War I: "While there is a lower class, I am in it; while there is a criminal element, I am of it; while there is a soul in prison, I am not free." Vonnegut then asks,

> How many of us can echo those words and mean them? If this were a decent nation, we would all find those sentiments as natural and easy to say as, "Good morning. It looks like another nice day."
> But the star system has made us all ravenous for the slightest proofs that we matter to the American story, somehow, at least a little bit more than someone else.

Reading these words, I thought about the Reality TV show Erin and I had watched the night before, something called *My Super Sweet Sixteen,* in which a teenage girl from Scottsdale celebrates her birthday with a $150,000 party, and two new cars. In one scene, she stands in front of her school in a tiara and presents invitations to the other cool kids, while the ugly and poor watch. Two undesirables begin to beg for invites and she allows them to dance for her on the sidewalk, while she and her friends insult them.

It would be natural enough to express disgust for this lunatic display. But all I felt watching that girl was the terrible misery inside her, her monstrous need to be popular, which has become our national aspiration.

INCLUDED IN THE speech file is a sheet of paper that includes random notes, mostly political rants of the sort Vonnegut produces at the drop of a hat, along with these two humdingers:

Something you should know about me: Geraldo Rivera
Question of the hour. Does penis size really matter?

I'm not sure what prompted the penis size question, though Vonnegut's obsession with this topic is well documented. I'm fairly certain he's the only writer (other than myself) ever to write a novel in which the male characters are identified by the length and girth of their johnsons.

The Geraldo thing is a little less cryptic; for a brief time Geraldo was married to one of Vonnegut's daughters.

That is so, like, *ick.*

BY THE SEVENTIES, Vonnegut was himself famous. (Not as famous as Geraldo. But who is?) He had written himself into his work. He had become a renowned speaker, an icon to malcontents and pacifists everywhere. Now came the deluge. Letters. Mountains of them. From Günter Grass and Herman Wouk and John Updike. From Marlo Thomas and Julie Nixon Eisenhower and Laurie Anderson. From Larry Flynt. ("My attorney is seeking a well-known and respected author who would be willing to offer expert testimony as to the literary merit of *Hustler.*") Mostly, from guys like me who fell in love with him and developed the absurd but inevitable notion that he might fall in love right back. Such tender notes of worship! They fill three boxes.

HONESTLY, I DON'T like this part of the movie. The stuff that excited me—Vonnegut's era of struggle, his lean and hungry ascent—is over now. We've reached the part where the privileges of fame overtake suspense.

Vonnegut continues to write novels, many of them quite good, but none feel groundbreaking, the way the early books did. He continues to say the right things, with tremendous eloquence, but his actions don't jibe. He divorces his first wife and takes up with a more glamorous model. He gets a place in the Hamptons. He writes a letter entreating Jack Nicholson to read a script for *Breakfast of Champions*.

Does Kurt Vonnegut sell out?

Sure. He sells out like hell. He's flattered by the money and the praise, by the innocent belief that commercial attention means his ideas are being heeded.

He gets himself a fancy New York lawyer, too, to sort through all the contracts and letters and such, the infamous Donald Farber. "I was dumb enough to join a health club," reads one of his notes to Farber. "It now bores me shitless. I no longer use it. I enclose my lifetime membership. . . . Would you take steps to break off the connection?"

How's that for mid-career decadence?

IT WAS NEARLY closing time at the Reading Room of the Lilly Library. I had not read four thousand documents in the allotted 840 minutes. More like four hundred. My eyes were burning. Soon, my wife would be waiting for me outside, gorgeously swollen, perhaps weeping at my inconsideration.

And so, at this point in my odyssey through Vonnegut's archive, I made a thoroughly stupid (by which I mean rather typical) decision. I watched Vonnegut on TV. The archive contained several programs, the most excruciating of which was a 1989 interview with Charlie Rose, during which Vonnegut admits that he watches TV "all the time," in particular *The People's Court*. Then comes this exchange:

VONNEGUT: People have two houses, one in the country and the city.

ROSE: Do you have that?

VONNEGUT: I do.

ROSE: I know, so do I—and we shouldn't want that?

VONNEGUT: No, I don't think so. And I mean, I wish I didn't own the house in the country, because I wonder what's happened to it over the winter.

ROSE: And you worry about somebody breaking in.
VONNEGUT: Yeah.

Huh?

I know. I know. This is what Americans do. We hold the right beliefs, then do the wrong things. It's been our national specialty, from *All Men Are Created Equal* to *Support the Troops*. Still, it hurt to see Vonnegut reveal himself like this. I had come to Bloomington in the secret hope that the guy would prove a worthy idol, that he had lived by his words, that my faith in him was well placed. And here he was, revealed as a limousine liberal. I felt like I was back at Wesleyan.

IT WAS ON THIS somber note that I left the Lilly Library and sped off into the sunset, or at least as far as the Indianapolis suburbs, where my old pals Gerry and Michelle Lanosga were waiting with a much-needed infusion of wine and a slab of salmon, which Gerry barbecued on a cedar plank. The fish tasted so much like bacon that I suspected he had performed some kind of religious transfiguration.

I'd met the Lanosgas twenty years earlier, at my first job after college. We were reporters in Phoenix. Michelle was engaged to another man and Gerry was stone cold crazy for her. The two of them spent the summer drinking to excess and attending AC/DC concerts and lusting after each other in the brutal, half-requited manner best suited to energetic twenty-two-year-olds. Now they had three boys and all the American bells and whistles.

After dinner, the boys took me down to the basement to meet the great variety of bugs down there. Then it was time for a pillow fight. Then Miles (age eighteen months) took a header from the lip of the fireplace. It felt a lot like the house I grew up in, in terms of unconstrained boy energy. And I wondered, as I lay next to my sleeping wife that night, if any of these boys would fall for Vonnegut in the way I had. The wine had made me hokey; that was true. But it felt like an important question. The world really was going to run out of oil. It might not happen in our lifetimes, but it would happen in theirs. And our citizens—so infantilized by abundance, so well armed—would then face a mortal challenge: to look beyond themselves, to care more for each other. It doesn't come naturally for most boys. They'd need someone like Vonnegut, someone smart and funny and forgiving, to show them the way. So I made myself one of those hokey, wine-soaked promises: to send each of those boys a Vonnegut book for his sixteenth birthday.

WE SPENT TWO MORE days on the road. Erin did most of the driving, while I glared at the gas guzzlers around us and imagined that I was somehow better than the drivers who glared back at me. It's one of my favorite pastimes.

I should have enjoyed the drive. I knew it would be our last for a long time. But we were racing to get somewhere, like always, like everyone. We were treating America like the big floozy she so frequently consents to be. In Ohio, it was surly road crews, chunked-up road, the stink of tar. In Pennsylvania, it was distant hills and shitty drivers. And everywhere, the same shining fast food symbols. This was America by superhighway: beautiful curves and no ideas.

Twenty miles outside Erie, we blew a tire at 70 mph. I needed to get the car onto the shoulder, but the drivers in the right lane wouldn't let me in and the shuddering got worse and finally the back of the car began to smoke and we lost speed and I knew for a moment that it was all going to end; I had a terrible vision of crushed steel and blood. Then some brave soul decided to take pity on us and let me into the right lane and I lurched onto the shoulder. The tire had shredded down to the rim. The sign directly in front of us read: *No Shoulder—½ Mile Ahead.* A semi screamed past. The blast of air nearly knocked me to the ground. Erin had gone white with dread.

"Stay in the car," I shouted.

I unpacked the trunk and laid her possessions on the weedy embankment and pulled out the feeble little spare tire and set about failing to change it. This took twenty minutes. Then I stood by the highway and watched the traffic whip past, clenched and joyless faces. From this new perspective, I could see the psychosis of our arrangement. We had become dependent on machines that allowed us to traverse the land without in any way experiencing it, and worse yet to feel this was the natural order of things. It was a kind of violence, to pass by each other at such speeds. Was it really such a surprise that terrorists had turned our vehicles into weapons?

THIS, IN CASE YOU'RE wondering, is how we wound up at the Wal-Mart in Erie, Pennsylvania, on the Friday before July 4. I had vowed never to give Wal-Mart any of my money, but they were the only place available to fix our tire at that hour, or anyway, they were the most convenient, so we gave them our dough, gratefully, and got back on the road and then we gave the assholes at Holiday Inn our dough, then the assholes at Exxon, and by 2 P.M. the next day we had arrived at our new house in the unsustainable suburbs, where I had vowed for many years I would never live. So this was me being an American, no better than my own purchases.

I should have felt a sense of relief at having conveyed my precious cargo safely home. But doing the Vulcan Mind Meld with Vonnegut for two days had upset me. I didn't know how to feel about the guy, if I still wanted to be him when I grew up. To sit there, day after day, immersed in the question of whether humankind would survive its own despicable conduct? God had proved an abject failure. Science, the great hope of his youth, had delivered us a hundred new ways to kill and a few spare miracles. Americans enjoyed unprecedented material comfort, and yet they grew sadder every day, more frightened and lonely and mean. Literary prophet wasn't seeming like such a dream job.

And here I can feel myself struggling for the happy ending, something inspiring about my daughter and the wish that our better angels might still prevail, how the empty fuel can will slow us down, humble us into empathy, maybe even help us reestablish those big, happy families we never had. But that's bullshit.

Kurt Vonnegut became a writer expressly to oppose such bullshit, to articulate the true woe of his circumstance. Most of this woe, incidentally, came not from Dresden or Vietnam or Iraq—not from the Family of Man, that is—but from his own family, from the insoluble loss of those he wished to love, and from those small, private moments when two people who should love each other fail to do so.

I remind you now what Vonnegut told the crowd down in Hartford: *I write again and again about my family.*

Vonnegut never got over those moments, and he turned to language to express his wrath and disappointment. He did so with such elegance and humor and mercy that he turned me into a writer, too. I love him for that. And I'll also never forgive him.

Postscript

On April 11, 2007, Kurt Vonnegut died of injuries sustained during a fall in his Manhattan home. He was eighty-four. When I received word, I couldn't help but think of that moment in Hartford when Vonnegut rose from his chair and stepped slowly, so gingerly, over that errant microphone cord.

Someone was cruel enough to send me a link to the Fox News coverage. The reporter cited Vonnegut's "unique brand of despondent leftism," which struck me as an apt reflection of Fox's unique brand of thrift-store fascism. I couldn't bring myself to scan any of the other obits. I knew what they said, all the praise mustered for such occasions.

Vonnegut would have been revolted. As a younger man, he had lusted after acclaim. He thought people were actually listening to him, a respectable Christian mistake. Vonnegut was an atheist, of course. No sweet dreams of heaven for him. No jokes tossed down to the suckers in purgatory. He leaves us his books, his pleas for kindness, his foolish hope for our salvation.

{

About
My Sexual
Failure

(Not that You Asked)

SHAME ON ME

WHY MY ADOLESCENCE SUCKED DONKEY COCK

Hot Tub

I am twelve. My parents, in authentic Northern California style, have installed a hot tub in the backyard, a sweet redwood job with a deck. I am vaguely aware of my cock at this age, nothing specific. I can't imagine a girl touching it. I can't imagine what it might do if touched. I haven't yet acquired that glorious pathetic byproduct of male socialization: cock consciousness, which is to say cock vanity, cock insecurity, cock *issues*.

One evening I jump into the tub wearing only thin nylon soccer shorts. It's just past dusk. The purple clouds are seeping off into black. My parents and brothers are gone for the night and I am feeling—I guess the proper word is *naughty*. I pull off my shorts and fling them onto the deck and stand before one of the jets and suddenly there's this, this . . . twinge. I sit down immediately. I try to keep still. My immediate suspicion is that I've done something very wrong. Then, somehow, I am facing the jet again.

I am facing the jet and I am rock hard and holding myself firmly around the base. I let the water pound that one right spot, which is—though I don't know this yet—where the nerves bundle below the tip. I push so close I'm blocking the jet, and nearly stumble with the feeling. The sensation inside my body is percussive, ecstatic, approaching violence. I reel backward and slam against the side of the tub.

Within a minute, I have assumed the position again. It takes longer this time and it stings and I could care less. By my fourth go-round, I am in considerable pain and sporting what looks like a cock hickey.

This goes on for months. One evening, I am almost caught by a friend of my mother's, who bursts outside to find me straddling a jet, my eyes shut, shorts clenched deliriously in my fist.

"*Oh,*" she says.

"I'm really sore from soccer," I yell quickly. "I pulled a muscle."

My brothers, like other normal boys, have already discovered the ardent tugging of terrestrial masturbation. Low-grade porn. Jergens. Kleenex. But it doesn't happen for me until the following year.

I am shocked, horrified, to discover the physical consequences of my habit, that something actually *comes* out when you come, and that (by rather unfortunate extension) I have been defiling the family hot tub for months. I am disgusted with myself and incapable of stopping. In the loneliness of youth, in the bruising doubts of boyhood, these moments become precious. With the fragrance of damp redwood thick around me and the jets blasting, I am precisely what I want to be: a brief ribbon of joy in black water.

Exam

I am sitting in the waiting room of our pediatrician, Joe Davis, with my brothers and our mother. Mike and I are thirteen. Dave is fifteen. We are all feeling vaguely embarrassed, not just by the ritual of our annual checkup ("Turn your head . . . now please cough . . .") but by having to sit on bright red chairs intended for five-year-olds.

Dr. Davis appears in the doorway and calls my mother over. Because she is also a doctor, he takes a certain professional pride in speaking with her personally. He glances down at his clipboard and announces the following results:

"Almond, David: pubescent male."

"Almond, Michael: pubescent male."

"Almond, Steven: *pre*-pubescent male."

Dr. Davis does not whisper these words. No, they come booming out of him, as if my mother were standing across a busy street instead of where she is actually standing—*right next to him.*

Becoming pubescent is all I have thought about for the last year. During this time, Dave has developed a set of shoulders worthy of Greek sculpture, while Mike, my upstart twin, has acquired facial hair and undeniable B.O. His body reeks of manhood. I, meanwhile, have remained stranded in some kind of post-latency limbo. Every evening before falling asleep, I pull down my pajama bottoms to check signs. I am so familiar with the hairs on the underside of my scrotum that I have considered naming them.

My mother is still talking to Dr. Davis, whom I now decide I will poison. I will poison him so badly that his tongue will fall out and it will be blue. Mike and Dave are sitting next to me, but neither one looks over. No smirks. No giggles. No innocent questions such as "Have you tried asking the tooth fairy for a real penis?" The brutality of the disclosure has preempted even their capacities for cruelty.

It will dawn on me only in the parking lot, as Mike and Dave launch into an earnest discussion of Estes Rocket technology, that the revelation of my pre-pubescence—which I have shouldered these many months, and which I have deluded myself into regarding as a private burden—is, in fact, so obvious, so taken for granted, that it no longer registers as a possible source of mockery.

Handjob

I am at Camp Tawonga. Tawonga is where Jewish kids from the Bay Area come to learn about creating community and respecting nature's harmony and getting handjobs. It is located somewhere near Yosemite. The word *tawonga* is derived from the Miwok Indians. In Miwok, it means "handjob."

I have been going to Tawonga since I was six. I am now fourteen. Girls at Tawonga look upon me favorably because I have a cool older brother and I once fell down a waterfall and because the standards of masculine pulchritude at Tawonga are frighteningly low. The guys in my cabin are a mess of acne and orthodontia.

At camp, I always find a girlfriend. This year, her name is Natalie. We slow danced at the costume party, though I had poison ivy all over my body and was therefore encased in a green polyester sweatsuit. She was dressed as a Playboy bunny. From a distance, we looked like a tree feeling up an underaged porn star.

Natalie has the nicest tits I have ever seen. They are big and brown and fluted at the nipple. I have spent hours rubbing and licking them. Sometimes, if we are in a private place, such as the dugout of the auxiliary softball field, I will lift her Lacoste shirt and gaze at them, so as to be overwhelmed by their perfect tittiness.

Natalie is a year younger than I am, but she lives in San Francisco. She is a city girl, and this means—if I have done my math right—she will touch my dick. She has already felt my dick with other parts of her body, such as mainly her belly and tush, because, unless specifically directed not to, I am grinding against her at all times. With my body I am saying to her: *You feel that? You feel that, baby? That's what we call in these parts a D-I-C-K!* The night before the session ends, our cabins go on an overnight together. We have been waiting two weeks for this chance. The campfire burns down. Natalie and I sneak off to a secluded patch of sand beside the Tuolumne River, where we dry hump ineptly for three and a half hours.

"This is our last night," she says, dramatically.

"It should be special," I say, dramatically.

"I know," she says, dramatically.

I pull down my underwear dramatically.

Natalie knows this is coming. She slips her hand under the sleeping bag and takes hold and begins, well, *yanking* is probably the best word.

I want to give her some direction, but I'm not in a very good position to do so because I am terrified that if I say anything she will stop, and because I myself don't really know how to jerk off, because my primary form of onanism has to date involved the use of the hot tub as sexual aid.

Natalie continues to yank, as if I were a particularly stubborn weed.

"How does that feel?" she whispers.

"Good," I say. "Really . . . good."

But her fingernails are scratching me, the tender skin is rending. Natalie is looking into my eyes and I am trying not to wince and playing with her epic boobs and wondering what happens if her nail actually slices through the thin skin that encases what I will later learn (in health class) to call the spongy tissue. I close my eyes and see a sausage slipping from its casing.

"Can you make it slippery?" I say.

Natalie dabs her tongue on the curve of skin between her thumb and index finger. My handjob now exudes the faint scent of Watermelon Bubble Yum, and things move much faster. Within a minute, I start to feel the unmistakable tremors. But the more excited I get, the more I squirm, and the more I squirm, the further in her nails dig, until, on the very threshold of release, I blurt out, "I better take over now!" and tear myself away from her just in time to inseminate the sand.

The next day, we hold hands on the bus the whole way and talk about how this isn't just a summer thing. It is something much deeper. We are soulmates. We have licked one another's souls. We are soulmate lickers.

Natalie is getting off in San Francisco, so we have our final farewell. All around us, other campers are singing about West Virginia, mountain mama, and Natalie is sitting on my lap, whispering, "I'll miss you, I'll miss you so much," and I want to thank her—for her shy foolish notes, for her feet, which are grubby and beautiful in yellow flip-flops, for the hickeys that ring her neck like plum skins, for the night in the arts and crafts shed when the lights blacked out and she fell against me without a thought.

But I am fourteen, so I say only, "That was the best handjob *ever.*"

Speedo

Back home, I am just another freshman. I wear knockoff polo shirts and Jacomo cologne from free sample bottles I forage at the mall. I try out for the soccer team, but get cut after I kick the ball directly at Scott Sutcher's head during a drill. "It was a mistake," I tell the coach. "My foot slipped." My brother Mike goes out for and makes the swim team. This makes no sense. I am the designated jock of the family.

I have no intention of ever attending one of Mike's swim meets. We do not attend each other's extracurriculars, as this would violate the unspoken Code of Fraternal Disregard. But I need a ride to my job scooping ice cream, and my dad says picking up Mike is part of the deal. We arrive just as the meet is ending. My brother climbs from the pool and huddles with his teammates.

Seeing his body is something of a shock. The uncoordinated pudge of our youth has grown into a swan: long, muscular, absurdly handsome. And then he is walking toward me and my shock redoubles. His Speedo. My God—there is something of great masculine significance in there, barely contained.

This should not come as a surprise. He is my twin brother. But strange as this may sound, I have never seen him or Dave naked. We are too fragile for such acts of self-exposure, though it now occurs to me, as Mike pulls a towel modestly around his waist, that perhaps he has been trying to spare me.

A few weeks later, I sneak into his room and try on one of his Speedos. I am thinking that maybe, just maybe, it is the suit that makes the man. I gaze at myself in the mirror and it takes me a few seconds to even *find* my dick.

Horse

Sophomore year, I develop a fierce crush on a girl named Suzie. But she takes up with a kid who is reputed to have a schlong on the equine scale. He is on the swim team with Mike. Apparently, the central qualification for this team is a *really big cock*.

Everywhere I turn, I encounter really big cocks. The focus on them is relentless, almost religious in nature. One of the enduring myths of these years concerns an alleged tryst between Tim Hollins and the unfortunately named Holly Kooch. As the tale goes, penetration is never achieved because Hollins is *too big* to fit inside. I fantasize about this attempted coupling constantly—I place them on a blanket at dusk, the light dreamy and sylvan—not because I have a raging crush on Holly (though I do), but because I envy Hollins. Too big to fit inside! My God! It seems the greatest male achievement one could hope for.

The Cult of the Big Cock is rampant. We all seem to know who among us has a big cock and we treat them with an unspoken deference. Eric Rulifson berates me after I tease another kid for having pimples: "George may have some zits, but he also has *a nine-inch cock,*" a defense so devastating I am left speechless.

My pal Jon Carnoy and I spend hours discussing the cock size of the guys on our soccer team. On those occasions when our homovanity revs high, we spank ourselves to a state of tumescence and measure. If you pie-chart my psyche at any point during high school, *big cocks and consequent ideation* will occupy 79 percent of my waking life.

Lizzie

I am in the backyard, playing Ping-Pong against the warped backboard. Neither of my brothers will play me anymore, so I make believe I'm up against Adolf Hitler, with the fate of the Jews hanging in the balance. To summarize: I am bored.

Dave appears at the back door. He has a look of barely suppressed joy on his face; I will soon endure humiliation.

"What?" I say.

"Mom wants to see you."

"About what?"

I find my mother in my father's study—not a good sign. She is seated at the desk. The recliner is for me. I am fifteen years old, a junior. I have been in my *awkward phase* for nine years.

"Well," she says. "Steven." She sets her hands carefully on her lap. "I want to say, to begin with, that I'm very glad you're using protection."

My mother is staring at me, having just made direct reference to my use of a condom and therefore, in my mind, to my penis, an action that strikes me as a betrayal of certain founding mother/son principles. But my mother is a no-nonsense type, a psychiatrist who spends her days listening to graphic kvetchings.

"I recognize that you and Pamela have become sexually active. I'm proud of you for choosing to do so responsibly."

I make a clucking noise.

I do not think to question how it is that my mother has figured out that I am having sex with Pam. That is way beyond me. I am still trying to fit my penis and my mother into the same room without puking.

"There is one thing we need to talk about," my mother says. "Yesterday when I came home from work Lizzie was playing with something on the oriental rug, chewing on something."

Lizzie is our new Labrador retriever. She is a frantic puppy who will soon grow into a frantic dog and be shipped off to a farm. She chews on everything. The only one of us who exerts any control over Lizzie is Mike, who French-kisses her with alarming frequency. My mother waits for me to make the logical connection.

I do not.

"I didn't know what Lizzie was chewing on," my mother says slowly. "So I went over to see what it was."

I am still not getting it, because my brain has a good habit of locking up when in the presence of large, mortifying revelations.

"I went over to see what it was," my mother repeats. "And, as it so happened, she was chewing on a condom. A, uh, *used* condom."

My reaction to this news is physiologically complicated. I begin sweating. My sphincter goes into a lengthy spasm. A vision comes to me of my mother walking over to Lizzie and bending down to figure out what she is chewing on and realizing what it is and *sighing* the sort of sigh that only the mother of three teenage boys can sigh and staring down at Lizzie and the condom, saying *Bad dog! Bad dog!* and trying to decide what the hell to do. She is a neat freak. She is a neat freak particularly when it comes to the oriental rug, which is hand-knotted and beautiful, with intricate designs I have spent many many stoned hours inspecting, a rug that frankly has no business in the living room, that belongs in a boy-and-dog-proof vault. My mother tells Lizzie to *sit* and to *drop it,* but Lizzie will not, so my mom finally grabs the edge of the used condom, which, to Lizzie, signals that it's time to *play.* She starts shaking her head like hyper dogs do and clamps down on the condom, which, thanks to the sharpness of her teeth, has punctured already, such that when my mother tries to pull it away the latex tears and my mother is spattered (perhaps in her actual face) with my semen.

So now I've got this invasive thought in my head (thanks, head!), which I know to be wildly inappropriate and, which I know, what's more, as the child of two psychiatrists, suggests some pretty unsavory things about me in terms of my Oedipal Complex and my hostility toward women and the likelihood (awfully likely) that I will grow into a sexual deviant who seduces women in the unconscious hope of staining them with my semen, and/or has sexual relations with dogs. I glance at my mother. She has that look that says: *I know what you are thinking, Steven.* So I say to her (in my head), *Oh yeah? What am I thinking?* And she says (in my head, quite calmly), *Your father and I have discussed the matter. We both feel these thoughts are within the normal range of adolescent neuroses, and nothing that thirty-five years of therapy won't cure.*

Back in reality, my mother is saying something like, "Lizzie must have found it in the bathroom . . ." But I am having trouble making out the words because I'm in the midst of what amounts to a grand mal seizure. At a certain point her mouth stops moving and I nod and mutter an apology. I am profoundly thankful she does not try to hug me.

I stumble back to my room. My brothers are standing in the doorways to their rooms shaking their heads, and I see now that I am not the first son called into the study; I am in fact the third and final son she has spoken to this afternoon, the one she has judged least likely to be having sex, an implied fact that only magnifies the horror of the entire Lizzie/used-condom episode, which is now—thanks to my brothers—public property to be invoked at their leisure.

Penis, Failing

Again, unfortunately, I am fifteen years old. I have somehow managed to become a regular on a program called *TV-20 Dance Party*, which features teenagers from around the Bay Area dancing to songs such as "99 Luftballons" and "Don't You Want Me." The year is 1982, so everyone is dressed in clothing that, just a few years later, will have to be burned.

It is unclear to me how I became a regular on this program, as there is only one dance I know how to do, which is that strange maneuver that Molly Ringwald showcased in *The Breakfast Club,* which requires one leg to be kicked out while the upper body jerks in the opposite direction. Imagine a Rockette with epilepsy. Now make the Rockette into a teenage boy with tapered tartan surf pants and chin acne. That is me. Hello.

It is a Tuesday in June and *TV-20 Dance Party* is taping live this afternoon, so I head over to Pam's house to pick her up. The moment I arrive she whispers, *My mom is gone.* This means we can have sex. It is our seventh time. We kiss deeply, madly, incompetently. We grope. We do the sort of spastic undressing expected of teenagers having sex for the seventh time. We're on Pam's bed. She is lying naked, her strawberry-blond snatch glistening. Summer has left an adorable scattering of freckles on her breasts. Pam is stroking me and saying *Put it in, put it in.* But I cannot put it in because I will come if I do.

"Let me put something on," I say.

This is the central benefit of condom use, as far as I am concerned: It helps me not come before intercourse. I am hoping to retreat to the bathroom and give my cock a few stern whacks with the back of my hand, which, I have been led to believe by Jon Carnoy, will draw me back from the brink. But Pam reaches under her pillow and hands me a condom.

"I want you inside," she murmurs.

"Let me taste you first," I say.

She shakes her head.

I stare down at her face, her lovely, blushing body. She raises her legs a bit, lets her knees fall apart, repeats that phrase, *I want you inside,* and I realize, with crushing clarity, that I will never enjoy a moment of such exquisite arousal again. I tear the package open and reach down. The simple act of touching the condom against the head of my cock—not unrolling, mind you, just touching—sends me over the brink. Pam's body lies unfurled beneath me. She is saying *I'm ready! I'm so ready!* I close my eyes and curse silently, then ejaculate into my cupped palm.

It is absolutely essential that Pam *not know* what just happened. I tell her I have to go pee, which is something that women—even recently postvirginal women in a state of extreme want—seem to understand. In the bathroom, I wash my hands. I glare at my dick for a while. I sit on the toilet and try to conjure an image from one of the porno mags that, thrillingly, has appeared under the sink of the downstairs bathroom at home. When this doesn't work, I grab a box of Pam's tampons. I am hoping—what?—maybe there's some kind of hot insertion illustration. But there is only a paragraph about Toxic Shock Syndrome, which does not help.

A car pulls up to the house and Pam's mom appears in the courtyard, humming the theme of her favorite soap, which would usually be a very bad thing, but which I now view as something akin to divine intervention. I dash back into Pam's room. She is off the bed, hurrying her tits into a bikini top. I pull on my boxers and we both head for the pool in her backyard. *Oh, hi, Mom. Nothing. Just swimming.*

Two hours later, we are standing around in a warehouse studio with two dozen other teens, waiting for "The Safety Dance" to start blaring, so we can enact moments of *spontaneous teen behavior.* The couple next to us is making out. She is a tiny blonde and he is a tall

Latin guy who (of course) appears to have some kind of large tuber in his jeans. It seems terribly wrong that I should be allowed on TV.

Assailant

I am in Long's Drugs, shoplifting with Tommy Tatum. This is a fairly routine activity, though, for reasons I cannot fully explain, on this occasion we are shoplifting items from the exhilarating *Health* section. Actually, Tommy is not stealing stuff; he is merely encouraging me to do so. I am wearing a tank top and soccer shorts. This is not appropriate shoplifting garb. It is possibly the worst outfit one could select for such a purpose. Nonetheless, I have come to steal, and there is very little that can prevent a troubled suburban boy from stealing if he has set his mind to the task.

I am not sure whether it is Tommy or me who picks up the Sta-Hard Gel, but I do remember that we are both instantly spellbound. The product comes in a sleek little tube and it promises we will give our partners *climax after climax* by helping the user control his *natural ejaculatory function.* It does this by *de-sensitizing the regions instrumental to male climax.* "It numbs the end of your dick!" Tommy observes helpfully. It is immediately implied that I must steal the Sta-Hard Gel.

I have already tucked a package of ribbed condoms into the lining of my soccer shorts, which should be enough. But Pam is not enjoying climax after climax when we have sex. In point of fact, she has not enjoyed climax. Naturally, this has become a source of angst for me. Unlike other boys, who are happy enough to be having orgasms with another person, I have come to see Pam's inability to orgasm as a reflection of my enfeebled manhood. I am always pressing the matter, working her body with a certain grim, unrelenting ardor, as if it were a new category on the SAT test. This is not working.

And so, while Tommy views the Sta-Hard Gel as a gag, I am secretly taken with the notion that it may be the answer to my dilemma. I fold the cardboard packaging in half and slip the tube into my shorts. We make our way to the register, where we buy packs of Big Red gum, so as to be viewed as legitimate customers.

The cashier is a girl named Becca. I attempted to scam on her freshman year. She says hello to Tommy.

We are heading for the exit when we hear a commotion behind us. A large black man is sprinting past the registers. He is shouting something I can't quite make out. During one of those wonderful racist half-seconds to which white people are so dependably prone, I decide that he must be an armed robber. Then it becomes clear that the guy is actually store security.

"Wow," I say. "Someone is totally busted."

Tommy nods.

We are rapt now, watching this guy sprint across the store. There is nothing more pleasurable for teenage boys than watching someone else get busted. It is not until the guy leaps past the register nearest to us that it begins to dawn on me: I am rubbernecking my own arrest.

"Don't move, don't even *think* about moving!" the guy shouts, and I say—oh, Christ, I have no idea what I say. I do know that I am *not moving*.

"Please take the products out of your pants," the guard says.

"What?" I say.

"You heard me."

Tommy shakes his head. He is muttering *dude* in a manner that is both sympathetic and deeply contemptuous.

I reach into my shorts and take out the ribbed condoms.

"The other one too."

"What other one?" I say.

The guard glowers down at me in a bored way. He has all day.

I pull out the Sta-Hard Gel and hand it over.

"Why did you steal these things?"

I say nothing.

"Do you have any money?"

"No," I whisper.

"Does your friend?"

Tommy nods.

The guard looks at both of us. He seems confused by our incompetence. He tells us to stay where we are and walks over to Becca's register and inspects the items I have stolen. The entire store—this is a big store, with a dozen registers—has come to a standstill. The guard could just hand the items to the cashier, but this is his moment in the sun. He has captured a criminal. He begins describing them for Becca, like they are suddenly doing inventory.

"Trojans. Ribbed. Twelve-pack. Got that?"

Becca nods.

The guard looks at the little tube in puzzlement.

"What is this stuff? Stay-Hard Gel?"

He is speaking loud enough for everyone to hear him. But what strikes me is how he pronounces the first word (correctly). I have been pronouncing the S-T-A phonetically in my head and wondering what it might stand for.

"What's the total?" the guard says.

Becca informs him.

He turns to Tommy. "Do you have enough money to pay for the condoms and the Stay-Hard Gel that your friend attempted to steal?"

Tommy nods.

The guard shakes his head. "Come with me," he calls out. "No, not you. Just the assailant. You pay for the items."

He leads me (the assailant) across the store and to a backroom. We climb some stairs to a little office and begin the formal interrogation.

"Why did you steal those items?"

"My girlfriend needed me to get condoms. I didn't have the money."

"But your friend had money."

"I know. It was stupid. I'm sorry."

"I understand you got yourself a little lady, you need protection. But you got to pay for that stuff. You know that."

"I know," I say. "It was stupid."

"You got to be *responsible*."

"I know."

"How old are you?"

"Sixteen."

"Sixteen. You should know better."

"I know," I say. "I *should* know better."

The guard nods, which I mistake for impending clemency.

"I gotta call your parents," he says.

This has not occurred to me.

"My parents are out of town for the weekend," I say.

Oddly, this is true. My uncle is in town, "supervising" us.

"I gotta call your house anyway," he says skeptically.

This is the worst scenario of all, because either Mike or Dave will answer the phone, and when they find out it's someone from Long's Drugs they will immediately sniff out the situation and the one who answers the phone will pretend to be my uncle, or will promise to fetch our uncle, then hurriedly explain the situation to the other brother, who will assume the role of my uncle on the phone. Thus the full story will emerge (caught shoplifting, Sta-Hard Gel), and my penis—tiny, ineffectual—will climb up inside my body and refuse to come out ever again.

I am close to tears now. My body slumps forward. I begin begging. This goes on for several minutes. My voice is shaky. I am offering him my misery. I am saying to him: *Don't you get it? I am my own worst punishment.* It feels like the logical culmination of my teenage years: to be so exposed before a stranger with a plastic badge.

At a certain point the expression on the guard's face softens. He shakes his head slowly and tells me he's going to let me off this time, though I am banned for life from Long's Drugs.

I begin slinking toward the door.

"Why you wanna steal that stuff anyway, man?" the guard says suddenly. "That's like putting Ben-Gay on your equipment."

"I wasn't thinking clearly," I say.

"You a young man," he says. "No need for that. Just do it once, then come back for seconds, you understand?"

"Yessir," I say.

I walk down the stairs bursting with gratitude. I have just received the most useful sexual advice of my life to date.

Becca waves as I exit the store.

Tommy is waiting for me out front. "That looked rough," he says.

"What do you mean?"

"We could see right into that guy's office, dude."

By turning on the light, the guard had transformed his one-way mirror into a full-length window, through which, as Tommy enthusiastically informs me, the entire population of the store watched the unfolding drama of my non-arrest.

"Were you crying?" Tommy says. "It looked like you were crying."

I do not answer.

CHESTFRO AGONISTE

Why, exactly, did I feel it would be "sexy" and "hot" to have my girlfriend wax my chest? I can offer no good answer to this question today, ten years after the event. I could offer no good answer at the time. What I could offer was a rather far-fetched fantasy, which involved (as far-fetched fantasies so often do) a byzantine set of sub-fantasies. They ran something like this:

1. My girlfriend and I would do a whole bunch of Ecstasy
2. At a certain point, she would disappear into her closet and emerge dressed like Catwoman
3. Warm wax would magically appear in her paw
4. She would caress said wax onto my chest, while purring nasties into my ear
5. She would pull my hair and tell me what a dirty little monkey I was
6. I would make monkey noises and rub my raging manbat against her
7. She would slap my manbat, but not so hard as to make me weep
8. She would pull the wax off and it would sting in an awesome, S&M way
9. My naked chest would look so manly that she would be compelled to lick the entire surface area
10. Some very serious fucking would ensue

I don't suppose I have to tell you that my expectations were a bit on the high side. What still astounds me is how spectacularly wrong it all went. And this wasn't your standard sexual miscalculation. The old whip-cream-up-the-cooter-begets-monster-yeast-infection. The I'm-feeling-crazy-tonight-are-you-feeling-crazy-baby?-back-sprain-mambo. The let's-do-it-in-a-public-place-Oh-Hi-Officer-deluxe. To which I say (and have said): Ho ho ho. No harm, no foul. *Kids*.

This was something darker, more ominous. At the risk of getting myself banned for life from the Church of American Sanctimony, I would characterize the episode as the Guantánamo Bay of sexual relations.

A few relevant notes to begin.

The wax. It was not the inviting substance I'd envisioned. It was, instead, a thick, pungent glop the color of earwax. I don't know where my girlfriend purchased the stuff. But she heated it on her stove (in a recycled soup can!) to the approximate temperature of lava.

My chest. And specifically the number of hairs upon it. I have not done an exact audit, but I am going to approximate a googol. To give you the proper mental image, I should note that a friend of mine once referred to this region, not unkindly, as my "chestfro."

My girlfriend. She was sweet. She was gorgeous. She was, rather sweetly, rather gorgeously, a sadist. She also happened to be Cuban-American, which lent her an unresolved self-dramatizing quality. There was a pronounced violent streak in her family. She worked out a great deal. Although she stood less than five feet tall and weighed a hundred pounds in sports bra and garters, I feel safe in observing that she could have kicked my ass sideways.

Me. I was frightfully insecure, with good cause, as I was living in South Miami Beach, where everyone was 3.5 times more attractive than me. My girlfriend had made considerable efforts to remedy my chronic gawkiness: new haircut, new glasses, new clothes. The chest waxing was, in part, one of these self-improvement projects. And this is where the problem began, I believe. Beneath the chest-waxing-as-hot-sexual-come-on lay a more problematic paradigm: the chest-waxing-as-elimination-of-excessive-Jew-hair.

Be that as it may, we went forward with the plan. She spread newspapers on the floor of her living room and put the wax on to boil, and I stripped to my skivvies and practiced monkey noises.

The problems began upon application. My girlfriend removed the can of wax from the stove *with a pair of tongs.* I lay on my back, giggling nervously. She dipped a tongue depressor and ran it along my clavicle. I felt I was perhaps burning. She moved down to the pectoral region. I tried to be stoic about this, while also suggesting (in a hoarse whisper) that we should maybe let the wax cool down.

My girlfriend scoffed. The wax *had* to be hot. She regularly waxed her own legs. And, as she had informed me regally, she had had her "twat" waxed—presumably for my benefit—on numerous occasions, so anything I might have to say about pain held no sway with her. Indeed, the process was already appealing to her sadism in profound and unwholesome ways.

Let me pause here to point out a physiological fact: Chest skin is *really* sensitive. I'm not going to put it up against twat skin (or whatever I should be calling it) but I will say that the chest, in terms of nerve endings, makes back skin seem like a hide. Even more delicate is the skin of the stomach, and specifically the strip that extends from bellybutton to pelvic bone (aka "the Highway to Hell") which, in the interest of consistency, my girlfriend decided needed to be waxed too.

About the wax, upon drying: I had envisioned neat little strips ready for the plucking. The reality was more like a small, turbulent sea of gunk. It felt like I had a great deal of gum stuck to my chest. I smelled like a giant crayon.

The real trouble started with the removal phase. I was prepared for a brisk temporary pain, of the sort one encounters when yanking off a Band-Aid. This was more like stabbing at road rash. Alas, my girlfriend, for all her experience in the leg department, was totally overmatched by my lush chestal thicket. For every square inch of wax, there were somewhere in the area of 19,000 hairs to be yanked. That is—to put it in technical terms—a *fuckuva* lot of adhesive force. The wax was slippery. My girlfriend couldn't get a good grip. She eventually hacked the wax up into slices. This did no good. (There was also the problem of my conduct; I writhed a fair amount.)

The result was a bunch of half-assed yanking, which loosened the hairs in such a manner than I suffered profound epidermal trauma while not actually freeing any of the hairs from their roots. I cannot remember precisely what was said during the ensuing twenty minutes. Here is an approximation, with the yelps edited out:

> ME: Ow! Please. Please, don't—Fuck!
> HER: It's almost out.
> ME: You have to do it faster, really—No! Ow! Fuck! Please move to another—that part really—Owwww!
> HER: Stop being a baby.
> ME: Please, sweetie. Please, I'm not joking!
> HER: Lie still. Just fucking lie still and let me—
> ME: Owwwww! You fucking bitch! You mean fucking bitch!

We were not communicating effectively.

The intrepid reader is, at this point, wondering when the nipple will hit the fan. Curiously, it will not. No, we didn't even make it to the nipples, though certainly my girlfriend had designs. What actually brought this sad ballet to a close was the initial (and final) moment of success: My girlfriend managed to tear free a single, mangled chunk of wax-and-hair. I climbed to my feet and marched to the bathroom and looked in the mirror and saw dabs of blood on my skin. It occurred to me at this point that we were probably not going to have sex.

I returned to the living room, encased in my hacked-up exoskeleton, and informed my girlfriend that I'd had enough. She looked at me with an expression that traveled beyond contempt, into the deeper regions of pity. "Fine," she said, and went to get Chinese takeout. It was unclear what I should do. I was furious and humiliated. She was fed up. We were in a fight. I considered placing a call for help, but to whom? Did the library carry a copy of *Waxing for Dummies*? Was there a local support group for the sadomasochistically challenged?

In the end, I found an old pair of scissors and cut away most of the wax, then shaved my chest and belly with my girlfriend's razor. And I must admit that I felt, for a few hours there, really young and hot. And gay.

Then the itching began. I spent the next month clawing at my chest. My girlfriend and I soon broke up. But I learned a valuable lesson. Namely, that most healthy relationships should not depend on the administration of hot wax for sexual enhancement. And, of course, that the enemy of my chest hair is the enemy of me.

What can I tell you about Vanessa Daws?

She had a pretty, impish face, a secret cigarette habit, a bosom of astonishing—and ultimately fraudulent—provenance. She was a southerner through and through, raised on peach cobbler and good manners, elaborate in her makeup protocols. She also had literary aspirations, which gave her one unfortunate thing in common with me.

Vanessa was the first woman I slept with during my two-year tour of duty in Greensboro, North Carolina, where I had come to study writing and alienate everyone on the face of the earth. It began like this: I walked into the office of *Triad Style* and saw a babe standing by the bulletin board. *Triad Style* was the weekly fishwrap (published by the daily fishwrap) for which I wrote freelance pieces under the nom de dork S. B. Almond. On balance, these pieces sucked ass. They were supposed to be wry accounts of various local attractions (the gun show, the monster truck show). I recall reviewing the local dumps at one point. All quite glamorous.

Nonetheless, within the *Triad Style* milieu the name S. B. Almond radiated a certain tragic cachet. This meant that Vanessa had heard of me. I know this because I sucked around the office long enough one afternoon to secure an introduction.

"So *you're* S. B. Almond," she said. Her accent was a smoky, teasing drawl. "What's the S.B. stand for?"

"Stupid bastard," I said. (It was my standard line.)

"Your mother must be proud," she said.

All our conversations were like this: the forced wit of the minor sitcom.

If I'd been a little brighter, I would have figured out that Vanessa knew who I was, that she'd already done a background check and decided I was her next Prince Charming. In the event, I was astounded when she invited me for a home-cooked meal. I spent the next week in a not-unpleasant tizzy of coital anticipation.

And I can remember driving south for that inaugural dinner, past the town of Climax, North Carolina, where I wished her to live, as this suited my slobbering poetic intentions. I remember, too, the nervous shuffle of my blood as I walked up the flagstone path to her door. She was dressed in an outfit I associated with debauched debutantes: the plunging velvet neckline, the tight mini.

Her house was fantastic, a *Southern Living* demo, down to the matte-and-copper accents. As it turned out, it wasn't her house at all. It was her mother's, but her mother was out of town and her dad had died when she was a young girl and so it was just us two and a meal of boggling proteinous complexity. I should note my habitual diet: Apple Jacks, cheese and crackers filched from readings, Progresso soup if I was feeling flush.

Vanessa lit candles and poured wine and praised my appetite. She ate little, drank much, and laughed politely at my horny-boy patter. The wine helped. By the time we were through dessert—some kind of viscid pudding—it was nearly midnight. I couldn't be expected to drive home in such a state, could I?

She led me upstairs. And I remember her pausing on the stairs to show me a photo of herself as a girl. Actually, it was a series, a kind of devotional gallery. In each, Vanessa was dressed in a leotard, flat-chested and beaming. She had wanted to be a dancer, but a bum ankle had done her wrong.

We proceeded to the bed in the guest bedroom, shared a cigarette. Vanessa asked if I needed to be tucked in. Then we were kissing, smashing our ashtray tongues together and grabbing for the junk. The tenor of these initial moments—lunging, impatient—seemed sexy enough to both of us. We'd seen enough movies in which such hostile incompetence passed for passion. It wasn't long before her shirt was peeled and her bra snapped open and there they were—great buoyant rondures in the *Playboy* register.

They really were something to see; my limbic brain went into an immediate suckling frenzy. The problem was they didn't feel right. Not to tongue, nor fingertip. They felt, rather, like croquet balls that had been upholstered in a thin layer of adipose and skin. Strangest of all was their appearance, the way each breast rose perfectly round from her chest, the skin so taut, all but her nipples, which drooped a little, as if suffering from poor self-esteem.

I couldn't figure it out. Were her pectorals really that toned? Did she have calcium deposits? I put the question aside for the sake of our unfolding sexual drama, which now proceeded to the damp lower regions and culminated in a panicky, partial fuck session, our bodies striking quick blows that knocked the breath out of us. Every few minutes, Vanessa informed me that her womanly virtue was in question, she wasn't just going to fuck me like that, in her mother's bed (we'd relocated), then she bit my shoulders and fucked me some more.

How was it, all this fucking? How was the fit? Did I come? Did she?

I don't remember. It is the hallmark of such doomed affairs: The sensations—ecstatic as they might be—have no emotional grounding, and one is left, years later, with a residue of peculiar detail. I do remember waking up with bruises on my shoulders, pale purple gnaw marks, and I remember strutting around for the next few days wishing it were summer so I could wear a tank top that would announce to my classmates the sexual abandon to which I might inspire a woman.

Instead, I arranged to meet her at the local dive bar. She showed up in a gauzy top that left no doubt as to her size, shape, and miraculous heft. The other guys in my program were stunned, and I was full of that heady pride that permeates guys who have not quite discerned that they are fucking for the esteem of other guys.

I managed to cajole the one fellow who could stand me into

coming back to my place, which meant he got to watch me and Vanessa neck, poorly. So this was nice. I had myself a trophy. She dressed well and flirted like a champ and tolerated my anxiety, which I suspect she confused with ambition.

The problem was those tits. I couldn't get past them. They were so big and so hard, so pushy for worship. But touching them sort of freaked me out. This wasn't any sort of political issue, merely an intuitive, tactile objection. It felt wrong to be groping at something inorganic. I'm sure we could trace this back to the fact that I was never breast-fed as a baby. But the truth is I've never been much for tits. In the end, they are secondary sex characteristics that have been elevated to fetish objects by our motherless consumer culture.

Vanessa didn't see it this way. She wanted me to regard her breasts with the reverence they deserved. They must have cost her (or someone) plenty, because I could never find any scars on the underside of them; I spent hours looking.

There were other problems. Conversation, for instance. Vanessa fancied herself something of a small-town rebel. She had all these ideas about herself. She was going to become a major magazine writer, head up to New York City. I was mixed up in all this—the restless Yankee novelist who would serve as her getaway driver. But the more she recited these dreams, the more hollow they sounded. Plus she had a flat ass and couldn't give head worth a damn.

And what of me? I was convincingly furious, but not in any compelling way. I sucked in bed, too.

We began to bicker.

I would assail her with my pathetic little list of enemies and plunk my elbows on the table and Vanessa would lecture me about manners, how they were in place to help people feel more comfortable. She had the whole Southern passive-aggressive thing down to a science. She had a favorite saying, too: *Fake it till you make it.* All I could think about was her hooters.

Within a month, we had hit the skids. We needed booze to bear one another, and started meeting up late, after a few drinks. The term "fuck buddies" might apply, except that we weren't buddies.

Our physical relations took on a cruel velocity. I called her once, toward the end, stoned out of my mind during a snowstorm. She was drunk and I was such a gentleman that I made her drive to my place. A little later, Vanessa climbed on top of me and pretended to enjoy my cock. She smirked and stage-whispered her dirtytalk. Then she took my hands and placed them on her breasts and my palms met that strange buttressed flesh and I thought of the photos of her as a lithe teen, spinning on her toes, how lovely she had been, how unadorned, and snowflakes floated down past my window and she saw the disappointment in my eyes as I gripped those sad saline mounds.

It would take a few more weeks for us to exhaust our shame, and a few more weeks for her to take up with a classmate of mine, which is about what I deserved. In my single surviving photo of Vanessa—taken on one of those chilly winter evenings when we were still enamored—she is dressed in black, grinning gamely from beneath the brim of a bowler hat. Her rack looks great.

HOW TO WRITE SEX SCENES: THE 12-STEP PROGRAM

Every single time I go to a party, or, at least, like, once every fifty parties, someone will approach me and say, "You sure do write about sex a lot, Steve. Any advice?" I usually tell them that I don't write about sex, I write about *desire* and *heartbreak* and I can't believe someone as intelligent-looking as him/her would reduce my *art* to lurid gymnastics. Then I ask for money.

This never works.

Thus, in the general interest of preventing more bad sex writing from entering the cultural jetstream and absolutely free of charge, I offer my *12-Step Program for Writing Incredibly Hot Sex Scenes:*

Step 1

Never compare a woman's nipples to:

a) Cherries
b) Cherry pits
c) Pencil erasers
d) Frankenstein bolts

Nipples are tricky. They come in all shapes and sizes and shades. They do not, as a rule, look like much of anything, aside from nipples. So resist making dumbshit comparisons. (Note: I am guilty of the last.)

Step 2

Never, ever use the words penis *or* vagina

There is no surer way to kill the erotic buzz than to use these terms, which call to mind—my mind, at least—health classes (in the best instance) and (in the worst instance) venereal disease.

As a rule, in fact, there is often no reason at all to name the genitals. Consider the following sentence:

"She wet her palm with her tongue and reached for my penis."

Now consider this alternative:

"She wet her palm with her tongue and reached for me."

Is there any real doubt as to where this particular horndoggle is reaching?

Step 3

Resist the temptation to use genital euphemisms, unless you are trying to be funny

No: Tunnel of Love, Candy Shop, Secret Garden, Pleasure Gate

Equally No: Flesh Kabob, Manmeat, Tube Steak, Magic Wand

Especially No: Hairy Taco, Sperm Puppet

I could go on, but only for my own amusement.

Step 4

Then again, sometimes sex is funny

And if you ever saw a videotape of yourself in action, you'd agree. What an absurd arrangement. Don't be afraid to portray these comic aspects. If one of your characters, in a dire

moment of passion, hits a note that sounds eerily like
Céline Dion, duly note this. If another can't stay hard, allow
him to use a ponytail holder for an improvised cock ring.
And later on, if his daughter comes home and picks up this
ponytail holder from his bedside table and starts absently
chewing at the thing, well, so be it.

Step 5

Real people do not talk in porn clichés

They do not say: "Give it to me, big boy."
They do not say: "Suck it, baby. That's right, all the way
down."
They do not say: "Yes, deeper, harder, deeper! Oh, baby,
oh Christ yes!"
At least, they do not say these things to me.
Most of the time, real people say all kinds of weird, funny
things during sex, such as "I think I'm losing circulation"
and "I've got a cramp in my foot" and "Oh, sorry!" and
"Did you come already? God damn it!"

Step 6

Use all the senses

The cool thing about sex—aside from its being, uh, sex—
is that it engages all five senses. So don't ignore the more
subtle cues. Give us the scents and the tastes and the
sounds of the act. And stay away from the obvious ones. By
which I mean that I'd take a sweet, embarrassed pussyfart
over a shuddering moan any day.

You may quote me.

Step 7

Don't obsess over the rude parts

Sex is inherently over the top. Just telling the reader that two (or more) people are balling will automatically direct us toward the genitals. It is your job, as an author, to direct us elsewhere, to the more inimitable secrets of the naked body. Give us the reddened stubble in the crease of a debutante's groin, or the minute trembling of a banker's underlip.

Step 8

Stop actually having sex

This is very important. Remember that the sexiest thing about sex is really desire, which is just a fancy word for *not getting laid.*

Step 9

It takes a long time to make a woman come

I speak here from experience. So please don't try to sell us on the notion that a man can enter a woman, elicit a shuddering moan or two, and bring her off. No sale. In fact, I'd steer clear of announcing orgasms at all. Rarely, in my experience, do men or women announce their orgasms. They simply have them. Their bodies are taken up by sensation and heaved about in various ways. Describe the heaving.

Step 10

It is okay to get aroused by your own sex scenes

In fact, it's pretty much required. Remember, the intent of any effective scene is to evoke in the reader the feeling state of your characters, including the aroused states. And you're not likely to accomplish this unless you, yourself, are feeling the same delicious tremors. You should be imagining what you're writing and—whether with one hand or two—transcribing the details.

Step 11

Contrary to popular belief, people think during sex

The body does its happy labor during sex, but the mind works overtime. And just what do people think about? Laundry. Bioterrorism. Old lovers. Sex isn't just the physical process. The thoughts that accompany the act are just as significant as the gymnastics (more so, actually).

Step 12

If you ain't prepared to rock, don't roll

If you don't feel comfortable writing about sex, then don't. By this, I mean writing about sex as it exists in the real world—an ecstatic, terrifying, and, above all, deeply emotional process. Real sex is compelling to read about because the participants are so vulnerable. When the time comes to get naked, we are all terribly excited and frightened and hopeful and doubtful, usually at the same time. You mustn't abandon your characters in their time of need. You mustn't make of them naked playthings with rubbery parts. You must love them, wholly and without shame, as they go about their human calling. Because we've already got a name for sex without the emotional content: It's called pornography.

Bonus Step!
Step 13

Read the Song of Songs

The Song of Songs, for those of you who haven't read the Bible in a while, is a long erotic poem that somehow got smuggled into the Old Testament. It is the single most instructive document you can read if you want to learn how to write effectively about the nature of physical love.

{ Why, Upon
Publication
of This Book,
I Will Have
to Leave the City
of Boston Under
Cover of Night

(Not that You Asked)

RED SOX ANTI-CHRIST

HOW ONE ASTONISHINGLY BITTER FAN
BROKE THE CURSE OF THE BAMBINO

I spent the last hours of October 27, 2004, burrowed beneath the blankets of my bed, engaged in an activity plainly definable as *cowering*. It was the fourth and final game of the World Series between the St. Louis Cardinals and the Boston Red Sox, and I was living in a dust-caked apartment in Somerville, just a few miles from Fenway Park.

The Sox were poised to sweep the Cards and thereby end the most ballyhooed dry spell in all of professional sports, dating back to the team's shipment of Babe Ruth to New York in 1918. I had received multiple invitations to watch this historic contest, and declined all of them. I was a man in possession of an excruciating secret, and I wanted very much to sleep.

It was dark and stuffy under the blankets. At a certain point, it also got loud. From next door came a noise of jubilation so primal I hesitate to place it in the humanoid category. Then car horns, the fizz-bang of bottle rockets, air horns, small arms fire. The beady red digits of my clock radio read 11:40 P.M.

Soon the phone would start ringing. My friends, proud citizens of Red Sox Nation, the loudest-suffering fan contingent on earth, would want to share their joy with me. Floodie would confide how he envisioned the final out moments before it was recorded. The Big Ruskie would describe, in slurred and loving detail, the lunar eclipse that painted the moon above Busch Stadium a blushing red. Young Bull would tell me, in that half-ashamed guy manner, that he loved me. If they considered the date at all, it would be to note that the Sox had lost a crushing Game Seven to the Mets on October 27, 1986.

None of them would grasp the true significance: October 27 happened to be the very day I was born into this world and called to serve as the Red Sox Anti-Christ.

TO BE A FAN is to live in a condition of willed helplessness. We are (for the most part) men who sit around and watch other men run and leap and sweat and grapple each other. It is a deeply homoerotic pattern of conduct, often interracial in nature, and essentially humiliating. In response, fans have developed what is most accurately diagnosed as a religious psychosis. We honestly believe that our thoughts and actions affect the outcome of games. And that an accumulation of these thoughts and actions, carried out over, say, thirty years, can shape the larger contours of history. So when I tell you that I, Steve Almond, am the primary reason the Sox won the 2004 World Series, I don't expect you to believe me. I'm just another Jesus freak when it comes to this stuff.

I can only humbly submit the facts for your consideration . . .

ON OCTOBER 22, 1972, the Oakland Athletics played the seventh game of the World Series against the Cincinnati Reds. In the sixth inning, Sal Bando hit a long fly to center. Bobby Tolan looked to have the ball in his sights, but his left knee—weakened by the laser malevolence of my glare—buckled under him. The ball fell in for a double, and the A's went up 3–1.

The Reds rallied in the eighth, putting two on with no outs. The A's summoned to the mound one Rollie Fingers. Fingers appeared unfazed by the 56,000 screaming maniacs at Riverfront Stadium. He wore a handlebar mustache, the tips waxed to impeccable upturned points, which, between pitches, he twirled with great élan. This mustache itself seemed to do most of the damage. Fingers induced two strikeouts to stanch the threat, then mowed down three straight in the ninth.

Five days later I turned six years old. I asked my parents for nothing. There was nothing to ask them *for;* I had been given the A's, the Series, a life.

LIKE MANY FANS, I grew up in a house full of men, the smallest of three brothers born to kind but overextended parents, and residing in a tiny Eichler home at the ass end of an affluent suburb. I attended school in a state of perpetual terror. Bullies could smell the fear on me. They did what bullies must. At home, I waited for my brothers to cast a healing glance upon me, and spent most afternoons alone.

That I turned to sport for solace should come as no surprise. It was one of the few areas in which I could engage the passion of my father, whose personal archive includes a yellowed box score of the first game he ever attended, a 1951 tilt between the Yankees and the St. Louis Browns.

Given our location—an hour south of San Francisco—I should have rooted for the Giants. But the Giants were dull. It was the Swinging A's who kidnapped my heart. They were a dashing bunch, brawny, headstrong, with a tendency to beat one another silly. My favorite book during this era was an illustrated version of the *Iliad,* and I thought of the A's lineup as a modern incarnation of the Greeks. They weren't a team so much as a reluctant coalition of superstars. Bert "Campy" Campaneris,[1] Billy North, Joe Rudi, the team's gallant left fielder—he would smash a grand slam in the first game I ever attended—and, of course, Reggie Jackson, with his tinted shades and biceps of bunched cable.

---

1. Campy remains my favorite baseball player of all time. A few inches shy of six feet and 160 pounds, he was a shortstop by trade, though he is the only player in the history of the game to have played all nine positions in a single game, *including pitcher.* He did this at the behest of the team's cockamamie owner, Charles Finley, who was crazier than any other man alive on the earth at that time.

The pitchers, equally imposing, bore names only a pro athlete could do justice: Vida Blue, Catfish Hunter, Blue Moon Odom, not to mention Rollie Fingers. I can still see Odom launching into the divine contortions of his windup, which, at its apex, tipped him over so far the knuckles of his throwing hand brushed the dirt beneath him. And those unis! Kelly green shirts with blingy gold sleeves. It will go without saying that my entire wardrobe was predicated on this unfortunate color scheme.[2]

For three autumns, I watched the A's destroy all comers. In 1973, they handed the Mets a Game Seven thrashing, courtesy of homers by Campy and Reggie. In 1974, they tamed the Dodgers in five.

None of this struck me as exceptional. It was merely the annual dividend of my devotion. My father and I would seat ourselves in front of the old Zenith in our den and watch destiny unfold, occasionally adjusting the rabbit ear antennae so as to remove excess snow from the unfolding destiny. At a certain point, Fingers would appear and induce a harmless grounder and the A's would converge on the mound and the two of us would leap up and briefly embrace. I was happy. My father was happy. The world was happy. It might have gone on like this. It *should* have gone on like this.

But then fate—or, as I prefer to think of fate, the Lord God of Sport—intervened. The instrument of His cruel intervention? None other than the Boston Red Sox.

IN THESE EARLY YEARS, I had nothing special against the Sox. My sense of the team was sketchy. They came from a place with snow. They wore old-fashioned uniforms. Their best player, Carl Yastrzemski, had a name I believed to be an exotic lunch meat. My interest was hardly piqued when, in 1975, Boston earned a spot in the AL Championship Series against the A's. They were just another team my boys would flatten on the way to a fourth title.

---

2. It should also be mentioned (though not dwelled upon) that I slept with a miniature kelly green bat under my pillow through my early childhood.

But the Red Sox had a mysterious effect on Oakland, an effect best summarized as *making them suck*. This was clear from the very first inning of their matchup, during which our sure-handed infield committed three straight errors. Game Two began in more typical fashion: Bando doubled and Jackson sent a bomb over the wall in right. But the Sox struck back for three runs against Vida Blue, then knocked the stuffing out of the unknockable Rollie Fingers, pushing Oakland to the brink of elimination.

I understood, even as an eight-year-old, that the A's sometimes lost. What the A's did *not* do was lose in the clutch. And thus it was clear to me, as I settled in before Game Three, that the A's were merely pretending to suck. This pattern of "pretend sucking" continued deep into the game, which I was watching (for reasons that escape me) at my grandparents' house. From time to time, my grandpa would stick his head in the doorway and offer me a mournful glance. He was a forsaken fan of the Brooklyn Dodgers and viewed the garish dominance of the A's as the inevitable result of my generation's moral degeneracy.

In the eighth, down two runs, Oakland finally woke from its slumber, putting men on first and third with Joe Rudi coming to the plate. The Sox went to the pen and extracted their closer, a right-hander with the absurd and villainous name Dick Drago. It was perfectly clear to me what would happen next: Rudi would pull a double down the line. I could see the ball's sweet humming path through the night, the cloud of chalk kicked up along the left field line; I could hear the crowd's grateful thunder. And then, quite abruptly, the ball was bounding to the shortstop and the Sox were turning a double play and Rudi was hurling his helmet to the ground and something inside me, some very early notion of faith, shattered.

AS AN ADULT, I have often found myself in the position of having to explain to women with whom I hope to sleep why I take such a maniacal interest in the Oakland A's. For years, it was my habit to trot out the story of the A's golden years, how they seduced me—

poor depressed child that I was—with those three sensational cam-
paigns. But the origins of my obsession reside in that first massacre
at the hands of the Sox. What characterizes the true fan isn't the
easy pleasure of rooting for a winner, but the struggle imposed by
loss.

There were, of course, plenty of rational reasons the team lost.
Catfish Hunter had defected to the Yanks, the A's bats had gone
dead, and so forth. But the true fan is unmoved by rational analysis,
and least of all the mercy implied by disappointment. We live in a
kingdom of shame and recrimination. Those who defeat us are to
be despised. And those who defeat us before defeat seems possible,
who pop the cherry of our omnipotence, become sworn enemies
for life.

Was this a healthy psychological posture to assume? I would say
no. My father made some effort to explain, in the face of my ban-
shee rage, that flying to Boston and murdering the Red Sox would
not actually solve anything. But I had trouble focusing on his lecture, what with my still beating heart torn from my chest.

The next year, the team shipped Fingers and Rudi to Boston.
Commissioner Bowie Kuhn (acting on orders transmitted from my
still beating heart) voided the deals. But the damage had been done.
The franchise went into a swoon that presaged and outlasted my
tortuous passage into adolescence. The A's were now losers, like
me. And the Red Sox were to blame.

I MUST HAVE SPENT a thousand summer afternoons in my room,
listening to Bill King narrate the drubbings subsequently endured
by the A's. My weapon of choice was an ancient silver Panasonic
weighing at least twenty pounds, with speakers that popped like fat-
back. The A's fan base amounted to shut-ins, the criminally insane,
and me. They drew fewer than thirty-eight hundred per game during the 1979 campaign (54–108), and I myself was perhaps the only
person on the planet who tuned in to the broadcast of a July laugher
that drew, if memory serves, 937 lost souls to the vast concrete bowl
known as the Oakland Alameda Coliseum.

Against all reason, I found reasons to root. That season it was the rookie center fielder Dwayne Murphy, who set his cap at a rakish angle atop his Afro, from which perch it would inevitably tumble as he dashed toward the gap to flag down one of the many drives surrendered by the team's pitching staff. Murphy was a lefty, like me, and a specialist at the drag bunt. I nearly wept the first time I saw him perform this elegant bit of legerdemain. He lowered his bat across the plate and drew it back just before contact. For a moment, he seemed to have caught the ball on the sweet spot, before gently pushing it between the mound and first base. Murphy himself was halfway down the line before anyone discerned the con. The drag bunt struck me as emblematic of those years: a way of improvising something from nothing, turning a gesture of weakness into strength, of locating redemption in the gaps.[3]

The next year, Rickey Henderson joined Murphy in the outfield. The adjective *electrifying* is shamefully abused in the sporting arena, but it does apply to the young Henderson. He looked like no other ballplayer alive: short and squat and endowed with a massive, rippled complex of muscles best described as the National Republic of Rickey Henderson's Thighs. I spent hours studying his batting stance, an osteoporotic crouch in which his legs cocked inward at the knee, creating a strike zone the approximate size of a Chiclet. He walked about 75 percent of his at-bats, and once on base he took over a game.

Henderson's steals were spectacular for their audacity—everyone knew he was going—and their improbable physics. The mechanics worked like so: About halfway between first and second, Henderson (now moving at the speed of sound) launched himself into a headfirst dive, covering the remaining yardage Superman style, crash-landing on his chest at the same moment his gloved hands hit the edge of the bag, bouncing in such a manner that his body slid across the top of the bag, decelerating by means of the re-

3. Murphy is to be forgiven, at least by me, for helping to fund and produce MC Hammer's first album.

sulting friction, then elegantly hooking the tongues of his cleats along that same front edge to keep from sliding into left field. As a thought experiment, I often speculated how far into left field Henderson would have traveled without this ingenious braking system. My general estimate placed him somewhere around the warning track.

AND WHAT OF my own derring-do on the diamond? For behind every fan there lives some private history of athletic ignominy. Mine began on the sun-baked ball field of Terman Middle School where, as a shrimpazoid eight-year-old, I showed up with my Reggie Jackson autographed Rawlings for a Saturday afternoon tryout. Along one side of the grass stood the coaches who would draft us, former jocks to a man, with round, scarred knees and beer guts cinched into golf shirts. Ladies and gentlemen, I give you Exhibit A: the Little League Meat Market.

Inexplicably, I wound up drafted directly into "the majors," a league composed of kids up to twelve years old. There should have been some rule forbidding this, a ban, for instance, on boys who still sucked their thumbs. But there wasn't. Big Jeff Wilkins, coach of Round Table Pizza, decided I was going to be a star, once he could find a pair of pants small enough to fit me.

This dream died rather quickly, thanks to Kathy Schindler, the league's only female player. Schindler was, to put it delicately, pubescent. She stood nearly six feet, wore two batting gloves, and, on occasion, spat. I was—just a reminder—an eight-year-old who still sucked his thumb. We had no business interacting. The only reason we were forced to interact is because I was playing second base at the precise moment Schindler (having been walked yet again by our terrified pitcher) broke for second.

I took the throw from home in plenty of time, but forgot I had to tag the runner. On came Schindler—blotting out the field of play, the sun, the sky above—and plowed into me, spikes up. The umpire threw his arms out and yelled *Safe*! "You gotta tag her, son," he murmured to me.

Coach Wilkins came roaring out of the dugout. He was perpetually sunburned, with a neck that belonged in the Fat Neck Hall of Fame.

"Do you understand what just happened?" he said.

"I forgot the tag."

"Is this a play we went over in practice?"

I nodded.

"And?"

I glanced down at my stirrup socks, puddled idiotically around my cleats. My spit had turned to paste. "I should have remembered."

"And who was counting on you to remember?"

"You."

The band of flesh that joined Coach Wilkins's cheeks to his neck flushed. "No, Almond. Not me. *Your team.* Your team was counting on you." He gestured grandly to my teammates, who were watching my humiliation with great satisfaction.

"Because what did we say, at the beginning of the season?"

For half a minute, I wandered the small corral of my mind for an answer. But it was all sheep shit up there.

Coach Wilkins glanced toward the stands and tried to shape his massive face into an expression of distress. He was experiencing something like ecstasy. This was one of the few pleasures granted the Little League coach: the right to publicly mock children under the guise of nurturing them. It stood as the sole reward for the hours spent lugging equipment bags, devising lineups, extending advice to children who, frankly, not only would fail as players, but would be lucky to escape major injury in the course of their woeful, stunted careers.

"There is no *I* in 'team,' " Coach Wilkins said. "Didn't we say that?"

"I guess," I said.

"No guess about it!" Wilkins roared. His rage was by now operatic. "There is no *I* in 'team.' Spell it out."

"*T-E-A-M.*"

"How many *I*'s in that word?"

"None," I said cautiously.

"You sure? You want to count again?"

I shook my head.

"That's right," he said. "None."

THUS BEGAN MY inexorable transition from failed jock to full-time jock sniffer, a transition ratified by my decision to apply for an internship as a sports reporter with my hometown newspaper following my sophomore year in college. Soon after, I received a letter on *Peninsula Times Tribune* stationery, informing me I had been hired for $60 per week.

"What do *you* want?" the editor said, when I showed up in June.

"I'm your intern."

"Already got an intern," he said.

This was a fair introduction to the world of sports journalism.

There are a good many bitter people on earth—I like to think of myself as one of them—but there are not many people quite so bitter as sports reporters. (Picture a locker room full of dorks. Now picture them tussling over a bag of Cheetos.) As the subintern, I had no desk. My first real assignment was an interview with Billie Jean King.[4] By August the editor, tired of tripping over me, dispatched me to cover an A's game. Why not? Everyone else was on vacation, and the team was awful.

I entered the press box woozy with the honor. A tray of free hot dogs had been set out for us credentialed reporters, but I was too frightened to eat even one. I sat in the back row scribbling notes furiously while the beat reporters discussed how many weeks it would be before the new manager, Tony LaRussa, took his own life.

After the game, I followed the veterans down to LaRussa's office, where he sat behind his desk, a grown man in a rumpled uniform, muttering glum assessments.

Someone mentioned the bullpen.

---

4. Or, as my colleagues referred to her, *Billie Jean Rug Muncher*.

LaRussa shrugged. He speculated that his newest relief pitcher—whose disastrous outing had just lost the game—might have arm trouble. (For reasons involving personal safety, specifically mine, I shall refer to this player simply as Pitcher X.)

When LaRussa was done, we were released to the main locker room, and here I found it difficult to concentrate. I was surrounded by naked A's, many of them my boyhood heroes, all of them much larger than they appeared on TV, their great penises bouncing as they strutted from the showers. Here was Carney Lansford, all-star third baseman, looking oddly bookish in spectacles. The mountainous Dave Kingman, moisturizing all eight feet of himself. And José Canseco, not yet bloated by steroids, a vainglorious rookie attending with much product to his *Tiger Beat* coiffure. *Autographs*, I thought. *I could get so many fucking autographs.*

But I was a reporter (remember!) so I hovered with the other supplicants. An elaborate code of rules prevailed in the locker room, developed to inoculate all parties against the inherent homoperversity of the ritual. You didn't interview a player while he was naked. You didn't look at their bodies. You waited quietly for them to complete what the French might call their *toilette*. Above all, you did not ask any questions that might offend, which reduced discourse to a safe zone of cliché (*tough loss, just keep battling, 110 percent*, ibid.).

I was unaware of this last restriction, and so I marched up to Pitcher X—thinking it vaguely odd that no other reporters wanted to talk to him—and asked him about the health of his arm.

X's face (a natively sweet-looking face) twisted. "*What?*"

"Your arm," I said. "I just wondered—"

"You saying something's wrong with my arm?"

"No," I said. "*I'm* not saying that."

X took a step toward me. "So who's saying that?"

"The manager," I stammered.

"Now you talking to the manager about me?"

X took another step toward me. I was obliged to take a step backward. The other reporters had noticed what was developing and gone silent. A headline briefly flashed before me:

INTERN FATALLY WOUNDED BY ENRAGED RELIEF PITCHER

BASEBALL BAT, BLEEDING FROM MULTIPLE
ORIFICES CITED AS CAUSE OF DEATH

I certainly didn't blame old X for wanting to kill me. He was at the tail end of a middling career and fresh from a performance that would send him packing from the big leagues with an official ERA of infinity. And so I slowly backed away, toward the main scrum of reporters. The players were watching me, too, all except Canseco, who stood before a full-length mirror, transfixed by his deltoids. He turned away from his image with reluctance, plainly heartbroken that, in the real world, there was only one of him.[5]

PITCHER X DID not in fact assault me. I survived the summer and returned to college only to discover Red Sox fever in full bloom. I should have mentioned this earlier: I had chosen a school in New England, just a hundred miles or so from Boston. Back then I was only vaguely aware of the pivotal role I would come to play in the fate of the Red Sox. This was my Anti-Christ-in-embryo phase. Or, to provide a more accurate visual, my young-Judas-Iscariot-with-a-mullet phase.

In either case, the year was 1986, and so I suffered the noisy exhortation of my classmates all that fall, as the Sox beat the Yanks for the pennant, then clawed back from a 3–1 deficit to top the Angels in the AL Championship Series. Dave Henderson's game-tying homer in the ninth inning of Game Five unleashed outside my dorm room a chant of *All Hail Hendu* that went on for 103 hours straight. I sat alone with only my ill wishes for company. I wanted the Sox to lose, as traumatically as possible.

5. I would later conduct an interview with Canseco himself, the full text of which, in the interest of historical exactitude, I now proffer:

    Me: "Mr. Canseco?"
    Canseco: "What the fuck are *you*?"
    Me: "I'm from the—"
    Canseco: "Get the fuck out of my way."

That being said, I refuse to rehash the details of the ensuing World Series, and specifically the Agonies of Game Six, a fervent recitation of which—Roger's blister, Stanley's wild pitch, Buckner's epic muff—has become the official Stations of the Cross in Red Sox Nation. All you need to know is that the Mets' comeback win in Game Seven (and the subsequent suicide watch issued for all Sox fans) transpired on the occasion of my twentieth birthday.

TWO YEARS LATER, my very own A's squared off against the Sox in the AL Championship Series and administered what I would respectfully characterize as an ass-raw whupping. I took this as further proof that whatever negative sway the team held over me in the past had been banished from this earth, or perhaps compacted into some kind of giant spiky lozenge, then stuffed up the ass of Red Sox Nation.

Yes, thanks to my unflagging devotion—those years of loyalty in the face of hundred-loss seasons—Oakland had been resurrected. Campy and Catfish and Reggie were gone. But now we had Canseco and Mark McGwire, the team's anabolic glimmer twins, and a ferocious pitching staff led by Dave Stewart, whose very plateward *stare* was registered with the FBI as a lethal weapon. The team was filthy with talent, and I looked ahead joyfully to the World Series against the meager Dodgers.

In the very first inning of Game One, Canseco bopped a grand salami. The only question in my mind was whether the A's would reach a hundred runs. But the team's bats fell silent, and they found themselves clinging to a 4–3 lead in the bottom of the ninth.

I was still not especially worried, because our closer, Dennis Eckersley, was the best in the league, the second coming of Rollie Fingers, right down to the mustache. He quickly retired two batters, then surrendered an uncharacteristic walk. Kirk Gibson strode to the plate as a pinch-hitter, though *strode* is the wrong verb. *Gimped* makes more sense. Gibson had a strained hammy on his left leg and a twisted right knee. Incapable of planting his legs, he flailed at two fastballs in the manner of a soused ballerina.

By all rights, Eckersley should have punched him out with high heat. Instead, as so often happens when you are pitching against someone who appears to need crutches, Eckersley got cute. He nibbled at the edges. Then, at 3–2, he delivered the lazy backdoor slider for which Gibson had been waiting. The pitch dipped toward the bottom of the strike zone and Gibson lunged batfirst, catching just enough on the barrel to send the ball sailing over the wall in right.

I was watching the game on a tiny black-and-white TV at the pottery studio my brother Dave managed in Berkeley, and my cry of anguish brought him running from the kiln he'd been loading.

"What's the matter with you?" he said.

"Is the kiln going?" I said.

"What?" he said. "Why?"

"I might want to stick my head in there for a minute or two."

"It's just one game," Dave said. "Calm the fuck down."

As wise and compassionate as this counsel was, I could not calm the fuck down. Instead, I stared at the screen, where CBS was broadcasting the first of 137 replays of Gibson's shot, all of which I would inexplicably watch.[6]

The truth is, I had never entirely trusted Eckersley, and it now occurred to me, in the same way a knife wound to the back might have occurred to me, why: because Eckersley was a castoff . . . from the Red Sox. He carried in his veins the doomed blood of that franchise, and he had now come and visited that doom on me. Or, no, perhaps Eckersley was a double agent dispatched directly by the Lord God of Sport. How else does the game's best reliever give up a homer to a man who was essentially crippled?

I wanted to explain this situation to Dave, to ask for his help in the performance of some kind of ritual sacrifice, perhaps. (We had

6. The current figure is closer to 137,000, as Gibson's homer has become inarguably the most popular highlight in the history of baseball. It is clearly a sickness that I cannot stop myself from watching these replays, and in particular that each time I see the play, some small, pathetic cavern of my heart truly believes it will turn out differently, that Gibson will swing through Eck's lousy slider or send a harmless pop-up into shallow right.

the purifying flames of the kiln at our disposal!) But Dave is not a fan. He would have insisted I was being "irrational."

The A's never recovered from the Gibson homer and fell obediently in five.

IN A GRAND history of my team, 1989 should have been an exalted year. Oakland stormed through the regular season, managed to avoid Boston in the playoffs, and made short work of their crosstown rivals, the Giants, to claim the title for which I had been waiting fifteen years. But that Series (if it is remembered at all) is remembered for the giant earthquake that struck the Bay Area minutes before Game Three, and sent the media into the sort of instantaneous frenzy triggered by natural disasters, which helpfully mimic action films. For the next week the entire world sat transfixed, watching the same stretch of I-80 collapse over and over, while baseball officials tried to explain exactly why playing the rest of the Series would restore hope to a stunned nation. Most of my family lived in the Bay Area, and though none of them had been harmed in the least, I was obligated to consider *just how tragically the tragic events of such a tragedy might trage.* It was not a lot of fun.

Like most people, I initially viewed the Loma Prieta earthquake as a freak occurrence. It would occur to me only later that the Occult Forces of the Sox were delivering one of their nasty Occultograms:

> TO: RED SOX ANTI-CHRIST
> *This is what we can do to you and*
>   *your team* STOP
> *Any time we fucking want* STOP
> *Enjoy!*

IN 1990, THE A's once again faced the Red Sox in the AL Championship Series. This time they outscored Boston 20–4. Any decent person with even a hint of clemency about him might have used this occasion to forgive Red Sox Nation for past transgressions.

I, on the other hand, gloried in the carnage, which I watched alone, on a borrowed TV, in my dank apartment in El Paso, Texas, where I was passing myself off as a newspaper reporter. Did I mind watching these games alone? Absolutely not. The true fan is always in a state of spiritual solitude when watching games of import. This arrangement also allowed me to devise and perform what might be loosely defined as a fight song, set (and I can now see how unfortunate this choice will seem to those not in the spirit of the thing) to the MC Hammer hit "U Can't Touch This." Please feel free to sing along:

> *A's beat the Sux!*
> *(Dooo-do-do)*
> *'89 redux!*
> *(Dooo-do-do)*
> *Beantown reflux!*
> *(Dooo-do-do)*
> *Swept again, ya fucks!*

The Series pitted us against the Reds, a rematch of the 1972 tilt that spawned my affliction. The A's had now swept three playoff series in a row, and everyone on earth assumed they would make it four against the Reds.

I don't have to tell you how this turns out. What unsettled me was how meekly my A's went down. Stewart got pounded in the opener. Eckersley gave up the lead game-winning hit the next night. In the fourth and final game, the fat and utterly average José Rijo reduced our mighty lineup to corned beef hash. It was as if the A's had been replaced by a squad of zombies.

My friend Holden—a well-meaning if deluded loyalist of the Texas Rangers—was the first to suggest what should have been obvious to me from the beginning: My anti–Red Sox mojo had boomeranged.

I MORE OR less took a pass on the A's for the rest of the nineties. I was in Miami for much of the decade, where the Lord God of Sport had decided to place not one, not two, but *three* shiny new franchises, in the hopes of seducing me. Instead, I turned for comfort to another of my Oakland teams, the NBA's Golden State Warriors.[7] The LGS also sent me a new best friend, a six-foot-five-inch Sox addict named Pat Flood, who spent many useless hours trying to explain to me why it was a mortal sin to refer to Carl Yastrzemski as "dumbshit Pastrami."

These were my years of alleged artistic growth. The Miami sun baked all sorts of delusions into my skull and I shipped off to grad school in the suburbs of the South, happy to pack my brutish fandom into a steamer trunk and ignore the occasional thudding. No, I was going to become the other sort of guy, who concerned himself with more refined matters, who wrote poetry and recycled.

I was pretending, of course, and poorly. I still read the sports section of any newspaper I could get my mitts on, still rifled the box scores for some sign of divine approval, still snuck off to a hidden dorm lounge every weekend to get my lonely fix. And then grad school ended and I needed to decide where in the wide world I might live.

Over the years, I've provided many semiplausible reasons for moving to Boston. I wanted to teach college. *Sure.* I wanted to stay far away from the kryptonitic effects of my family. *Understandable.* I wanted to be in a city with lots of single women who might not see through my fraudulent sensitivo routine. *Well, two out of three ain't bad.*

In fact, I moved to Boston in the autumn of 1997 not of my own volition, but as a matter of prophetic necessity. I had a score to settle with Boston and its baseball fans. This is how it works with us Anti-Christs: We blow into town confident of our own righteous mission. It never quite occurs to us that our presence might serve as a prerequisite to the salvation of our enemies.

7. Anyone who knows the history of the Warriors—a franchise that had not, until this season, smelled the playoffs since the early Clinton years—will confirm the idiocy of my conduct. Rooting for the Warriors is like dating a Mormon with bad breath.

—

ON MY SECOND day as an official Bostonian, I scalped a ticket to Fenway Park and watched from behind a large green girder—the scalper had promised a seat along the third-base line, he just hadn't mentioned the girder—as the Royals thumped the Sox, 9–2.

Fenway was gorgeous. So gorgeous that I raced home and wrote a barfy poem. I still hated the Sox, but I was also trying to fit in to my new hometown. Both our teams sucked and I saw no reason to allow old ghosts to curdle my goodwill. Besides, Boston seemed to have enough problems. Half the streets were being torn up on behalf of an absurd automotive boondoggle called the Big Dig. Some goon squad of developers had punched the Boston Garden in the mouth so as to put up a parking lot (another barfy poem). Revelations began to emerge that some of the local clergy subscribed to the Mark Foley School of Teen Mentorship. Overall, the city trudged along in its un-official capacity as New York's Bitch.

Thus, I tolerated Sox fans as a minor irritant, something like the college students who seize the local street corners every September, spewing smoke and nonsense. Many of these fans were my friends, and therefore difficult to escape. But it's also true that I became qui-etly and horribly fascinated with the sports talk radio stations of Boston, and specifically WEEI, which broadcasts an array of noisy blowhards genetically incapable of pronouncing the letter *r*. I lis-tened to these gentlemen mostly in the car, and found their indig-nation oddly soothing while I was mired in traffic.

Then something bad happened. In 1999, the Sox made it all the way to the AL Championship, where the Yankees summar-ily thrashed them. The ensuing uproar was not soothing. It was more like the inconsolable wailing of many children betrayed. I could hear, in each rant and squall, the echoes of my own doomed loyalty. It might be said that I had met the enemy and they was me.

This was not how I saw things, of course. Sox fans did things I would never do. They booed their own players. They hassled fans from out of town. They waddled about righteously in shirts bearing logos such as "Yankees Suck." Most annoying of all, they regarded themselves as *underdogs,* forever pitted against George Steinbrenner's "Evil Empire" (their term, not mine). To those of us who root for poor teams from small markets, the notion that the Red Sox would lay claim to the holy mantle of underdogdom is beyond loathsome. A friendly reminder: the team has the second-highest payroll in baseball.

No, it was *my* team who represented the little guy. What I couldn't figure out is why the LGS kept smiting them. For three years running (2000–2002) the A's reached the playoffs only to collapse in the first round. They blew six straight clinching games, three against the Yankees. It was as if the LGS *wanted* to see Goliath stomp David, as if he were gazing down at me through his cruel oculus and cackling, *Having damned the citizens of Red Sox Nation, I shall make you feel the sting of their lamentation!*

AS THE 2003 season opened, I was in no shape to listen to more moaning, particularly because the Sox had just nabbed our gutsy center fielder Johnny Damon by offering him a perverse salary of the sort the A's cannot afford to pay.

My foul mood was exacerbated that spring by another event, which I cannot fairly neglect: The United States was in the midst of invading Iraq. This was a discretionary war, launched under false pretenses by foolish cowards and covered with reflexive obedience by all available media, which confused the war—an event in which the resources of our vast and powerful nation were mustered to murder the people of a much smaller nation—with a sporting event. Nightly highlight reels charted the day's major offensive drives. Correspondents offered sandswept on-the-field interviews with our burly combatants, while generals served up bromides fit for a head coach.

As an opponent of the war, I felt an oddly familiar sensation watching all this. It was like being a disgruntled fan, helpless before the slaughter. Although it was worse than that, because I had played a distant but undeniable role in the proceedings. As a fan, I had helped foster a culture governed by the sports mentality, in which winning mattered above all else, and the application of violence was seen as a necessary means to that end rather than a betrayal of our democratic standards.

The man we (almost) elected president in 2000 bears much of the blame,[8] but I'm going to tread lightly here, as I've got my own crucifixion to attend. The point is that another season in hell was upon me and I was in my car, enduring war propaganda, then Sox propaganda, then more war propaganda, and this, compounded by my own choker-identification-misery, caused me to snap. On April 10, 2003, I published the following, uh, editorial in Boston's alternative weekly:

> A couple of weeks ago, at my weekly poker game, the host, a guy we call The Big Ruskie (though he is, in fact, a mid-sized man of German/Irish extraction) looked at me during a lull and said: "You know, Stevie, I've never believed in ESP or any of that kind of crap. But I really do have a feeling, a deep feeling, a feeling in my soul, that this is the year the Red Sox will win the World Series."
>
> I love the Ruskie. But looking at him across that poker table I felt I was gazing into the bloated, half-cracked heart

---

8. If the Reagan presidency marked the apotheosis of politics as entertainment, the reign of Bush II has marked the ascendance of politics as sport. The man himself, a failed athlete and baseball owner and a notorious cheat, has shown an astonishing talent for reducing the complex realities of the modern world into the only duality he cares to understand: the win/loss record. His manner—the cocksure gait, the coy bullying, the juvenile solipsism—derives not from the frat house he commandeered in college, but the locker room he wished to occupy in those years that he was (let us pause to remember) a cheerleader. To speak of his political philosophy is foolish, for he has none. He follows the code of honor held to by all failed athletes: *It's not how you play the game, it's whether you win or lose.* Iraq, he felt, would be an easy win. Viewed in this context, one can see his Mission Accomplished photo op for what it was: a premature end zone dance.

Yes, I'm aware that was a political rant; that's why I snuck it into a footnote.

of every single Red Sox fan on earth. Because every single Red Sox fan on earth (whether or not they say this out loud, though most of them do) truly believes that this is the year the Sox are going to vanquish the Yankees, break the curse, win it all. So let me be the first, on the eve of yet another opening day, in this blessed year of 85 A.S. (After Series), to deliver to the entire Red Sox Nation the same simple but timeless message: *Shut up.*

Shut up about Pedro and how he's the greatest pitcher on earth if his shoulder holds up. Shut up about Manny Ramirez not running out ground balls. And for God's sake, shut up about how we got nothing in return for Roger Clemens seven years ago.

Shut up.

Shut-up-shut-up-shut-up.

Now look: I've been a sports fan my whole life and rooted for the Oakland A's during the darkest days of that franchise. I am on intimate terms with the agonies of fandom. What's more, I've traveled this fine country of ours and witnessed the behaviors of numerous sports habitats. It's true that most fans are prone to complaint. But I hope you'll believe me when I observe (with no intention to offend) that I have never encountered a group of fans as whiny, sanctimonious, and unforgiving as Red Sox Nation.

I have, of course, asked Red Sox fans to shut up on an individual basis. I have frequently asked my friend Zach to shut up. This is especially important because Zach is that saddest species of Red Sox fan: the rabid optimist. Last year, when the team leapt out to a 27–9 record, he was ready to set the rotation for the playoffs. Then, of course, the team did its usual late-summmah swoon.

This is generally how it goes with the Sox. They start strong and finish weak. Part of the reason for this—according to me—is that the players simply get tired of listening to the fans, who are always one strike out, one bonehead error, one gopherball away from crying bloody murder. In short: The players would like the fans to shut up.

They can't say this, though. Because if they did, the fans would go into that self-righteous how-dare-you-I-pay-good-money-to-watch-you-spoiled-brats mode that is even more tiresome than their usual tirades.

And here I think of my pal Artie, who actually does pay good money to see the Sox and occasionally (senselessly) invites me along to games. Oh, Artie! How sad it is to watch his transformation, from the guarded optimism of May to the disconsolate rage of August. This is a man, after all, who tapes every single Red Sox game he can't watch live and gets furious if you tell him the score before he has a chance to watch.

Artie is the more common kind of Red Sox fan, the fatalist, and he knows he's locked in a terrible cycle of self-punishment, but he's helpless. He's given a significant portion of his heart to the Sox and they have inflicted the standard crack down the middle, and there's nothing he can do but yell at his television in blind aggravation.

The thing is, to a true Red Sox fan, the idea of shutting up is simply impossible. It's become the entire raison d'etre of their allegiance. To allow the team's flagrant and repeated misdeeds to go uncriticized would be, by their own twisted logic, to let the team down.

And the sort-of-beautiful-but-really-more-pathetic thing about being Red Sox fans is that they'll never run out of things to bitch about. Because baseball is a game of endless mistakes, miscalculations, misfortunes; so sure, Varitek may go three for five on Tuesday with a nifty basket catch in front of the backstop. But on Wednesday, he'll muff the throw down to second and the ball will go bounding into centerfield and Red Sox Nation will rise as one to denounce him.

It's such a dysfunctional relationship.

In closing, I'd like the Red Sox Nation to consider a simple exercise in logic:

a) The Red Sox do not seem to improve when bitched about.

b) You bitch about them incessantly.

If you agree that a and b are true, then:

c) Shut up.

WAS THIS A WISE THING to write as a resident of the Greater Boston metropolitan area? I would say no. But I felt at the time it was a necessary (and long overdue) declaration of war. Fate had drawn me into the chilly bosom of Red Sox Nation. It was time to go public as the team's Anti-Christ once and for all. We'd been on a collision course since 1975. The Lord God of Sport was in full agreement.

Which is why, as autumn came to New England, as the maples rid themselves of leaves, turning the sidewalks as bright as Van Goghs, I found myself in the dank interior of Casey's Bar and Grill watching the A's take the field against the Sox. (I was not watching with one of my Soxchotic friends, because we had all agreed—without exactly discussing the matter—that I had best seek other venues.)

Game One was a humdinger, pitting our ace Tim Hudson against his counterpart Pedro Martinez (known to Bostonians as Saint Pedro of the Contract Holdout), a wily flamethrower with a Jheri curl that dripped duende. The A's scrapped out a run in the ninth[9] to send the contest into extra frames where, in the twelfth, with two outs and the bags full, catcher Ramon Hernandez did something no A's player had done since the heyday of Dwayne Murphy: He laid down a bunt of transcendent beauty. The ball dribbled down the third-base line. The entire bar let out a howl. Eric Chavez scampered home for the winning run, a walk-off bunt.

The clientele at Casey's was by this time quite drunk and ex-

9. The key single supplied by Erubial Durazo, whose mellifluous name I sang in my head for the next thirteen hours.

tremely belligerent, though I'm not sure that's ever not the case, and I was careful to hold off on any celebration until I hit the sidewalk, at which point I ran down the street windmilling my arms and pounded the hood of my car repeatedly.

I switched bars for Game Two. The A's pitched Barry Zito, whom I refer to as Baked Zito, based on my wishful theory that he smokes a lot of dope. Zito throws the most beautiful pitch in all of baseball, a curveball that loops toward the batter's frontal cortex before diving into the strike zone. It's a great deal of fun to watch a Zito curve, because hitters often buckle as they fight the impulse to bail out of the box. The Sox spent most of the afternoon in this mortifying posture. Zito struck out nine, and the A's breezed.

I had enjoyed the first two games about as much as a human being can enjoy two sporting events, a pleasure prolonged by listening to the meatheads on WEEI, who, taken as a single sound track, produced the ferocious whingeing of a large machine with broken gears. It took a great deal of willpower for me not to call the station.

I watched Game Three in the lobby of a hotel in Brattleboro, Vermont. I was in Brattleboro for a literary festival, and this meant I was eating dinner with a large group of writers, some of them cute lady writers. It seemed to suggest some sad, uncultured things about me that I would choose to watch a baseball game rather than flirt with cute lady writers. And so, as is often the case in my life, I watched on the sly, sprinting back and forth from the table to the TV at the bar, offering as an excuse an unspecified family crisis, which, pathetically, for my dad and me, an A's playoff game does constitute.

Of the many strange plays in this game, the strangest of them occurred in the sixth. Eric Byrnes, who had replaced Damon in center for the A's, wound up on third with one out. The Fenway masses absolutely reviled Byrnes. This had something to do with his ostentatious high-kneed gait (the verb "flounce" seems to apply) and even more to do with his flowing blond locks, which I will admit lent him the aspect of a slightly effeminate wrestling villain. Nonetheless, he stood ninety feet away from knotting the game at one, and when shortstop Miguel Tejada hit a high bouncer, he bolted toward the plate, where Jason Varitek awaited him.[10]

Byrnes came screaming down the line. He had the throw beat by several feet. But Varitek, who was standing in front of home plate, did something, well, evil: At the last second—and I must emphasize this temporal aspect, *at the last second*—he stuck his left leg out so that his foot, in clear violation of the rules of baseball, as well as common sportsmanship, was blocking the base path. Unable to change course, Byrnes slid directly into the side of Varitek's foot, which, anchored by his Brobdingnagian thigh, did not budge. Instead, Byrnes's knee crumpled, and he went tumbling headfirst *over* home plate. The ball now arrived and bounded past Varitek (understandably distracted by his effort to cripple Byrnes) and skittered toward the backstop. Byrnes hobbled to his feet and initiated a spastic jig behind home plate. He did not pause to consider whether he had touched home plate, or whether he might wish to, for he was in the thrall of a primal playground drama: *That motherfucker just tripped me.* For ten long seconds, Byrnes hopped around behind the plate, shaking his blond locks in anguish and reaching down gingerly to confirm that his lower leg was still attached to the rest of his body. Nobody could quite figure out what was supposed to happen next. And then suddenly the cameras picked up Varitek, who had run to retrieve the ball and now bustled toward Byrnes and tagged him. In any sane universe, the ruling here would be obvious: Byrnes should have been awarded home plate and been granted the right to administer a lethal charley horse to Varitek. This being Fenway Park, and the opponent being my own A's, the umpire called Byrnes out.

"Tough luck," the bartender said.

10. Varitek is often referred to as "the heart of the Red Sox." I think of him, however, as "the thigh of the Red Sox," owing to the Hendersonian dimensions of his quadriceps. In moments of morbid speculation, I have wondered whether these thighs are larger than my own torso. Those who detect an immature ad hominem in the foregoing observation, please note that Varitek's physical deformity plays a central role in the drama about to unfold.

Luck had nothing to do with it, but I nodded and returned to the table, where the writers were busily flinging bons mots and sniffing each other for coital ambitions.

The game ended in the bottom of the eleventh, when Boston's Trot Nixon deposited a fastball into the right-field bleachers. Nixon had missed three weeks with a strained calf muscle, and thus the announcers were quick to compare this blow to the Gibson homer of 1986. Nixon himself, interviewed after the game, awarded the RBIs to God. *It was Jesus up there swinging that bat,* he told America, in the timeworn tradition of athletes who view the Kingdom of Heaven as an upscale suburb of Las Vegas.[11]

I LEFT VERMONT with my back in spasm (in retrospect, it may have been my soul) and drove directly to an establishment called the Good Times Emporium, which looks something like paradise as conceived by a juvenile delinquent. It is the size of an airplane hangar and contains 50,000 video games, most involving Uzis. Also: pool tables, paintball, batting cages, air hockey, bumper cars, a wide array of fried foods, and a service staff legally required to wear blouses that make visible the tattoos on their boobs. The TVs are the size of billboards.

I was aware of the looming psychological danger. The Lord God of Sport had announced His presence to me the night before in that exquisite tableau of injustice. My hope was that He had gotten it out of His system.

In the second, the A's loaded the bases with no outs. Byrnes himself stepped to the plate and hit a towering fly ball down the right-field line. The fellow next to me produced a noise like a horse being punched in the stomach. But the ball tailed off at the last in-

---

11. I realize you expect me to launch a diatribe here about how modern sports culture—with its implicit reliance on aggression to generate unholy profits—marks a precise repudiation of the moral code Jesus expressed in the Beatitudes and, in this sense, a vital adjunct to the perversion of His message being carried out by the medieval bigots who populate the Christian Right of this country, but I'm not. So there.

stant, and he missed his grand slam by half a foot. Byrnes went quietly, as did the next two batters.

This was a squander of the first magnitude, a very bad sign. But we still had Tim Hudson on the mound. As the A's took the field for their half of the second, in fact, Hudson had gathered a small retinue around him. And then suddenly, Hudson was trudging toward the dugout while various Boston fans loudly speculated as to testicular endowment. The announcers eventually identified his injury as a strained oblique muscle. This struck me as appropriately oblique.[12]

On came Steve Sparks, a journeyman knuckleballer who had been released by the Detroit Tigers earlier in the year, not before helping that team set a major league record for losses. He promptly served up a gopher ball to Johnny Damon. It was now clear what was happening, no crystal ball necessary, and I began rooting—rather hysterically—for the Sox to break the game open.

Instead, the A's fought back and found themselves up 4–3 with six outs to go. At this point, I turned to the least felonious-looking guy at the next table and said, "Don't worry—the Sox will come back." I was attempting a move patented by Floodie down in Miami: the rare double-reverse judo jinxball. Keith Foulke, the A's closer, came on for the save. He retired his first two batters, then allowed the next two to reach base.

Up came David Ortiz. Because of his girth and jovial on-field demeanor, the Boston DH is often compared to the animated character Shrek.[13] Because he is also Dominican, the lily white Fenway

12. It would emerge that Hudson had sustained the injury the night before the game, during an altercation at a bar where he and another player had gone to unwind, apparently unaware that opposing players who enter Red Sox Nation surrender their civil right not to be hassled by shitfaced asshole fans.

13. In his recent Sox hagiography, *Feeding the Monster,* author Seth Mnookin portrays Ortiz as a locker-room clown who regales the press with prognostications such as "We're going to kick their ass, drink their beer, and rape their bitches."
   Adorable!

rabble have taken to calling him "Big Papi," one of those charming nicknames that no doubt make them feel very ethnic. Hitless in the series thus far, Papi whiffed at Foulke's first two offerings. Foulke now drew a deep summoning breath and prepared to slam the door.

But that is not what happened. Instead, Ortiz began fouling off pitches, settling into his swing, timing Foulke. I could see this with agonizing clarity. Foulke, meanwhile, was descending into that invisible panic that afflicts A's closers on the brink of a win that will deliver me unreasonable happiness. In the end, Ortiz worked the count full, then turned on an inside fastball that went screaming from the shaded infield into the blinding sun of right. Jermaine Dye, stationed ten yards too shallow, sprinted back toward the track. All around me, Sox fans rose to their feet. I could hear them cursing softly, making choked sounds of prayer. Dye turned first one way, then the other. He raked the air with his gloved hand, like a man frantically searching for the ripcord to his parachute. It was a very long line drive. At last, Dye leaped, a valiant and hopeless gesture. Ball met earth at the base of the wall and thudded and jittered. Both men aboard scored and Shrek the Rapist pulled into third, panting.

The entire population of the Good Times Emporium began chanting *Paaaapi! Paaaapi!* Young toughs of various ethnic flavors, boys who, on any other occasion, might have been happily knifing one another in the parking lot, were instead exchanging high fives and sloppy hugs, while I sat in a putrid cloud, breathing in the fried cheese sticks and chicken wings left to sit and the thousand happy beer burps offered up into the smoky air.

THE NIGHT BEFORE Game Five, I had a dream, and in this dream my father called to say the A's had lost 7–2, but that it was all right, they would be allowed to go to the Series anyway, an assurance that suffused me with irrational serenity. The amateur psychoanalysts among you will recall that '72 was the first of the A's three consecu-

tive championships, and the year my condition was born. Thus, the
dream marks the wished-for return to a prelapsarian state in which
father and son are reunited and the A's always win, even when they
lose.

I woke with a swollen tongue and October in my heart. This was
a Monday in Somerville and my apartment smelled of bachelor. The
novel upon which I had diddled away the past two years of my life
lay rotting inside my computer. I was supposed to visit a class of college students that night, to speak to them about how to survive as a
writer without actually selling your plasma, and I couldn't quite
bring myself to cancel, despite the fact that half the class (the Sox
fans) ditched anyway.

At precisely nine, I sprinted back to my car, intending to lunge
for the radio. My cell phone rang. This would be one of my friends
calling to inform me that the A's were down by nine runs and that
Eric Byrnes had been placed on dialysis. But no, it was a woman. A
very jiggly woman, as it should happen, who, I suspected, would let
me smell her neck. She wanted to see a movie.

I thought: *Yes, this is fate.* This is fate instructing me to go see a
movie and smell this woman's neck. Fuck the A's. Fuck my whole
messianic fan complex. The game was going to happen, no matter
what I did. The Lord God of Sport would carry out His merciless
will. There was no reason for me to suffer a third straight loss. So it
was settled. I was off to the movies.

But I couldn't bring myself to call this woman back. Instead, I sat
gazing at the shitty little radio in my shitty little car and imagining I
could hear the dull roar of the crowd, as I had on those many afternoons of my youth. And then (somehow) that roar was filling my ears
and it was a sweeter sound—more human and comforting—than
any I had ever known. Zito and Pedro were locked in a scoreless tie
through three.

I knew then that I would listen to the game, all the way to the
bitter end, because rooting simply doesn't work in retrospect. It requires an instantaneous response, the building of hope, strike by

strike, hit by hit, the gradual release of anxiety as your pitcher works his way out of a jam, the adrenal surge at the sight of a drive to deep left, the delicious horrible whiplash of a screamer snagged at the hot corner. The true fan, in other words, does not merely sit back and receive the game. He or she is working every moment, crafting fantasies, second-guessing, storing up regrets, tempering the unwanted equity of pain. This is the essential experience, the reward and punishment rolled into one, the sad duty of our sad disease.

So yes (of course) I blew off the tootsie and joined my friend Tim, who was at yet another bar with our pal Young Bull, a good-natured Texan stoner whose unseen darker regions had drawn him to the Sox long ago. In the sixth, Zito began to tire. His curve bit into the dirt while his heater, as if to compensate, rose slowly into the fatal latitudes. He gave up a dinger to The Brute Varitek, walked Damon the Apostate, then plunked Todd Walker. Zito was unraveling (as my students might put it) *like a tortured ball of yarn.* With the game tied and two on, Manny Ramirez stepped to the plate.

Since his arrival in 2001, the citizens of Red Sox Nation have enjoyed no greater pleasure than treating their dreamy left fielder as a communal chewtoy. His performance against the A's was not helping matters. He had gone 3-for-18 without an RBI. His last confrontation with Zito, in the fourth, had ended with Manny waving nostalgically at a fastball on the outside corner.

This was cause for hope, of course, which, if you have been paying any sort of attention so far, is cause for dread. Zito delivered a strike, then a ball, then a strike, then another ball. His fifth pitch was a fastball dispatched, unwisely, to the same spot he had tried last time. Manny was waiting.[14] A gruesome and unmistakable

---

14. It struck me as plausible that his feeble swing in the fourth was in fact a setup, a point Young Bull and I argued to the point of causing Tim to place his head on the bar and attempt to sleep.

crack rang out. The ball soared high into the air, did a couple of loops around the moon, and landed twenty rows into the bleachers. Young Bull jumped from his barstool and performed a tribal dance involving anointing his shirtfront with beer.

Here, down 4–1, I should have tipped my cap to the LGS and gone off to find a cat I might quietly torture. But I didn't want to be alone, so I hung around just long enough to witness Sox second baseman Damien Jackson and Johnny Damon engage in a vicious collision that knocked The Apostate cold for several minutes. What secret pleasure I took at the sight of his unmoving body! It was probably time to leave the bar.

Back at Tim's, I started smoking pot. I don't know why I thought this would make things better. (Drugs almost never make things better.) Young Bull ran inside and turned on the radio. But I was feigning indifference. I stood on Tim's porch and smoked and feigned and occasionally glanced through the window, where Young Bull was perched before the radio, clutching his head. He came outside a few minutes later to announce that the A's had knocked Pedro out of the game and put the tying run on first with no outs in the eighth. In I went, fuckheadedly, and listened to the heart of the lineup squelch the rally. Durazo: pop out. Chavez: lazy fly ball. Tejada: grounder.

I returned to the porch, pipe in hand, intending to scrub my short-term memory clean. Soon Young Bull would burst outside, wearing the grin of a miracle winner. It would be terrible for a few seconds. Then it would be over and I could return to the proper miseries of my life—the losing struggle with words, the quest for a woman stronger than my self-hatred.

As it happened, Young Bull did appear before me. But he looked stricken.

"What?" I said.

"You should come," he said.

"A homer? What. *What?*"

Young Bull went back inside.

A homer, of course, would have been far too definitive. You can't blow a homer. No, the A's had runners on second and third with one out in the bottom of the ninth. A base hit of any sort would win the game. They didn't even need a base hit to tie the game. A bunt would do it. Or a sac fly. Or a feeble little bleeder to the right side. These did not seem like unreasonable hopes.

The Sox manager, Grady Little, brought in his volatile sinker-baller, Derek Lowe. Due up was Dye, the A's best fly-ball hitter. But the A's manager, Ken Macha, called Dye back from the on-deck circle and pinch-hit Adam Melhuse, the backup catcher, who had collected three hits in Game Four. It was one of those moves guaranteed to make Macha seem like a genius, by which I mean it made absolutely no sense. Melhuse struck out.

Lowe now did the obvious thing—given that his true intent wasn't just to win the game, but to do so in a manner that would inflict maximum pain on me. He walked the bases full. Ellis, the second baseman, was due up. But he'd been pulled from the game in favor of Billy McMillon, who'd been pulled in favor of Frank Menenchino, who had exactly zero at-bats in the series. Eric Byrnes was the logical choice to pinch-hit, as he was batting nearly .500. But Macha had just inserted him as a pinch runner. So Macha stared down his bench—I like to think he did so with a funereal air—and came up with Terrence Long.

A reserve outfielder, Long had perhaps the most graceful swing of all the A's. The problem was that his bat never actually hit the ball. At least, I had not *seen* it hit the ball. He was being asked to rescue the A's and, by extension, to rescue me. To say that I smelled trouble would be like saying that Custer, upon reaching the Little Big Horn, smelled Indians.

Nonetheless.

Nonetheless, the Series had funneled down to a single batter. He reaches base safely, we win. He makes an out, we lose. The crowd out in Oakland was agape, athrum, ahowl, as was every member of Red Sox Nation. I myself spent the endless interludes between pitches pacing around the room, yelling out a series of increasingly demented bets—*twenty bucks says Long knocks himself un-conscious with his own bat!*—none of which Young Bull would ac-cept. No, he was busy hyperventilating, bent in the posture of a man waiting to be examined by prison guards.

To call this at-bat "a dramatic showdown" somewhat overstates actual events. Lowe made short work of Long, finishing him— if memory serves—in four pitches, the last a nasty sinker that dropped onto the inside corner.

In the moment that followed, Young Bull rose up and bounded over to shake my hand. Then he closed his eyes and smiled. I was working furiously to minimize the impact, telling myself this was just so much silliness, a juvenile attachment, setting over my burred raiment the flimsy and unconvincing robes of a New Testa-ment fan. "Nice comeback," I said.

Young Bull's phone rang and he gazed into the tiny blue screen. "It's my dad!" He flipped open the phone and began speaking as if he were five years old. "Wasn't it beautiful, Dad? I know! Gosh! I'm so happy!" Down the porch steps he wandered, out onto the side-walk to receive his dose of fatherlove. I followed him, merely to eavesdrop on his joy. The sky was a chalky purple and horns were blaring everywhere.

TIM HAD SHUT off the radio, in the interest of sparing me the postgame interviews. I would only read about what happened next, how Derek Lowe strutted off the mound and made an obscene ges-ture toward the A's. And how, in the A's locker room, Miguel Tejada raged against Lowe and vowed revenge to the assembled reporters. At a certain point, he was led away from the jackals to a private al-cove where he broke down altogether, for this was the ninth straight playoff clincher he had lost, and the weight of futility had finally crushed his athlete's pride. Tejada wept.

As for me, I was stoned and depressed, mired in a classic sports hangover, the period after a harsh loss during which you revisit all the ways your team chunked it while simultaneously feeling like a fool for revisiting all the ways your team chunked it. Psychologically speaking, the A's hadn't lost. They had refused to allow themselves to win. And this struck me as my own crisis, the white-hot shame at the center of my fandom. I kept holding myself back in matters of love and literature, swinging through the fat pitches, forgetting to touch home plate, choking. How is it, I wondered, that I might rid myself of this hex? Was there some sort of operation? Or maybe a blood transfusion. I even called my father, hoping to swear off the A's out loud, like they teach addicts to do. But he wasn't around.

I had reached the stretch of the Mass Pike that runs beneath the Monster, and as I passed into the shadow of that great green wall a terrible shame seized me. The Lord God of Sport had led me into exile, led me into battle against my sworn enemies, led me to the brink of victory a dozen times—and each time forsaken me. Or, more accurately, He had allowed me to forsake myself. What if there was no lesson here, merely an exercise in pain?

THOSE HOPING FOR a recitation of the ensuing Sox/Yankees series can pretty much fuck off. I did everything I could to ignore the affair, by which I mean I caught only five of the seven games. I am trying to think of the most appropriate metaphor for what it was like to watch. The best I can do is to say that it was like having to choose between Bush and Cheney.[15] The rivals bashed each other around for six games, taking three apiece, to set up the expected showdown: Pedro versus Roger Clemens.

I watched the game in a bar called Rocco's, on the shores of Lake Erie, the western extremis of New York State. The crowd was split down the middle, the Sox fans loud with pilsner and anguish, while the Yankee partisans remained quiet, churning inwardly. Clemens lacked his fastball, and exited after four. Pedro pitched superbly. He entered the seventh with a three-run lead, at which point Fox

15. This is what we in the lit game call *hyperbole*, for Bush/Cheney were—even as the series was being played—rapaciously ruining democracy as we know it, whereas the Sox/Yanks were merely ruining a week of my otherwise frittered leisure time. Still, I trust that A's fans will understand what I mean.

flashed a graphic onscreen, noting that he was 84–3 in such situations. The balloon of hope within Red Sox Nation swelled almost painfully.

Everyone assumed Grady Little would yank Pedro before the eighth inning, and allow his bulletproof bullpen to finish the matter. But this he did not do. No, Pedro remained in the game for another five batters, suffering what probably ranks as the most notorious meltdown in the history of baseball.

I should have considered this pleasure enough. But I was (and am), after all, the Red Sox Antichrist, and thus in this, my shining moment, I made what would turn out to be a momentous decision: I wrote a seven-thousand-word letter to my friends in which I broke down Grady's refusal to pull Pedro, and the ensuing disaster, in excruciating (and psychologically tawdry) detail. It was a florid glop of prose, bristling with the sort of false empathy that Iagos like me conjure at the drop of a ballcap. I knew my friends would read every word and that they would suffer deeply in doing so, while I, an alleged friend, an alleged *sympathizer*, derived some demonstrably sick pleasure at the thought of their deep suffering.

SO MY FRIENDS were in a shambles. The callers to WEEI had descended into sociopathic ideation. It was, in this sense, a return to the known world of glorious victimhood—for Sox fans are never happier than when they are pursuing despair.

As the 2004 season opened, my own expectations were humble: I wanted a final confrontation between the A's and Red Sox, with a culminating contest at Fenway Park, during which my Oaktown heroes would decimate the Old Towne Team, and, if necessary, I would be torn limb from limb on the infield grass by a raging mob. The key to happiness resides in such compromises.

But the A's missed the playoffs by one game. And the Sox, after losing three straight against the Yanks in the AL Championship, came roaring back to take four straight, then four more against the lethargic Cards. Damon the Apostate smashed the winning run in the Series finale and their new closer, Keith Foulke, recorded the final out, while I cowered beneath my blanket, waiting for my birthday to be over.

THE SOX FANS among you will find this summary cruel in its brevity. The rest of you need not shed too many tears. For the Red Sox, upon finally winning the Series, have launched their own cottage industry of Soxporn, a torrent of books and videos documenting the fortnight in question. My friends have watched and read and rewatched and reread all of this crap. They have wrung from the experience every precious drop of vindication, and turned ahead to disappointments yet unborn.

I think now of the recent conversation I had with a cabbie named John, on the way to the airport. The radio was tuned to WEEI, so I had to shout to be heard.

"You a Sox fan?"

"Since Yaz was in short pants," he said.

I asked him where he'd been when the team won the Series.

"Didn't watch the game," he said. "Didn't watch any of them."

"Wait a second," I said. "Not even the comeback against the Yankees?"

John the Cabbie glanced at me in the rearview mirror and shook his head. "Would've jinxed them," he said calmly. His cheeks were a deep scarlet, his white pompadour stained by a lifetime of smokes and cheap pomade. "Anyway, they won't win again, not in my lifetime."

He spoke the line with proper vehemence, but there was something hollow in his delivery. Without the curse, after all, he had lost the exaltation of martyrdom. In winning the Series—a triumph he hadn't even allowed himself to enjoy—he had suffered the ultimate loss. The secret wish nestled within his stated fear was obvious: He wanted to return to the way it had been before the Sox won, to recapture the ecstatic grievance that had defined him (and his fellow Soxchotics) as special.

It was at this precise moment, as I stared into the bloodshot eyes of John the Cabbie, as together we were swallowed by the blackness of the Callahan Tunnel and the babbling menchildren of WEEI fell abruptly silent, that I hung up my cleats as the Red Sox Antichrist. My work, I guess you could say, was done.

AND WHAT OF me and my Athletics? I keep meaning to quit them. Really I do. I have personal matters to attend to, and a growing list of moral qualms. I can't help feeling that sport has become a fueling station on the road to war.

It is also, in my view, a form of slavery. However we might seek to obscure this truth, the modern sports complex has reduced the most abject precincts of this planet to ad hoc plantations, harvested each year for specimens. The strongest and fleetest may win a few years of lucrative idolatry, but they are discarded soon enough, when their bodies break down. The peculiar sickness of the American mindset may be located in the peculiar notion that the professional athlete—rewarded all his life for a capacity to defeat and harm others—should serve as a moral exemplar. (The common parlance is *role model*).

Having said all this, I am left to explain why I can't quite quit the A's. My fancy excuse runs something like this: In a world in which our politics, our entertainment, our very waking lives have come to feel preordained by corporate masters, sport offers a last vestige of unscripted experience. True pressure, true grace.

The simple excuse is that I feel alive when I watch the A's. This vitality often takes the form of misery. But the chance to surrender my will is not without its sacred pleasures—a language, however primitive, with which to seek the solace of other men. Maybe it makes more sense to think of sport as the dominant religion of our age, the discovery of faith within ourselves by an allegiance to gods we can see, all those lovely bodies making miracles of air.[16]

16. I say none of this in an effort to whitewash the future of our nation. Our obsession with sport is clearly a symptom of imperial doom. We must remember: All that held Rome together at the end was spectacle.

I'm not suggesting that a stadium is a church. A stadium is just a place for people to gather close together, one of the last, ripe with longing, exposed to the risks of hope and its duties. I'm not naïve. Only I am. Sometimes I need to pretend. Sometimes I need a broken-down old stadium, stinking of beer and mustard, and rain falling like flour before the sodium lights.

Concerning the Laughable Nature of Literary Fame

(Not that You Asked)

HOW REALITY TV ATE MY LIFE

AKA INVASION OF THE RED BULL CONQUISTADORS

(A Melodramatic Farce in Twelve Brief Acts)

Act One

In Which I Make the Acquaintance of P. Diddy's Personal Trainer

A couple of summers ago, a woman named Angela Bosworth sent me an e-mail asking if I would like to appear on a new "documentary style" VH1 show called *Totally Obsessed*. I'd just written a book called *Candyfreak,* which was about, among other things, my obsession with candy. Ms. Bosworth had not actually read the book. She had, rather, "read a ton of articles" about the book.

This did not entirely surprise me. I had done a good bit of TV for *Candyfreak* already, so I was used to people not reading my book. I knew that TV producers came on hot and heavy but rarely followed up. And I knew they had a tendency to exaggerate the length and potential impact of any appearance.

My strangest TV experience to date had been on a show called *Cold Pizza,* ESPN2's answer to the *Today* show. They asked me to come down to their New York studio to discuss Halloween candy. I was booked onto the same show as P. Diddy's personal trainer, with whom I spent a good half hour in the green room and who, I don't mind telling you, has absolutely great delts, as well as a stunning grasp of the metabolic effects of a low-carb diet, though I can't remember his actual name. Let me be blunt: I'm not sure I ever knew it.

He got about twenty minutes on the air, in which he discussed his employer's upcoming entry into the New York Marathon, his training regimen, his blisters, and other pressing issues within the greater Diddysphere. My appearance lasted five minutes. I was paired with a host whose on-camera persona called to mind a particularly frightening anxiety attack I'd suffered in college. At one point, he stuck his mic inside his mouth so viewers could hear the Pop Rocks he had just inhaled. I know that at least one person saw this segment, because the guy who manages the bar where I go to drink off such experiences told me his wife had seen me. This is what's known, in the writing game, as fame.

To be clear, then: I had what I want to call a *bad feeling* about the request from VH1. I was almost certain it would mean a lot of time and effort, and some mild humiliation, that it would only invite stress and disappointment into my already stressed, disappointing life, that, in other words, I should delete the message, pretend it never arrived, and get back to work.

Act Two
The Things We Do for Love

Why, then, did I forward this message to my publicist—knowing that this act alone would essentially require me to appear on *Totally Obsessed?*

I want to say that I had hope. I want to say that I truly believed appearing on this TV show would lead viewers to seek out my work and that some of them would dig what I was up to and would tell their TV-watching pals, so that, in a sense, eventually, there would be a whole army of viewers awakened to the pleasures of literature. I want to say this. But of course it's complete bullshit.

My reasons were sadder—more abject and narcissistic. To begin with, I was worried that the VH1 folks would eventually contact my publicist anyway and that he might get angry at me for not passing this message along, which was not what I wanted because I worship the ground my publicist walks on, because he is the only person (other than my mother) who cares passionately about the fate of my books.

That's really a very small sub-reason, though. The main thing was that I was flattered and star-struck. I enjoyed casually mentioning *the VH1 thing* to friends of mine, which forced them to ask me what I meant, so I could then say, "They want me to be on this new program, the pilot, whatever. It's such a *drag*."

Yes, they needed to know that I considered the VH1 thing a *drag*. I was doing it only because my publicist forced me. My friends were remarkably, disturbingly, impressed. Their attitude toward me (generally one of informed skepticism) gave way to something more like awe. They wanted to know what the show was about, what I'd be doing, and especially whether this meant *they were going to be on TV*.

And all this helped mobilize within me a belief complex familiar to anyone who has attempted to put art into the world. It worked like this: I would appear on the show and be brilliant. I would get famous. Everybody who ever called me a loser, privately or publicly, would suddenly feel like losers themselves. I would actually travel back in time, to my childhood, and enjoy the love and regard of my entire family. All my insecurities would evaporate.

For purposes of brevity, I am excluding the more obvious, quotidian perks of fame, by which I mean the opportunity to ejaculate on Paris Hilton's face.

Contemplative Interlude I
A Brief Discussion of My Relationship to TV

I have never actually owned a TV, a fact I mention whenever possible, in the hopes that it will make me seem noble and possibly lead to oral sex.

As we all know, TV is a cesspool of mediocrity that sucks precious time and energy from those who fall under its spell. In other words, I am an addict. Anyone who has seen me in the presence of a television knows this.

As children, my brothers and I developed a TV loyalty so fierce as to occasion its own vocabulary. The brother who turned on the set first was said to "emanate." When another brother entered the room he would immediately ask, "Who emanates?" I should stress that we were using this word from the time we were eight years old, despite the fact that we had no idea what it meant, which, regrettably, is still the case. Most of the 1,739 fights we got into as kids related to some issue of emanation, such as whether the act of fixing oneself a banana with peanut butter constituted a voluntary surrendering of emanation and thus empowered the emanator-designate to assume control. I don't suppose I need tell you we could have done with a bit more parental supervision.

My point is that I would have suckled the cathode tube, given the chance. I can remember in vivid detail particular sessions of TV watching, as the gourmand might recall an epic meal. At the tail end of the *Candyfreak* tour, for instance, after five weeks on the road, I lay down on my hotel bed and watched consecutive episodes of a show called, I think, *Extreme Blind Dating,* in which the girl wears a hidden earpiece so that two of the guy's ex-girlfriends can, from a remote location, advise her as to the most humiliating things she might say or do during the date. At the end of the program, a limo shows up. If the girl is inside, he gets a second date. If he's failed the test, his exes are in the limo and they get to jeer at him and, in a gesture that is apparently fixed *Extreme Blind Dating* protocol, flash him their breasts. As I watched this program I began to believe that it was my duty to contact the producers—I took down the 1-800 number—and audition. I considered which of my exes would agree to be on such a show (none), and what they might tell my date (make him dance), and whether I could muster the necessary poise (probably not), and whether I really wanted to see my exes' boobs (yes), and which ones (any of them, actually), and would it be possible, in the absence of real exes, to hire fake ones (probably). It was, though I don't think I'm quite doing it justice, a glorious and deeply tragic afternoon.

Let me say also that TV has—like marijuana—gotten much more powerful over the past thirty years. There is almost always something compelling on, something I truly want to watch, often more than one thing, which is why my older brother Dave, when he gets access to a TV and emanates, actually watches four or five shows simultaneously, till he reaches a point of *narrative saturation* (i.e. his eye sockets start to bleed). I take it as a fixed law of cable TV that one of the *Rocky* films is on at all times, most often the fifth and worst *Rocky*, which I adore.

In short, when it comes to TV I have evolved a hard exoskeleton of moral distress and intellectual snobbery, which is in place to protect the squishy, defenseless flesh below.

Act Three
Introducing the Candy Monkey

You would think launching a show about obsessives would be pretty straightforward. Find the nutbags, turn the camera on. But you would be wrong. *Totally Obsessed* had an elaborate casting process. I was asked to send videotapes of previous TV appearances. I was asked to send photos. And I began speaking on the phone, nearly every day, with a young woman named Rakeda, whose job it was to "pitch" my segment to the higher-ups. She had a long list of questions: *Is candy more important to you than sex? Have you ever fought anyone over candy? If candy ran for president, would you vote for it?* She also began to interview my friends and family. I got lots of calls from loved ones, all of whom were terribly excited, but also a little baffled by Rakeda. "What's the deal?" my brother Mike asked. "Is she mentally handicapped or something?"

No, she was not. She was working toward a particular need: the need to supply her bosses with evidence that I was *totally obsessed* with candy. The fact that I had written a book about candy didn't really count. They needed something they could film.

Weirdly, stupidly, my segment was eventually approved, which meant I started getting calls from Simbi, the segment producer, and her assistant, Dana. I liked Simbi right away, because she seemed to recognize that her job was basically absurd and she laughed a lot and because she claimed I was her favorite subject so far. Dana I liked less. She spoke quickly, often incoherently, and tended to call at times that really weren't appropriate, such as 10 P.M. on a Friday night. When I closed my eyes, I could see her résumé and the words *associate producer* in a dignified font. It made me very sad.

Simbi told me the show wanted to capture me in my native habitat. I explained to her that my native habitat involved me sitting around in my underwear, avoiding writing. I did throw chocolate parties, and brought candy to poker games, and sometimes, if I was feeling crazy, I brought a few bars to my morning squash game. Simbi tried to sound encouraging about all this, though she clearly had hoped my schedule would involve praying to a large Candy Godhead, bathing in chocolate, and the liberal use of lollipops during sexual high jinks.

She spoke about one of her other subjects, a fellow from New Jersey who was *totally obsessed* with professional wrestling. "What's so great about him is that he jumps all over his furniture, kind of like a monkey, imitating all the wrestling moves."

"How did you find him?" I said.

"He sent in a tape."

Yes, as it turned out, most subjects had actually *applied* to get on the show. It was at this point that I should have realized I was out of my league. This was my competition: a guy who jumped on furniture.

But no. Instead, I concluded that there was a way for this to work. I was going to have to camp it up. I was going to have to become *The Candy Monkey,* a frantic, fraudulent, joyously undignified version of myself. The idea I had was that the smart viewers would embrace my shtick as cleverly ironic. They would recognize that I was actually a deep, thoughtful guy who was just playing a Candy Monkey on TV and they would admire my subversive irreverence.

In other words—and here we are coming to a key factor in the ensuing failure—I developed the dangerous fantasy that *I could defeat Reality TV.*

Act Four

Some Initial Bitchslaps

Based on the phrase "documentary style," I assumed the crew scheduled to arrive at my apartment in the middle of July would consist of Simbi and a camera person, who would probably have one of those little handheld digital numbers.

I had underestimated Reality TV, rather seriously. The crew numbered six: Simbi, a cameraman (Jay), a sound guy (Derek), a gaffer (Andy), a site coordinator (Charlie), and Simbi's cell phone (Phone), by which she was in near-constant contact with the home office. We met for a get-to-know-you dinner and they ordered without regard to price, and when I asked Charlie what a site coordinator did exactly, he said, "I'm the one with the Gold Card!" then laughed diabolically.

They'd been on the road for a couple of weeks already, filming other *Totally Obsessed* people, and displayed the kind of forced camaraderie that derives from spending hours together in hotel rooms and far-flung bars. I liked their vibe—laid-back, eager to party, not terribly attentive. In a word: L.A.

And yet, when they arrived at my place the next morning, what emerged from their van was more like a military unit. The guys, though all impressively hung over, hauled in case after case of equipment, light stands, cameras, tripods, monitors, boom mics, dimmers, extension cords. Charlie was dispatched to fetch coffee and returned with twenty quarts and two dozen Dunkin' Donuts.

Simbi took me aside to discuss the filming schedule. "Scene one will be the basic interview, then we'll move to a scene in the kitchen . . ." I didn't really get it. *Scenes?* What had happened to the poker game and the chocolate party? Didn't they want to capture me in my habitats?

My friend Eve explained this to me later. "When I mentioned your chocolate parties to Dana, she said the only way they would be interested was if you were the only one who ate chocolate. Like, if you invited people over for the party, but you were so obsessed with candy that you wouldn't let them have any."

Had I known this a little earlier on, say, before the crew had occupied my home, I would have been given pause. But it was too late. I was seated on a small black chair. The camera was rolling. Simbi was asking me the first of forty-one questions, all of which I'd already been asked many times.

Simbi's shooting script called for me to provide an extensive tour of my apartment. Fortunately, in the spirit of the Candy Monkey, I'd gone to the trouble of redecorating. I'd put Rocky Roads on the mantle, lined the wainscoting with caramels, filled my cabinets with Smarties and Neccos, taped wrappers to the walls, mounted chocolate porn on the fridge. The pièce de résistance was a thirty-five-pound Chocolate Pagoda, which my friend Karl (an engineer) had spent four hours constructing the night before. It was the most beautiful thing I had ever laid eyes on. In short, I had transformed a somewhat grubby bachelor pad into a somewhat grubby *Candy Lair*.

Act Five
Squeezing Poop

I had assumed (again, stupidly) that filming would be a breeze. But between lighting and sound, it took more than an hour to set up each shot. There was a lot of standing around while Jay and Andy had conversations like this:

> JAY: Squeeze a little more poop on the dimmer.
> ANDY: There?
> JAY: No, now there's a bounce off the fill.
> ANDY: What do you want, a Gary Coleman?
> JAY: Try a beaverboard, maybe raise the main.

ANDY: Good?

JAY (*checking
the monitor*):   No, we need a dickhead. Actually, try a
buttplug.

ANDY: You want me to Dutch those barneys?

JAY: No, just Hollywood it.

ANDY: There?

JAY: Yeah, that's good. We're speed.

I know you think I'm making this shit up, which, actually, I am. But those guys did use every single word in the above dialogue. It was part of their film production slang, a way of aggrandizing what would otherwise be grindingly dull work. They had a special term for everything. A clothespin was a *C-47*, or a *bullet* (a backward clothespin, naturally, was a *C-74*). The sandbags used to secure equipment were called *beach,* unless they were over thirty-five pounds, in which case they became *ballbusters*. One did not take a bathroom break but called for a *10-100* or, in more extreme need, a *10-200*. (It will go without saying that I later forced Andy to make me a glossary of terms, which now hangs on my wall.)

I found the whole experience hopelessly cool—for about six hours. When it was time for lunch, Charlie went out in the van and returned with enough deli to feed the Red Army. He'd already gone to the market and brought back copious amounts of fruit, vegetables, nuts, chips, beef jerky, energy bars, soda, water, beer, and, of course, Red Bull. (The production team drank tremendous amounts of Red Bull. I'm not sure I can overstate the amount of Red Bull they drank. Over a two-day period, I would estimate a million cans.) There was about the scene something endearingly profligate.

Between shots I would wander into my kitchen and stare at all the food on my counters, the donuts, the Pringles, the soup and sandwiches, the coolers brimming with Cokes, and I would think: *This is free! VH1 paid for this!* I wanted to grab someone off the street and hold up each item for him and shout: *They bought this! VH1 bought this for me! I am not being had for cheap!*

Act Six
Waiter, There's a Sound Guy in My Shower

Because my bathroom was too small to accommodate more than two people, particularly if one of those people (Jay) was toting a camera the size of a small atomic bomb, Derek had climbed into my tiny shower. He stood under the spigot gamely, trying to ignore the nest of hairs clogging the drain at his feet. His fuzzy boom mic was poking over my white plastic shower curtain, which has been described by more than one friend (in fact, by every single one of my friends) as the ugliest in the short human history of shower curtains.

Let me say: I was embarrassed.

The bathroom was not somewhere I wanted to be filmed. I was concerned that my mother would see the segment and catch sight of the rust-stained toilet bowl and the somewhat bacterial sinktop and that she would weep.

But Simbi had insisted that I give a full tour of the apartment, and this included the bathroom. In my capacity as Candy Monkey, I had stashed some taffy in the medicine cabinet, along with a confection called Lobster Poo, which seemed, at the time, to make sense thematically. Jay called out "Speed" and I began holding forth on the need to "fortify nontraditional candy venues," a sermon which culminated with my recitation of the couplet on the bag of Lobster Poo:

> I went to the Cape and here's the Scoop!
> I came back home with Lobster poop!

It was at this point that the bloom came off the rose. Some more serious version of myself (standing behind the actual, blathering version of myself) whispered into my ear: *What in God's name are you doing?*

To which I responded: *I am lifting American minds from the muck of ignorance.*

My Student, Under Interrogation

I put in eight hours as the Candy Monkey that first day, explaining why I kept candy in my laundry room and demonstrating how I ate M&M's, while Simbi barked out helpful instructions such as "Can you open your mouth a little wider?"

Again: American minds, lifting, muck of ignorance.

Late in the afternoon, I went to do some errands, and the crew set up to interview a few of my friends. I can remember returning home at dusk and catching sight of a disquieting tableau through my bay window. My former student, a shy, brilliant kid named Simon, was sitting under a harsh bank of lights. The boom mic hovered over him. His pale forehead shone like the surface of an egg. He was sweating and blinking. I wanted, right then, to walk into my house and tell the crew to turn off the lights, let the poor guy go. But I waited until the interview was over and ushered him into my bedroom, which was the only place that wasn't overrun with equipment.

I kept asking him if he was okay and he kept saying yeah, he was okay, but in a dazed manner, like a boxer taking a standing eight count. We spent a few minutes talking about his writing, his plans after graduation. But the noise from the other rooms was distracting. The crew was breaking down the set, swilling Red Bull, discussing how hammered they hoped to get.

"I should probably go," Simon said.

"Thanks," I said. "Thanks for coming by and doing this."

"No problem. It was fun."

"It didn't look like too much fun," I said.

"I don't think I was what they were really looking for," he said. "I probably should have made you sound a little crazier."

"That's ridiculous," I said.

A whoop went up from the next room. Simon glanced at me and grinned sheepishly. He was an exceptional young writer, a maker of stories with real human depth. And I could see now that he actually felt guilty. Reality TV had made him feel guilty for failing to be disingenuous enough.

Contemplative Interlude II
On the Nature of Power in Hollywood

It was a given, among the crew, that working for VH1 was strictly a money gig. They all harbored bigger dreams. Simbi had a short film making the rounds at festivals. She was working on a screenplay. So was Derek. So was the rest of Los Angeles County. They talked about all this over lunch, their projects, their writing partners, the nervous chatter of who knew whom.

They knew the fundamental truth of Hollywood: that the big money is made by films and TV shows that are patently stupid, though these products are made by people like Simbi and Derek, who are not patently stupid, and who must therefore exist in a state of creative and moral limbo, justifying their hackwork by perpetually citing higher artistic ambitions.

I came to like Charlie best because he just didn't give a fuck. He had no grand yearnings, no life plan. He was thirty-five and looked like a cross between a young Martin Sheen and The Dude from *The Big Lebowski*. He liked to party. He liked to get naked. He liked to spend The Man's money. He was probably clinically hyperactive. And yet there was this fetchingly maternal aspect to him. Here was a guy who, while the other guys struck the set, cheerfully scrubbed the soy sauce off my kitchen counters and carefully affixed a white plastic garbage bag to my oven door. I thought: This man is going to make someone a hell of a wife someday.

Act Eight
Andy Is in Play

Day Two began with a scene in which I went candy shopping at my local Brooks pharmacy. I had already explained to Simbi a few dozen times that I didn't shop for candy at my local Brooks, that I didn't shop for candy at all, really, but that was beside the point. She had a very clear idea of what she needed, and I, your humble Candy Monkey, did my best to oblige her. This meant walking down the candy aisle while Simbi issued directives such as "Fondle the candy like you're choosing a melon!"

It was, however, genuinely fascinating to see the way the world interacted with Reality TV. They were in awe. Little kids would wander up to the crew and stare at them in wonder. The braver ones would mug for the camera. My haircutter, Linda, whose shop is next to Brooks, came by to watch. Best of all, Andy, the gaffer, when he wasn't squeezing the poop, went over to ply his charms on the Brooks cashiers.

In contrast to Jay, who was tall, sloe-eyed, undeniably hunky, Andy was ill-kempt and stubby. He looked like a Metallica roadie. But he knew he had the Hollywood mojo on his side, and this, along with being a stranger in a strange town, endowed him with swagger. His rap and the attendant giggling from the heavily mascaraed clerks were far more interesting than anything I was doing. I wanted to turn to Simbi and say, "Listen, you're missing the action! Andy's showing that girl his tattoo!"

In watching this drama unfold, I could see precisely how those *Girls Gone Wild* videos came into being, because everyone in this country shares the same not-very-hidden desire: to be the star, the one who becomes known under the lights. There was no real reason for Reality TV to contrive elaborate plot lines. All they had to do was to head out into public with a camera crew. Was this not the transcendent lesson of *Cops*? That Americans were so desperate for fame they'd agree to be arrested on TV?

And here it seems worth mentioning an incident that had taken place on Day One. During my initial interview, the woman who lives next door began to scream at her grandkids. This was not unusual. It was, in fact, their central daily activity. The problem was this woman's voice, which might be compared, favorably in terms of decibel output, to heavy munitions. What struck me was the alacrity with which my landlord, Stephen, who'd been watching my interview, marched outside onto the porch.

"Quiet down!" he bellowed. "We're trying to film a TV show over here!"

Act Nine

In Which I Am Afforded a Brilliant Opportunity to Forfeit Any and All Legitimacy I Might Ever Earn as an Artist

Now it was late in the afternoon and I was hunched in my bedroom closet where, in my capacity as Candy Monkey, I had stashed candy. We had filmed, to this point, some nine hours of me yakking about candy, fondling candy, gobbling candy on demand. Simbi had one more request. She asked that I seat myself on the bed. The crew fell silent.

"We need to talk about something," she said quietly. "I didn't tell you this before, but every segment of *Totally Obsessed* has what we call the *reveal*. That's the part of the show that we tease at the beginning and then, at the end of the show, we do the reveal, okay? So what we need for your segment is to get you on your bed, rolling in candy."

"Excuse me?" I said.

"We need you to roll around in candy on your bed."

"On my bed?"

"Right."

"Roll around on my bed?"

"Right."

"In candy?"

Simbi nodded.

"I don't really feel comfortable with that," I said.

"But you told me you rolled around in candy!" Simbi said. "I remember, because that was the exact moment that I said to myself, 'This guy really *is* totally obsessed.' "

I should confess that I had told Simbi I rolled around in candy, because when I was a little kid I used to roll around in candy. And she very well may have asked if I still rolled around in candy as an adult, and I very well may have told her yes. If I did so, let that stand as a precise measure of my shamelessness.

But the issue now was whether I was willing to roll around in candy *on camera,* and my answer was a polite no. It was impossible to fully explain my reluctance to Simbi, but it went something like this: I had written a book, which I believed in, but also feared was gimmicky. Rolling in candy for a national TV audience was only going to reinforce this latter notion, and also, in truth, I already had done my duty as the Candy Monkey, attempting to persuade people to buy this book by flying around the country handing out free candy bars, and I was distressed, in some more fundamental way, at the notion that writers should have to do this sort of shilling at all, particularly on TV, the medium that had done more than anything to kill reading in this country.

Simbi looked at me with real hurt in her eyes. Or maybe the word I want is *betrayal.* She looked at me like I'd betrayed her. Then she began to argue with me. She argued that I had promised her this, that I would be letting her down if I refused to roll in candy, breaking a personal covenant, and also that I shouldn't be self-conscious, I should just "let myself go" and have a sense of humor about the whole thing. "That's what we're really looking for," Simbi said, "people who aren't afraid to just be themselves." Her voodoo was very powerful.

And because, in my own Vichy way, I was still hoping to collaborate with her in construction of my own supposed fame, I began to waver. Maybe I could do this, lighten up, play along. Then I would conjure an image of myself actually rolling around in candy and think: *No fucking way.*

Act Ten
In Which Simbi Does Not Accept No for an Answer

"All right," Simbi said. "Hold on. I need to make a call." She went outside to contact the Executive Producer. The crew and I could see

Simbi marching back and forth in my driveway, speaking urgently into her cell phone. We couldn't hear her, but I imagine the conversation ran something like this:

"Hi, it's Simbi. We're here with the candy guy. Yeah, well, there's a problem: He won't roll in candy."

"What?"

"He says he doesn't feel comfortable rolling in candy."

"But he told you he rolled in candy."

"I know, I told him that. But he got cold feet. He says he's afraid it will make him look like a fool."

"So what, he thinks he's an *artist* now? He's too *good* to roll around in candy?" [Sound of fist smacking desk.] You get in there and convince him! Capiche? I didn't send you three thousand miles just to film some jackass *talking* about candy."

"What if I can't?"

"Simbi, what's the name of the show you're working on?"

"Totally Obsessed."

"Which of those words don't you understand? Now you go talk to this punk and get me that reveal!"

Simbi came back inside and announced that she had a plan. I didn't have to roll my *whole body* in candy. But maybe I could just show her the kind of candy I liked to roll in; I could roll my arm in candy. So I got a bunch of different kinds of candy and put them on the bed and I offered a brief lecture on candy rolling. Simbi kept saying things like, "Now, doesn't that just make you want to roll your *whole body* in that candy? Come on! It'll be fun!" This went on for an hour.

Eventually, Simbi gave up on the candy rolling thing. But she still needed a reveal, so I agreed to lie on my bed while Jay filmed a close-up of my face as I delivered an earnest monologue, ostensibly to a lover just off camera. "You know how I feel about you," I said. "You're special to me, and together, we're really kind of magic. But I have to tell you, the time has come for us to take this relationship to the next level. I have certain *needs,* like any man."

At this point, the shot widened and it became clear that I was addressing a piece of candy, specifically the Valomilk, a chocolate cup with runny marshmallow filling, which I bit into. As the white filling ran down my chin, I grinned and said, "You only eat the ones you love."

I had hoped this super-quasar of glibness might be enough, but Simbi demanded a second reveal, which consisted of me dispensing pillow talk to an invisible lover—again a Valomilk, this time set atop the pillow next to mine.

Act Eleven
Chicks Dig Scars, They Don't Dig Grafts

By early evening, the crew had run out of rooms in my apartment, but they needed to film a few more of my friends, so they had taken over my landlord's place upstairs. They now controlled the entire house. I watched them ferrying equipment up and down the stairs and decided that the most effective way to take over a country was not to bomb them at all, but to send Reality TV crews.

It was close to midnight before the interviews were done. This is when the serious drinking started. Charlie had made a liquor run and come back with enough beer for homecoming at Mississippi State. Jay began mixing Red Bull and Absolut. I kicked in some decent-grade *mota* and started cranking the tunes. Pretty soon, we were into the chocolate, the good stuff, and things got very sloppy.

Andy pulled a slip of paper out of his back pocket and showed it to me. There, in loopy script, was the name *Cristal*, and a local phone number.

"Scored it at Brooks," he said.

"Fuck yes!" Charlie said. "Call her, dude!"

"I already did," Andy said.

"Well, call her again! Come on, get her over here. You can do her first and I'll take sloppy seconds."

"Fuck no," Andy said. "*I* got the number. Anyway, I already called her. She was making all these excuses. I'm not calling her again."

He went to call her again.

Jay began to tell a funny story about Charlie's last Christmas party, during which Charlie had fed his cats an entire baked ham.

"You know what my favorite thing is?" Charlie asked me. "Jehovah's Witnesses. This kid came by my house a few weeks ago and he started talking about how Jesus Christ was my only hope of salvation. I said to him, 'Do you get to have sex as a Jehovah's Witness?' He said, 'Only for the purposes of procreation.' I said, 'Dude, they've got you *brainwashed*. You're a young guy. You should be out there fucking.' He was trying to get away from me, but I wouldn't let him go. That's what I love. I *love* when phone solicitors call me. They say, 'Do you have a minute to talk?' and I say, 'Oh, listen, I've got *all day* to talk.' "

In the other room, Simbi was crashed out on my couch, listening to Etta James at maximum volume. My pals Boris and Austin were doing shots with Derek and Andy and talking about what guys so often talk about: slang terms for degrading sexual acts.

Charlie began telling me about a motorcycle accident he'd gotten into and pulled up his pants to show me the damage. He grinned down at his leg, which was the color and texture of corned beef hash.

I told him it looked pretty bad.

"Let me tell you something," he said. "Chicks dig scars. They don't dig grafts."

Then we all gathered around my coffee table and I cut up a bunch of Lake Champlain Five Star Bars.

The party went on and on, more booze, more chocolate, more pot, more music. Toward the end of the night (which is to say, toward dawn) we all started getting a little sentimental. We took pictures. We vowed to stay in touch. I felt like I'd become an honorary member of the crew. I knew this was mostly bullshit. But there was something real in it, too, the drunken riffs, the music, the fine chocolate on our tongues. It felt wonderful to be a part of such a spontaneous gathering, as if I had finally managed to show them the true dimensions of my life, which would never appear on TV, to be aired and commemorated in syndication, but would live in our collective memory as a wondrous and fleeting human communion.

Act Twelve
The Ax Falls

It began with Dana. It began with Dana and her insufferably frantic phone calls, which beset my life a month later. She wanted to know if I had any more footage of myself. I e-mailed her back a message that said, in essence: *What in God's name are you talking about?* I and my friends had already provided some fifteen hours of footage, for a segment that Simbi eventually informed me would run four and one half minutes.

Dana kept calling, demanding "more footage," so I called Simbi.

"We need shots of you eating candy," Simbi explained. "What we got is great. Everyone here loves it. But the Executive Producer wants more shots of you actually eating candy."

"Didn't we do a lot of that already?"

"Yeah," Simbi said. "But she wants more."

"If I say no, does this mean they cut the segment?"

"No, not at all. It would just make what we have stronger. And no one is going to ask you to roll in candy. I promise."

I had that same bad feeling, like I was Montezuma being asked to invite Cortés back for a nightcap. But I also felt that my publicist and my friends were counting on me. And, of course, some of that same fame panic set in, the dumbshit hunch that I would be perceived as a failure if this fell through. So I told her okay.

Simbi followed up with an e-mail in which she noted, matter-of-factly, that a new crew would arrive in three days, and that they needed to reshoot all of the scenes in my house, along with the scene at Brooks.

In great confusion, I called her.

Simbi explained that the Executive Producer wanted more of a feeling of "us just being a fly on the wall." She went on for several minutes, until it became clear that she had no idea what the Executive Producer wanted. I told her I'd be available from 10 A.M. to 4 P.M. on Sunday, and happy to reshoot anything inside my apartment, but that was all.

Simbi called the next day to tell me the segment had been cut. I had expected she might be apologetic, but she sounded more self-pitying than anything. I don't suppose I blame her. She was the one, after all, who had to wake up each morning and go to work at *Totally Obsessed*.

So I was pissed off. But that actually lasted only a minute or two. After that, I was merely relieved. I was so tired of dealing with Reality TV, tired of their tireless manipulation, tired of my own willingness to go along with what had clearly become a bad charade, just plain tired.

Contemplative Interlude III

The central illusion of Reality TV, the notion that the viewer is merely "a fly on the wall" watching life unfold, is, as you have seen, bogus on virtually every level. The people who appear on Reality TV are carefully vetted. The producers put them in artificial situations and goad them to behave in ways they wouldn't normally. Indeed, the main criterion for those who want to appear on Reality TV is the extent to which they will allow themselves to be humiliated—the Shameless Quotient.

I hadn't realized it at the time, but throughout the filming of the segment I (and my friends) had been engaged in an unstated power struggle. We hoped to represent my obsession with candy not as a pathology, but as an exaggerated—or perhaps liberated—version of the obsessions that live within all of us. All that is fine and well, but it's not what Reality TV is about.

So what is Reality TV about? It's about the careful construction of two central narratives: false actualization and authentic shame. The nubile bachelorette on the brink of true love with one of several men she has known for seven hours. The brazen cad who manipulates his beloved on cue. They need actors who can ignore the contrivances, who can put their tears and howls on public display, who will roll in candy when asked to do so.

The success of the genre is certainly a measure of Hollywood's imaginative failures. Even more, it reflects our unrequited yearning for the authentic. Americans are drowning in a cesspool of fake emotion, nearly all of it aimed at getting us to buy junk. But we really do want to feel, even if that means indulging in the jury-rigged joy and woe of others. It's quite a racket, actually, to feel so truly moved, even as we fall farther and farther away from the truth.

BLOG LOVE

A ROMANTIC WEEKEND WITH
MY VERY OWN CYBER NEMESIS

A couple of years ago, a writer friend of mine sent me a link to a weblog in which a guy named Mark Sarvas posted the following statement, under the headline THE TRUTH MUST BE TOLD:

> The adulation accorded Steve Almond constitutes one of the blogosphere's enduring mysteries. From the very first days of this site, I've shaken my head in a sort of dazed wonder at the wake of overheated prose stylings the guys [*sic*] leaves behind. So I am, of course, delighted that the *Washington Post*'s Jonathan Yardley finally steps up and speaks the truth.

An excerpt from Yardley's review followed. Then this summation:

> If Almond devoted a fraction of the efforts [*sic*] he brings to self-promotion to his writing, he might finally be on to something. But I doubt it.

Who was Mark Sarvas? Well, he was a writer of course. You could tell this because there was a portable typewriter right next to him in his photo, which was taken outside. So he was clearly dedicated to his craft. But he was also a cool writer, the kind who wore a leather jacket and shades while hanging out next to typewriters outside.

Sarvas lived in Los Angeles. This meant he was a novelist *and* a screenwriter. Somehow, between novel drafts and pitch meetings, he managed to produce a blog which he had named, unpretentiously, *The Elegant Variation*.

His entries were literary gossip items for the most part, links to articles, an occasional belch of schadenfreude. His prose style stressed elevated diction, convoluted sentences, serial use of the royal "we," and, in an effort to convey a stream of consciousness . . . lots . . . of . . . ellipses. Writing like Henry James (or at least Henry James for the learning disabled) apparently helped Sarvas preserve the fantasy that he was not just a wannabe writer bravely dedicated to long-distance slander.

A FEW MONTHS later, I received an e-mail from another friend, directing me to an online forum in which Sarvas described the birth of his blog:

> I launched The Elegant Variation in a fit of madness on October 14, 2003 with a declaration of my love for James Wood and my loathing for Steve Almond. Nine months later, my positions remain unchanged.

Given my formative role in its creation, one might expect his blog to be brimming with critical insights into my work. Nope. In fact, it was not clear Sarvas had read any of my work. In this sense, it wasn't quite fair to call him a critic. He was more like what the young people call a *hater*. And not just your garden variety hater. No, he was special. He was President of the Official Steve Almond Haters Club. I considered writing him a congratulatory note and sending along a signed photo. Sadly, I do not possess any signed photos.

Indeed, it struck as me as one of the dinkier titles in the history of belles lettres to be President of the Steve Almond Haters Club—

like being an ambassador to Liechtenstein, or maybe an ambassador *from* Liechtenstein. Pynchon. DeLillo. Foster Wallace. These were authors one might be proud to revile. But me?

Poor Sarvas! As I considered the guy from afar, I began (almost involuntarily) to feel sorry for him.

OF COURSE, ANY SERIOUS writer needs to preserve the bulk of his pity for himself, so I put Sarvas out of my mind.

That changed in spring 2005, when I was invited to the Los Angeles Times Book Festival. Knowing I was headed into town, a guy named Jim Ruland asked me to read at his series, "Vermin on the Mount." I said sure. His next e-mail listed the lineup, which included . . . Mark Sarvas. Ruland also asked me to come by the Vermin booth to sign books. Among the features of this booth: Sarvas would be "live blogging."

The idea of not doing these events never occurred to me. On the contrary, the third-grader who thrives inside me very much looked forward to accosting Sarvas.

When I told my pal Pete about this plan, he shook his head.

"What?" I said.

Pete paused. "He's in love with you."

"Please," I said.

"Hatred is a form of love," Pete said. "Look at it, dude: He founded a whole website based on his feelings for you."

"It's a blog," I said.

"He's obsessed with you."

"He hasn't even read my work."

"It's what you represent. You're like his big, sexy daddy."

I took a moment to let this sink in. "Are you saying I should fuck him?"

"No," Pete said slowly. "What I'm saying is that you should fuck him and film it and post the video on the Web."

"That is *so* hot," I said. "I'm getting hot just thinking about it."

Pete put his hand on my shoulder.

"So is he. I guarantee it. So go. Go make magic with your secret online fucktoy."

BUT OF COURSE I could not make magic with my secret online fucktoy. Life is never that simple. For one thing, I had a girlfriend (Erin) out in L.A. For another thing, my discussion with Pete had hipped me to the idea that Sarvas wanted my attention, rather desperately. Whether he knew it or not—chances are not—he was toting around a whole scrotum full of fantasies: The basic one in which he mustered the courage to insult me to my face. The exalted one in which he read so brilliantly at our shared appearance that I would be forced to admit I was just a self-promoting hack. The kinky one in which we slapped one another with silk gloves, then slipped into tights and fought a duel.

It was my job not to gratify this shit. Any sign that I knew who he was, that he mattered to me in any way, would simply give him too much pleasure. (Let me be honest: I was concerned he might ejaculate in his pants.) So I had to be very *detached*.

My plan was simple—I would pretend I didn't know who he was. When introduced, I would say a few nice, disingenuous things about blogs, and if he, or someone else, mentioned his antagonism, I would smile and say, "Thank God someone is out there keeping me honest!" Then later, if it felt right—and only if it felt right—I would pull down his Underoos and spank him on his hot little blogger bottom.

MY PLAN TO show restraint didn't last long. I had been at the Book Festival for barely an hour when I made a beeline for the Vermin booth. I walked right up to Sarvas and stuck my hand out and said, in a loud, friendly voice, "Hi! I'm Steve Almond!"

He looked up, startled.

"Jim's over there," he said, pointing to the tall fellow on his left. My hand hung in the air, waiting for the shake that would initiate our *supercharged literary smackdown*. But Sarvas took a swift step to the side, sat down in front of his laptop, and refused to look up again.

I felt oddly preempted. It had been *my* plan to pretend I didn't know who Sarvas was, and here he was pretending he didn't know who I was, even though I had just introduced myself to him.

I stood there for another few seconds, staring at Sarvas as he stared at his computer screen. I wanted to say something to him, something like, "Does anyone around here smell blog pussy?" But this would blow my cover, give him that gift of acknowledgment, so I shook hands with Jim instead and waited (in vain) for *him* to introduce me to Sarvas, who remained hunched over his machine, live blogging.

THAT NIGHT MY GIRLFRIEND—against her best intentions—checked his blog. She wanted to see what Sarvas had been writing as I stood in front of him.

Here is a direct transcription:

> 1:41–Steve Almond is standing right in front of me . . . We haven't spoken; he's talking to Jim . . . Wondering if he'll punch me out . . . I think I could take him . . .

As sad as this might seem, even sadder was the response of his fellow bloggers. One of them, a guy named Robert Birnbaum, sent the following response:

> *Yo! Fo! Shizzle!*
> *Almond b a wus. He gotz to be got.*

Remarkably, Birnbaum is not a young African-American blogger from Compton who goes by the street handle OGB (Original Gangsta Blogga). He is a paunchy middle-aged Jew who conducts long interviews with writers for *his* lit blog, often mentioning himself and his dog Rosie. Having been interviewed by Birnbaum myself, I tend to think of him as the Regis Philbin of the lit game, though that may be overstating his charm.

It was not entirely clear how I was supposed to be got (or perhaps gotz) but the presumed method of execution seemed to involve Sarvas and his keyboard: I would be live blogged to death.

THE VERMIN READING was at a bar in Chinatown. I arrived early, to make sure I got to hear Sarvas, but what struck me was Jim Ruland's introduction. He described Sarvas as a selfless champion of literature. It was especially disheartening to hear this, because Ruland was smart enough to recognize how little Sarvas actually cares for art, the extent to which his blog was an elaborate and indulgent plea for regard.

At the same time, Ruland was running a reading series in Los Angeles, a town where books were a minor cultural curiosity that occasionally spawned depressing movies and, more often, sat on coffee tables, suggesting intellectual depth and accenting the color scheme. His desperation, in other words, endowed Sarvas with some perceived power, which explained why he was on the bill in the first place. It was a kind of sponsorship showcase.

The piece Sarvas read exuded a dismal semicompetence. One of his characters *spoke through clenched molars.* Later on, he (or she or it) did something *to no avail.* He didn't much care for his people, and it showed.

There was an intermission, during which the readers milled around downstairs. Amazingly, none of the local lit trash on hand had enough gumption, or plain old mischief-making instincts, to engineer an introduction. Most knew who Sarvas was, and that he hated me. But none of them would acknowledge the dynamic. Instead, they all stood around in a cloud of unrequited rubbernecking.

MY READING WAS a letdown. Ruland got the name of my new book wrong. Sarvas failed to rush the stage. I read a story, stupidly, that expressed my predominant feelings about Southern California:

The sun was gone now; the purple smog of dusk was upon them. This was a summer evening in L.A., just the way they drew it up all those years ago. A breeze came rolling in and the streetlights began to come lit. The very thought of the city beyond his hotel exhausted him: the knotted freeways, the vast, flat valleys of porn, the hot distance of everything from everything else.

A few hours after the event (ah, the joys of the Internet!) Sarvas offered his readers the following assessment of our respective performances:

We're pleased to say the reading was a smashing success . . . Folks even seemed to like our offering, laughing more or less where they were supposed to . . . and we can report that Steve Almond's reading did nothing to alter our opinion of him . . .

Later he added:

. . . We found his story to be wholly not our cup of tea, its literary sensibilities a bit too informed by the pages of Penthouse Forum for our tastes . . . We're scarcely prudes but Almond's work is all assfucking and facials without much to commend itself for . . . we're struck by an absence of context . . . of character . . . of depth . . .

Sarvas couldn't have known this, but my response to his entry was a distinct sense of arousal . . . thinking about him typing those words . . . *assfucking and facials* . . . with his actual fingers . . . we wondered what Sarvas might have been wearing when he posted . . . was he dressed in his leather jacket? . . . maybe nothing *but* his leather jacket . . . might he be whispering my name? . . . through *clenched molars?* . . . we were trembling . . . yes, trembling . . . *entry* . . . the very word dripped . . . *assfucking* . . . *entry* . . . *We're scarcely prudes* . . . was Sarvas trying to tell us something? . . . we tried to keep from touching ourselves . . . honestly, we *did* . . . alas, it was *to no avail* . . .

THANKFULLY, SARVAS AND I had one more shot at love—my Sunday morning visit to the Vermin booth! He would have to be there (live blogging!) and, with an hour to kill in the same small booth, he would *have* to talk to me. I wore something low-cut, but not slutty, and curled my hair.

But he didn't show.

Devastated, I proceeded to the VIP area, a sun-dappled veranda where I stood around nibbling canapés with the other authors, all of us feeling thoroughly fluffed by the star treatment. This was L.A., after all, a town that runs on the bad Kool-Aid of fame. The problem was that every ten minutes or so some minor film celebrity like Eric Idle or Michael York would drop by and we would all stop talking and stare and recognize, at once, how sadly un-famous our little kingdom is.

I had two official gigs at the festival. The first was serving as moderator of a nonfiction panel. My four authors had written books on the following subjects:

- 1968
- Political activism
- The development of penicillin
- Anal sex

I am going to spare us all the embarrassment of detailing this particular panel.

My second gig was as a panelist on a roundtable discussion devoted to the short story, which played to a full house. Sarvas had grabbed a seat up front and brought along his computer. Just before the panel began, I walked over to him and set my hand on his

shoulder and said, in a soft voice, "Hey, I really enjoyed your reading last night." I was hoping to get his phone number, obviously. I
was hoping to be a part of his next *entry*. (I am so transparent!)

Okay, that's not true. My intentions were a bit less prurient. I
hoped this comment might teach him something: that it was best to
conduct yourself like an adult, to exhibit grace even when what you
wanted to do (maybe even had the right to do) was tear someone a
new asshole. But the lesson didn't take.

I'll explain why, but it's important first to talk about the panel itself, which was sensational. My co-panelist, Merrill Gerber, talked
about what it was like, as a woman of the fifties, to write stories
about domestic life at a time when her colleagues—men like Robert
Stone—were offering up accounts of war and drugs and politics.
Aimee Bender, whose stories are often fantastical, helped me see
plot in an entirely new light. "When you write outside of realism,"
she observed, "plot becomes the internal life of the character." Bret
Anthony Johnston spoke eloquently about the practice of writing. "I
don't believe in the idea of talent," he told the audience. "I don't believe in the idea of inspiration. I don't believe in a muse or anything
like that. I believe in work. I believe in dedication. . . . Your job is to
try to make a piece of art, and the way you do that is by going to your
studio every day." There wasn't a single comment that didn't smack
of the truth, that didn't make me think about my own work and the
larger role of writing in the present culture. I took notes.

Of course, Sarvas was also taking notes. Aside from bashing
me, here is the sum total of what he had to say on his blog:

> On the subject of the short story, the panel is moderated by
> Novelist/Blogger and former The Elegant Variation guest
> host Tod Goldberg; the other participants include Aimee
> Bender, Bret Anthony Johnston and Merrill [*sic*] Joan Gerber.
>
> Tod keeps it light, querying the authors on everything
> from peanut butter preferences to whipped cream refer-
> ences . . . We also learn Tod has a short story collection com-
> ing out in September . . . but apparently *Tin House* won't

publish him . . . Aimee Bender apparently brought a cheering section, as the room erupted into cheers at her introduction . . . Tod identifies her as crush-worthy for smart 13 year
olds . . . The most notable thing to us is that Gerber has published seven collections of short stories . . . seven collections . . . we wonder how on earth she manages to get them
published . . . (Forget the seven novels she's also published . . .) Over the years, Redbook published 42 of her stories . . .

ATTENDING THE PANEL had forced Sarvas to confront his actual
role in the literary order: He was a pretender, a person who lacked
the dedication Bret Johnston spoke of, and who therefore had created his own narrative (the blog) in which the essential topic was
not literature at all, but his own towering envy. *Why them? Why not
me?*

It came as no surprise that his "coverage" of the event read like
a Page Six dispatch. Nor that his loyal readers felt well served by this
summary. What astonished me was that Tod Goldberg, our moderator, responded. "Thanks for providing coverage," he wrote. "And
wonderful as always to see you out causing trouble."

Why would Goldberg—a fine writer and genuinely thoughtful
guy—offer such a comment? I suspect because he views Sarvas as
someone who might help his career. The same is true of Jim Ruland. Whatever they think of his ad hominems, in the end they kiss
his ass.

Publishers have started doing the same thing. If you want an
index of just how desperate the industry has grown, look no further
than the rise of the lit blogger as a phenomenon. Some are even
parlaying their blogs into book deals. Why? In part, because publishers are drawn in by the mystique of the Internet and the notion
that an author has a built-in—what is the word the marketing people use? Ah yes, here it is—*platform*.

To be clear: Some bloggers also happen to be terrific writers.
They use their blogs to undertake the honest labor of self-reflection.

The improvisational form activates their love of the language. But many bloggers are simply too lazy and insecure to risk making art, to release their deepest emotions onto a blank page with no promise of recognition. So they launch a blog instead.

I can understand the temptation. It's one I feel every day. Sarvas horrifies me precisely because he represents certain desires that live inside me: the desire to avoid the solitude and humiliation of sustained creative work, to find a shortcut to fame.

Does that turn you on, Sarvas? You're *inside* me.

THE LIT BLOGGERS out there will, I suspect, eagerly interpret the foregoing as a blanket condemnation of blogging. It is not. My beef isn't with the medium, but those who glibly abuse its privileges. (Or, as I prefer to think of them: assholes who blog.)

Twenty years ago these guys were, for the most part, struggling writers whose assholic notions were limited to friends, family, and those unfortunate souls they encountered at cocktail parties. Today, they get to broadcast these notions to the world, under the banner of "lit blogging."

All of which raises the question: Why do so many people read lit blogs?

To begin with, not *so many* people read them. Instead, a very concentrated population read them over and over. Namely, other bloggers. They all read one another, in the hope something they mentioned on their blog will be cited on another blog. It's a kind of Ponzi scheme in which the object is attention, and the shared illusion is one of relevance.

Of course, plenty of aspiring writers and publishing folks also read lit blogs. With coverage of books all but disappearing from corporate media, these sites serve as instant clearinghouses for news items, local readings, and reviews. Many (Sarvas's included) advocate for favorite writers. They allow people to feel connected to the world of letters.

All this is perfectly commendable. At their finest, these blogs contribute to a serious discussion of literature and the world at large, which is why I happily write pieces for the more thoughtful ones. But lit bloggers also have a tendency to boil that world down to a series of conflicts and controversies. Reading them often becomes a legitimized form of scandalmongering, a chance to revel in the failings of others.

The impulse is natural enough. The modern writer is engaged in an enterprise almost guaranteed to crush the spirit. Blogs merely serve as bulletin boards for the resulting feelings of despair and envy. Their chosen topic happens to be literature, but it could just as well be sports or politics.

In this sense, Sarvas has less in common with his hero James Wood than he does with Rush Limbaugh. Both are part of a burgeoning culture of grievance. They engage their audiences not through serious critical analysis of their alleged domain (policy, literature) but through a demagogue's excitation of spite. If this era has proved anything, it's that the demagogues win unless you smack them back.

FOR THOSE OF YOU wondering why I would lavish all these words on a twerp like Sarvas, there's your answer. I am well aware that in the process, I have made a dream come true for the guy. Yes, he has officially infiltrated my world. And all it took was two years of sustained slander.

He hasn't realized this—and he never will—but his subconscious motive for attacking me was the hope that I would someday write this very piece. He envisioned something truly vicious, something he could feed off for a good long time. I've tried to oblige. But I'm also going to offer him something he wasn't bargaining for: my forgiveness.

I don't mean pity. I do pity the guy. But that's a condescending posture, and it only gets you halfway to the truth. I mean *forgiveness*. I forgive the guy for hating me so much. If I were in his position, I would feel the same way. And I have. I've felt the same burning jealousy he has, toward those writers whose artistic and commercial success shames me. If I haven't broadcast those feelings to the world, it is only because my act is a little more polished than his.

But we're basically the same guy. We both face the same doomed task: to write in an era that has turned away from the written word. I wish Sarvas the best. May his finest motives win out in the end. That would be a triumph no one could ever take away from him, or diminish. Shit man, it might even be a work of art.[1]

1. Last winter Sarvas sold his first novel. Mazel tov, *mon blogamour!* Here's to the hope you take up fiction . . . full-time.

I can't remember the particulars, how it started with Barry Hannah. I'm pretty sure I was in grad school, turning my tender ambition at words into an endless feud. Nothing made much sense. I lived in the South (how had I wound up in the South?) in this crappy carriage house with a mattress on the floor. I cooked quesadillas over an open gas flame and drank cherry Coke from the big bottle. From time to time, a lady spent the night, but she always smelled the loneliness and I couldn't bring myself to beg. My stories were great gray puddles of blah.

I was working so hard at being a laudable young writer, but no one was giving me any eggs. I wasn't getting what I deserved. I was getting *ripped off*. So every day I sat there in that broiling apartment, in a fog of resentment, pumping out B.O. and wondering when things were going to change. Someone must have read the symptoms, or maybe I had the good sense to go to the library on my own—whatever the case, I found myself with a paperback of *Airships,* dating to 1979 and showing all of those years.

The first line I read was this:

"My head's burning off and I got a heart about to bust out of my ribs."

You'll have to remember that this was in grad school, where, by no exact fault of anyone on the premises, the herd was pushed (and pushed itself) in the direction of serious and subtle prose, where the high crime of any workshop was overt emotionalism, the abject declaration that what we were up to *mattered.*

So there was Barry Hannah and his weird, scampering, unstoppable blood leaping against all that.

"I got to be a man again," he wrote.

And: "When it comes off, I see she's got great humpers in her bra."

And: "Everyone is getting crazier on the craziness of simply being too far from home for decent return."

He was a guy in whose presence I could actually, finally, *breathe*. It didn't matter that his stories were loose and Southern and baroque—things I would never be—only that they were authentic. And this wasn't because of his great bulging brain (like Faulkner) or his macho restraint (like Hemingway). It was because he used language to express extreme feeling states with such naked precision. Or maybe it would be more accurate to say that his extreme feeling states summoned the language. I knew this much: His insides were soft and red, like a tomato. It was that way for both of us. Only he was able, somehow, to make gorgeous frescoes where I made only pulp.

I read *Airships* chronically, maybe a dozen times, and each time I wanted to lick the pages. Those stories! All full of death and sex and grotesque types chewing to the end of their tethers. What kind of world was this? Why, in the face of such pain and humiliation, did I want never to leave them?

I can remember the long August days of nothing, the dumb, stoned parties, my idiot heart clutching at anyone who came close and driving them off. I was living in the Bible. Everything was wrath and betrayal. I took it all twice as hard. I shaved my head. I wanted to look like the freak I was.

There was one party in particular, later on, in autumn. This was the night I was supposed to consummate matters with my love interest, a fraudulent poet with a nice big caboose. The energy between us was deep and crazy. We were going to electrocute one another with desire. We were going to bleed the same blood. But before I could touch her in any real way, she turned away and fled into the sticky night, and another friend, just about to dump me also, stared down at the concrete pilings of my porch and said, "Well, you know, you *are* kind of a train wreck."

Everyone else left too, off to be happy and normal, to dream in placid colors, and I went inside my place and looked at the mess from the party, the beer bottle ashtrays and burnt tortillas, and my ears were ringing with the hurt. I was disgusted with myself: my dull sentences, my social failures, my inability to feel less about the world.

Those were the nights I sought out *Airships*. I'd sit there and read a sentence like "I'm going to die from love" and start crying. And what's strange is that it felt so good to cry, there was a kind of joy in it, because all feeling is joy, because the capacity for feeling is the great unstated human achievement, and because somewhere, off in the distance, I could see that my capacity to feel wasn't going to mess me up forever, and that someday, if I kept at it, the writing thing, if I kept myself open to the lashings of the world, the true, brutal hurt of the place, I might start to get somewhere.

So that's what *Airships* was about for me: coming out of hiding as an emotionalist. Realizing that, amid the vanities and elisions of the Southern literary tradition, there was a deep, Christian possibility: that confession might actually cure, that love might act as a revolutionary force, that the chaos of one's past and present, if fully experienced, might portend some glowing future.

All of which sounds hopelessly lofty. All I mean is that reading the guy made me a more forgiving person. There's room in this world for all of us freaks.

PRETTY AUTHORS MAKE GRAVES

There's a helluva lot more of us . . . than you.
—FRANK ZAPPA

I was an ugly kid. Buck teeth. Fat cheeks. Bad hair. *Terrible* hair. You look at the old albums and it's a museum of bad hair. I should have had myself shellacked.

But listen: Most of the good writers out there are ugly. Butt ugly. Plug ugly. *Fugly.* I'd give you a long list of examples, but I'm not interested in research. Research bores me. You know what I'm talking about, anyway. All that literary dogmeat. Except for Faulkner. Faulkner was hot. But he was a drunk, and he was mean to his kids.

I only trust the ugly writers, anyway. Deep down, those are the ones who have earned their wrath. All the rest of them, the pretty boy and girl authors, fuck them. Or, better yet, don't fuck them. Get them all hot and bothered. Tell them you know Terry Gross, you once dated her former personal assistant, then leave them there, lathered up and grinning in a hot cloud of their own fabulous bone structure.

As for author photos, they're a goddamn fraud. The photo on my first book is Exhibit A. It's the most pathetic sensitivo-beefcake shot of the century. My friends tell me I look like a gay porn star. Maybe I am a gay porn star. Maybe my gay porn star name is Maxi Spray. Doesn't matter. Anyone who's seen me in person knows the truth.

If you want to make art in this culture, if you want to shake people down for their feelings, you're ugly by proxy anyway. All that's going to happen is this: You'll sit down and decide you're *profound* and you'll write a lot of dreck for a long time and various people along the way will feed you little niblets of praise, which you deserve, but not for what you're actually writing, which is still a stinking heap of narcissism. Then, eventually, you'll start to send your work out to the bad parents of the world and they'll find it (and you) ugly and send you little slips of paper with passive-aggressive inscriptions printed by machines and you'll start to see yourself, finally, as they do: an ugly little wannabe freak with a car that makes guys stop you in the parking lot of your supermarket and offer body work for cheap. This is called progress.

Because what you're aiming for here is to rediscover that inconsolably ugly little kid inside you, because that's what triggers the beauty jones.

One measure that will help: *Stay away from healthy romantic interaction.* The worst thing you can do is to use the funk of sexual success as a hedge against the appropriate depths of self-horror. Remember, you're probably clever enough to fool someone betterlooking for a while. But in the end, you're ugly. That's where you live, and you live there alone.

The rest (bad news!) consists of the dogged, lonely work. You sit there. You push your characters around. And when you, or they, feel ugly enough, have felt ugly enough for long enough, a little thrush of beauty unfurls to rescue both of you. Then it disappears.

If you're truly unlucky, some of the bad parents out there will start to accept your crap and you'll move on to the next set of bad parents until finally you're dealing with the world of New York Publishing, which is inhabited by bright, ambitious people who hate your guts for still trying. They will make you feel worse and worse and uglier and uglier and *in the end* you'll need to thank them, because they, too, are helping you find that inner ugly schmuck kid I keep mentioning.

It is perfectly reasonable to fantasize about punching these asswipes. But they are only emissaries from the world of commerce, bit players, pimps and petty tyrants, and they have only the numbers to defend them, which is to say they have no defense, whereas all of us, the artists, we have our ugliness and the resultant beauty pinned to our lapels.

Are you picking up what I'm putting down?

Let me tell you a little story.

When I was in seventh grade I fell in with a crowd of pretty people. At my school, they were called *rah rahs*. They were viewed with derision by the rest of the population, who were either physically ugly or wrongly colored or suffered from the ultimate form of disfigurement, which, in this culture, is poverty.

I myself was plain ugly, but I'd gone to a grade school that nobody recognized and so I was a novelty and eager to please and, as such, was adopted by the rah rahs. There was one girl in particular, Nicole Taylor, and she was absolutely stunning: blond hair, blue eyes, ski jump nose, just what you'd expect. She was also—and I'm not sure why I'm mentioning this, but it seems obscurely relevant—a Mormon.

One night, we were at a party up in Los Altos Hills, the wealthy part of town, and we started playing spin the bottle. Nicole spun the bottle and it pointed at me. I was absolutely terrified. She kneewalked over and she set her lips to mine and stuck her tongue out. What I'm telling you: She pried my mouth open with her hard little tongue and jabbed it around once or twice and then pulled away and returned to her place with an icy expression. She never forgave me for that indignity, which was the indignity of the beautiful having to embrace the ugly.

At a party some months later, at her own lavish home, I and a kid named Troy took part in an impromptu chugalug contest. Troy was as boring as a stump, but he was also the most handsome boy in the history of the world. He was so handsome you wanted to lick his skin. So we chugged our bottles of Sprite and let the carbonation burn our throats and suddenly Nicole appeared in front of us and said: *Steve Almond, if you spit that soda on me I'll have my boyfriend kick your ass!*

I spat the soda on her.

I didn't mean to. It was a reflex. Nicole burst into tears. She spent the rest of the party in a state of puffy bereavement. Everyone shook their heads. Nicole got what she wanted; I was neatly expulsed from the rah rahs.

The lesson is this: Justice can be its own form of beauty. And this: The ugly are doomed to a certain kind of solitude. All right, fine. What else is the life of a writer? We're all frauds waiting to be found out. We're all cowering dogs. We're all hoping to wring a little beauty from the neck of shame. Fine. Fine fine fine.

Let me tell you another story.

When I was in tenth grade I went to see a play at the local high school auditorium. It was a play about Vietnam, something righteous and tragic. I got there late, so I had to sit in the front row. (Do I need to tell you that I was alone? That I could not find anyone to accompany me?) Just at the end of the second act, during the big, tense soliloquy by the star—who was supposed to be ugly, mangled by the war, but was in fact as handsome as James Dean—I cut a fart. It wasn't a very loud fart. Just a quiet little fart that slipped out. But it came during one of those hushed, actorly pauses and caused the people sitting in the front three rows to start laughing in soft convulsions. When the lights went up I hurried from the theater and went to get my bike from the racks. A bunch of kids were behind me, laughing. When I turned around they stopped abruptly and one of them, a sweet homely girl named Kendall, came over and asked me how I was doing. She felt bad for me. I was *The Boy Who Farted.* For the rest of high school, I would be *The Boy Who Farted.* I would be renowned, in the small, merciless universe of my high school, for having let a little cloud of ugliness escape my body in public.

When people ask me how I came to write and why I write so much and why there's such an embarrassing yearning for beauty in the shit I write, I often feel like telling them this story. Asking them: What would you do if you were *The Boy Who Farted*? Wouldn't you want to persuade the world to regard you in some more flattering light?

A few more items:

Buy art. Quit mucking about like a cheapskate and wolfing down burgers from Fat Food. Stop throwing your money down Hollywood's sewers. Vote with your dough and vote for the stuff written or sculpted or sung by the ugly. Actually concentrate on who you're fucking. Hold your one and only heart to a higher standard. And so on. I'm proud to be ugly, and proud to make pretty things.

What are you?

{

A Recipe
to Die for,
A Band to
Worship

(Not that You Asked)

DEATH BY LOBSTER PAD THAI

A COUNTERPHOBIC PAEAN TO FRIENDSHIP, CRUSTACEANS, AND ORAL TRANSCENDENCE

I am frightened of many things: death, Mormons, Stilton cheese, scorpions, Dick Cheney, the freeways of Los Angeles. But I am perhaps most frightened of lobsters. The spiny antennae, the armor-plated cephalothorax, the serrated claws—they are, to my way of thinking, giant aquatic cockroaches who can snap your finger off.

I mention this because for the past few years now I have been heading up to Maine to visit my pals Tom and Scott, and specifically to partake of the transcendent Lobster Pad Thai that they prepare together, lovingly, painstakingly, over the course of a long, drunken summer afternoon. And because this past summer I played an unwitting (and reluctant) role in the preparation of the greatest single Lobster Pad Thai in the history of man. And lobster.

It began with a simple request: Would I be willing to stop by an establishment called Taylor Seafood to pick up some things?

Of course I would.

"We'll need a pound or two of shrimp," Tom said. "And some lobsters."

I swallowed.

"They're selling four-pound lobsters at a great price."

I now spent perhaps half a minute trying to imagine myself picking up a four-pound lobster, with my actual hands, but blood kept getting all over the lens.

"Hello?" Tom said. "Hello?"

"Yes," I said miserably.

"Did you get that?"

"Yeah. I got it. Four-pound lobsters."

"Four of them. We'll reimburse you when you get here."

You'll reimburse me, I thought, *if I live that long.*

I'M NOT SURE how many of you out there have seen a four-pound lobster. (Most of what you see in the grocery stores or restaurants are less than half that.) Neither my partner in crime Erin nor I was quite prepared.

The creatures were—as Tom would later observe unhelpfully—larger than many newborn infants. Their tails were Japanese fans. Their claws were baseball mitts. They squirmed unhappily as the guy working the counter packed them into flimsy plastic bags. The biggest one swung toward me before he was lowered down and I am here to tell you there was murder in those beady stalked eyes.

Yes, of course the claws were bound with thick bands. The animals had been rendered sluggish by ice and air. They were in no condition to attack. And yet . . .

And yet the true phobia is marked not by the threat of actual harm, but a fantasy in which the subject imagines harm into being. Thus, as Erin drove north, as the bags rustled about in the backseat, I felt certain the lobsters were merely *pretending* to be sluggish and out of sorts while in fact communicating with one another via their antennae, biding their time, preparing to launch a coordinated attack. How would this happen? I didn't know exactly. I envisioned them using their tails in a sort of ninja-pogo maneuver, bouncing from dashboard to emergency brake while nipping at our fragile extremities.

Thus I kept close watch over the bags until such time as we arrived at the home of Scott and his wife, Liza, Tom's sister. Also on hand for our arrival were Tom's lovely wife, Karen, and their two darling children Annabel (age: *almost* eight) and Jacob (age: four), all of whom gathered in the kitchen as we lugged the four heavy bags inside. Scott immediately opened one of them and hoisted out one of our purchases. He whistled admiringly while Jacob—perhaps the only other one of us who realized the danger we were in—took a step backward.

SOME BACKGROUND IS IN ORDER.

Fifteen years ago I flew down to Miami to interview for a job at the alternative weekly and, after two days of vapid schmoozing, decided not to take the job. Then two things happened: I ate my first bowl of black bean soup, and I met Tom, the managing editor, for a cup of coffee. I felt almost immediately that I had found a long-lost older brother, the kind of guy who might rescue me from my own glib excesses—both as a writer and a human being.

There is plenty to explain this. We're both Jews, suburban depressives, painfully susceptible to the song of language. In the four years we spent together in Miami, Tom taught me most of what I know about writing. He also taught me how to eat.

I can remember practically every meal I've eaten with him over the years: not just the epic five-course AmEx-buster partaken at Kennebunkport's hallowed White Barn Inn, but the pillowy gnocchi in vodka sauce ordered from a tiny Miami trattoria called Oggi, as well as any number of grilled fryers exquisitely prepared by Tom himself, using butter, rosemary, and sea salt.

The man has always been a foodnik. But in recent years, his culinary interests have bloomed. Part of this is due to Karen, whose abilities are of such a caliber that she regularly enters (and wins) national recipe contests. But it is Scott, his cheery brother-in-law, who has been his most concerted enabler. The two of them are deeply in love, and cooking has become the purest expression of their devotion. For a number of years, they prepared crab cakes together. A few years ago, they decided to undertake Lobster Pad Thai.

Tom's reasoning was based on the following factors:

1. He refuses, on principle, to eat lobster outside the state of Maine;

2. His central goal, therefore, when visiting Scott and Liza each summer, is to eat lobster every single day;

3. The rest of his family, particularly his children, do not care to eat lobster every single day;

4. The pad thai format is one way of sneaking lobster past these ungrateful philistines;

5. The recipe plays to Scott's strength as a cook: the ability to organize and prep tremendous numbers of ingredients (what the French call, somewhat grandly, *mise en place*).

It is Liza's contention that her brother Tom employs one additional factor, namely that this recipe calls for the use of every single utensil in her kitchen.

TO RETURN TO the scene of my terror: The lobsters had arrived. Scott was holding one in his hand, waving it about so that its claws clacked like castanets. Jacob and I were not amused. Eventually, the lobsters were shuttled down to the basement fridge. The people rejoiced. (At least, I rejoiced.) Erin and I were fed many scones. A miniature-golf excursion was initiated, then a long discussion concerning Liza's latest sandwich creation, a lobster roll Reuben, which sounded obscene, delicious, capable of clogging a major coronary artery at fifty paces.

An hour or so after noon, Tom and Scott stood up and looked at one another and announced (in the same way I imagine the lead climbers announce an assault on the summit of Everest) that it was *time to get started*.

I feared this would mean a reappearance of the lobsters, but there was a good deal to be done before that. The chefs use a recipe from Jasper White's noble volume *Lobster at Home,* one White attributes to Gerald Clare. As with most Asian recipes, it calls for various esoteric ingredients (shrimp paste, fish sauce, Thai basil, cilantro), all of which must be precisely measured, poured, mixed, whipped, and sliced.

It may well be true that Tom and Scott use every single utensil in Liza's kitchen. But it is equally true that they have a fantastic time doing so. Indeed, for me, the second great pleasure of the Lobster Pad Thai ritual (after the eating, at which we will arrive in due time) is watching these two commandeer the kitchen. Their style, in terms of grace and economy of motion, calls to mind Astaire and Rogers, though in terms of alcoholic consumption, Martin and Lewis might be closer to the mark.

Scott does most of the blade work, and it says something profound both about his skills with his trusty eight-inch Wüsthof Classic and my own culinary incompetence that I have watched the man julienne lemongrass for a full ten minutes.

Both chefs do a good bit of punning, with Tom—a longtime headline writer—taking the lead. (To give you a flavor of his style, consider this groaner, which topped the review of a particularly dismal Chinese eatery: *Wonton Neglect.*) These shenanigans compose a kind of theater in the round, given that the kitchen is the home's central hub, and given that their pace is, to put it charitably, a leisurely one. It is not uncommon to hear Liza and/or Karen mutter that *they* could prepare the same meal in an hour, rather than six. Scott and Tom are entirely impervious to such kibitzing.

This is what I find so enchanting: that two men should lose themselves in the spell of collaboration. My own experience, growing up with two brothers, did not include group food prep. The closest we came was the time Dave stabbed Mike with a fork.

so scott and tom were having a swell time cooking, and I was having a swell time watching them, and Liza and Karen were having a swell time both not having to cook and gently mocking their husbands for being slowpokes; the kids were climbing all over Erin. The afternoon was cooling off. The ginger had been minced, the scallions finely chopped.

"Is it time?" Tom said.

Scott nodded and went out back to fire up the propane-heated turkey fryer that he and Liza bought a few years ago (I believe I've conveyed that they're foodies). This could mean only one thing: the reappearance of the lobsters.

Yes, up they came from the basement. Scott carried two of them outside and lowered them, tailfirst, into the scalding water. Erin, who is a vegetarian on moral grounds but eats seafood, wanted no part of this. None of the females did, actually. Scott and Tom were interested in a purely scientific sense: How many four-pound lobsters could fit in your standard turkey fryer? (Answer: two, just barely.)

In the end, Jacob and I were left to watch the pot and its unhappy crustaceans. I am sorry to report that they did not die immediately. One in particular did a good bit of writhing before giving up the ghost.

"Is it still alive?" Jacob said.

"No," I said. "Those are just death throes."

"But it's *moving*."

"Yes, that's right. But sometimes an animal makes little movements after it has already died."

Jacob looked at me skeptically.

"What's that stuff?" he said finally.

The lobsters were emitting strings of pearly, coagulating liquid.

"That's . . . that's . . . I don't know exactly."

Jacob had been curious about the lobster boiling in the way of all morbid four-year-olds, but this latest development exceeded his tolerance. He headed back inside.

The lobsters were dead now, no question. Their shells were turning a luminous red beneath a veil of briny steam. I had watched them perish. I felt bad about this. They were innocent creatures, after all. Terrifically ugly and potentially lethal, but only if I found myself on the ocean floor, a place I did not often find myself.

Tom and Scott reappeared. Their only concern was timing. How long did it take to parboil a four-pounder? Scott poked at one of the lobsters. I decided that I probably needed a beer.

IN TERMS OF lobster guilt, the cooking phase was only a prelude. For the central scene of the entire pad thai drama resided in the gathering of the partially cooked lobster meat, which required the complete destruction of each animal's exoskeleton and the scrupulous removal of every single morsel therefrom.

To bolster this effort, Tom had bestowed unto Scott several Christmases ago an implement which has since come to be known (to them, at least) as *The Eviscerator,* a pair of truly fearsome kitchen shears used to cut through the shell of a lobster. Also deployed was the traditional claw hammer. The other members of the family gave the kitchen a wide berth.

I'm not sure that I can describe the action adequately, other than to observe that it made open-heart surgery look tame. This was nothing like the dainty dissections performed by casual diners on restaurant lobsters. It was carnage, an orgy of twisting and snapping and hacking and smashing and the emission of numerous fluids. To say that Scott and Tom enjoyed this ritual is to understate the case. They conducted their operation in a giggling ecstasy. This was a treasure hunt, with gratifying elements of gross-out humor.

Tom peeled off the top of one tail to reveal a dark, veiny line.

"What's that?" I said.

"Back end of the digestive system," Scott said.

"It's full of shit," Tom said.

"The shitter," Scott said.

"The poop pipe," Tom said.

They had each drunk about a six-pack.

There was also a great deal of green gunk, which is called *tomalley* [insert your own pun here] and is technically, somehow, the lobster's liver. Scott would later inform me, rather against my wishes, that he and Tom sometimes smear tomalley on a piece of bread, a snack he touts as "pungently tasty." (On a related though unnecessary health note, Scott felt compelled to warn me that tomalley should not be consumed by pregnant women or children, because it contains toxins, which he claims, implausibly, can be counteracted by the consumption of beer.) The harvest went on for nearly an hour, because the four-pounders were so incredibly large and because both men pride themselves on a thorough excavation of all body cavities.

It is a strange thing to see the source of your phobia systematically disemboweled. It made me feel guilty again. These lobsters were senior citizens, after all. They might have been grandparents. For all I knew, they had been involved in the labor movement. I saw them scuttling feebly along the ocean floor, muttering curses at the agile young lobsters, lining up for the early bird specials on krill.

It was time for me to go into the living room.

When I returned a half hour later, a large silver bowl sat on the counter brimming with glistening lobster meat. It was more lobster than any of us had ever seen. We took turns lifting the bowl and trying to guess how much was in there.

The formal weigh-in: 5.7 pounds.

DUSK WAS NOW approaching. The shadows on the back lawn had grown long. Tom and Scott took some time to clean up the kitchen, then devoted themselves to the preparation of a batch of Vietnamese spring rolls, which were being served in honor of Annabel's upcoming birthday, along with *nuoc cham,* a tasty lime-juice-and-fish-sauce dip, which the birthday girl (predictably, according to Tom) refused to eat.

This was, in its own way, an involved process, one that required wrapping noodles, shrimp, vegetables, and cilantro in fragile rice paper. I was even more impressed by the notion that a nine-year-old child would request such a delicacy. My own ideal meal at that age consisted of Chef Boyardee Beefaroni, Ho Hos, and Orange Crush.

With the spring rolls done, Tom and Scott turned to the main event: stir-frying. Owing to the sheer volume of the batch, this had to be done in two shifts. Scott made sure the right ingredients were going into the wok at the right intervals, and Tom stirred, somewhat frantically. First peanut oil and the lobster (the smell was dizzying), then ginger, lemongrass, chili paste, shrimp paste, sugar, rice stick noodles, fish sauce, lemon and lime juice, scallions, and egg.

The formal recipe calls for this stew to be dished up in separate bowls, with peanuts, bean sprouts, and cilantro. Then, and I quote, "Garnish with lime wedge and sprigs of Thai basil and *crisscross the lobster antennae over the top.*" (Italics mine.)

Thankfully, Tom and Scott dispensed with the frou-frou approach and simply made up two huge communal bowls. We gathered on the screened-in porch. For a few moments, we could only stare at the Lobster Pad Thai. It was like the gastroporn on the Food Network: too beautiful for our mouths. Then someone (I suspect me) spooned a portion onto my plate and all hell broke loose.

I must note here that I am not generally a fan of pad thai. Because often, in restaurants, the pad thai has been sitting around for a while and it gets dried out and—owing to some strange alchemy of, I think, the rice noodles and the fish sauce—smells like old socks.

This pad thai, however, was so fresh, so exquisitely prepared, as to explode on the tongue: the aromatic herbs, the loamy snap of the bean sprouts, the citrus juice, the chewy noodles, the crunchy peanuts, and, at the center of the action, the sweet succulence of the lobster. I can't begin to capture the experience of this pad thai; words are inadequate, because all of these flavors and textures were being experienced simultaneously, interacting in the course of each bite.

AND HERE'S WHAT made the whole thing so special: Tom and Scott were right in front of us, downing significant quantities of wine and beaming. They had cooked this feast for us, for our enjoyment, and just as much for themselves, for the sheer pleasure of a thing created together.

It made me think of all the stories Tom and I had worked on

over the years—more than a hundred. It was what Tom thrived on: the chance to guide a process, to help headstrong schmucks like me get my sentences in order, to usher beauty into the world. And I thought of all the Monday nights we drove out to the Miami Shores Bridge Club for three hours of cutthroat duplicate under the yellow lights, how deftly Tom played and how patient he was in the face of my incessant overbidding. It choked me up a little to think of all the history between us and how we could never have that back.

People were offering toasts now. To the intrepid chefs. To the lobsters. To "The Eviscerator." We had been at the table for nearly two hours. The candles were burning down. The kids had gone to bed. I was on my fourth serving.

There was some debate over whether this was the best pad thai Tom and Scott had ever prepared. I did not see how one could make a better pad thai, and said so. Then, after checking with the proper authorities, I began to eat directly out of the serving bowl.

The rest of the evening begins to get a little blurry. I believe I suggested that Tom and Scott consider opening a restaurant dedicated exclusively to Lobster Pad Thai (proposed name: Booth & Claw) though there is some chance I merely thought this to myself. I know there was a dessert that involved chocolate. We eventually went inside and played a rather silly game of something or other. For the most part, we sat in stunned gratitude, digesting. The next morning, Erin and I had to return to Boston. We did so reluctantly, and only after securing a large plastic container stuffed with pad thai. It was half gone before we left Maine.

I spent three years as a rock critic in El Paso, Texas, which was where I lived at the tail end of the eighties and where I came of age in a sense—grew old enough, that is, to recognize that heavy metal was essentially tribal in nature and that it had everything to do with rhythm and aggression and desire and conquest and physical release and death, which is to say, with sex.

But I'm not here to lecture on sex, or "The Social Mores of the Headbanger Subculture, Circa 1989." My agenda is to make clear how heavy metal saved my life, which it surely did, and not by inspiring me toward complex thought, but by the opposite process: the complete annihilation of thought in favor of instinct. To live dangerously, absurdly, even fallaciously—this was the legacy of my metal days. To believe one might get laid, sucked off, gulped down, on any given night, anywhere on earth, a hidden stairwell, a crowded bathroom, your neighbor's porch, anywhere.

But please don't ask me *Did it happen, and how, and what did she smell like,* because you're missing the point. It isn't the facts I'm speaking of here, but the desire. Not the deed, but the possibility. What is a piece of art, after all, but the possibility of a particular truth? And what are artists but suckers talented enough to win a few converts?

So there it was for me to grab on to, once a week. Metallica. Slayer. Cinderella. Poison. Vixen. Kiss. Winger. Queensryche. And there was me in my reporter's garb (off-brand chinos, white oxfords) scribbling down song titles and adjectives in the dark, while ten thousand kids, skinny boys mostly, surged and howled around me.

There were girls, too. Metal chicks. Always with the big tits, the swirling tits—no bras!—the tops spilling out of their blouses like pale fruit, bouncing like crazy on the balls of their feet, or up on some boy's shoulders, calling out for more, louder, harder, with their red red lips.

I was sure metal chicks knew how to screw, could have screwed me into the ground, and I screwed hundreds in my mind, thousands maybe, pleasuring myself in one or another of the lousy apartments I lived in back then, the basement jobs with iffy plumbing and stale air, until the sweet guilt of completion softened me.

Hell yes.

Went to see Ratt headline a triple bill, with Britney Foxx and Kix, and wound up baked out of my mind because someone, some young *vato* with one front tooth, handed me a joint. I was just standing there taking notes and the joint appeared and I did my civic duty. This was in the El Paso County Coliseum, where they held the rodeo, and the place still smelled of rodeo—burnt popcorn and the sweet earthy reek of manure—and Kix rocked the place pretty good (far better than one might expect from a band that shares a name with an obscure cereal brand), and then Ratt came on and they had the drums rigged so that every time the drummer took a whack the stage lights changed configuration; I was sure I was watching a giant pinball game.

That show was just one of many, part of something larger, what I would now refer to, ingloriously, as a *lifestyle*.

Not that I got myself all snagged up in the trappings—the clothing and the albums and the lighters—because I was, after all, a good suburban kid from a progressive California city, with a couple of parents who had dabbled in hippiedom and raised me up on a steady diet of Beatles and Stones, a kid who had thrown his lot in with the Police and the Smiths and the Fixx, who dabbled in prog rock (*Domo arigato, Mr. Roboto!*) but remained officially an acolyte of New Wave, which seems somehow more embarrassing to admit than anything else I've told you.

Well.

The point being that I thought of myself as slumming. Observing El Paso's metalheads as they thrashed and banged against their own bleak prospects, as they closed their eyes and hoped for a way out through the music—all this was a matter of professional duty.

But I was more like those kids than I would ever have admitted to myself, as insecure about my manhood, as desperate for affirmation, as hungry for touch. Didn't matter that I wore skinny thrift-store ties and wingtips, or carried around business cards with my name printed on them. Didn't even matter that I had a girlfriend who read Nietzsche. What mattered was my insides, which were in a state of continuous, riotous want.

Did I mention Tesla?

They were my favorite metal band, probably because they weren't even really metal, just five burnouts from Sacramento who knew enough to play loud. The lead singer, Jeff Keith, grew up eating government-issue cheese in Broken Bow, Oklahoma. Before he joined the band, he drove a septic truck. His job was to transport rich people's shit around. He was a shit transporter. You don't think this guy knew his way around a wish fantasy?

The rest of the guys, they were all shit transporters of one sort or another. They lacked pretense, because they lacked access to the world of ideas, which is the laboratory of pretense. What they knew was that life sucked most of the time, but that music (along with sex) was the only sure path to joy.

I got to see Tesla only once, opening for White Snake. Went to see the show with my pal Hank, a lawyer at one of the big downtown firms. We got us a bottle of MD 20/20—pink grapefruit, as I recall—and drank the whole thing sitting on a curb outside the arena, Hank still in his dark suit. We also smoked a big, fat blunt. Shit yeah. At one point, a Latin woman walked past in jeans so tight that we could see everything and Hank said, "Jesus, man, that's one of our paralegals." He couldn't believe that she was dressed like that, right out in public.

Sometimes you had to explain this kind of stuff to people like Hank, because they wanted to believe that El Paso was pretty much what they saw, a dried-out suburb with chain restaurants and a friendly brown underclass. This was easier than facing the city as it actually existed—a head-on collision between the First and Third Worlds, the sort of place where the day maids had to sneak across a toxic river every morning at six. Where, if you got up early enough, you could watch the whole sad drama, the Border Patrol agents cruising around in puke-green vans, deciding whom to deport back to the insatiable hunger of Juarez. Though actually El Paso was what all cities are (only more so): a factory of lurid dreams.

All I could think of as this woman walked past us was how much I wanted to strip those jeans off—I knew it would take some doing—and hump her on the fine leather chair in Hank's office. *Squeak-squeak-squeak.*

This night I'm talking about was, if memory serves, a Friday in early spring of 1989, and Hank and I were juiced up on sugary wine and downtown brown, and we streamed into the arena just in time to catch Tesla wailing through "Heaven's Trail (No Way Out)." No one was listening that carefully. They were just the opening band, relegated to the front third of the stage, looking a little naked, almost earnest up there without the fancy costumes and fireworks. But it was a beautiful thing to hear the sweet clamor of all that art.

And I did manage to have sex with that paralegal.

Or no, maybe it wasn't her exactly, but the teller from the bank with the same dyed ringlets of hair. What I remember is the lovely curve of her in the moonlight, and the desperate mashing of our wine-soaked bodies.

Now, as a grownup, well into my reasonable thirties, it would make sense enough to disown the excess of metal, the dopey hairstyles and costumes and tragically stupid lyrics. I don't listen to the stuff anymore, aside from Tesla. Never did listen to it much. But what I can't rid myself of is the yearning, the dumb yearning of the body and the heart's frenzy, that sense of what might happen at any moment, the sex that might happen at any moment, the skin and the wet parts, the utter absence of shame.

Metal was always about this—shameless hope—and this seems in keeping with the best spirit of rock and roll. I find it hard to get turned on listening to the minor-key bombast of alt-rock (which sells us self-indulgent misery) or hip-hop (which sells us black self-immolation in a thin, shiny wrapper of self-celebration). But I still stiffen up at the sound of a good, overblown power chord. I still look around and try to spot any stray tits in the room, and later, in the privacy of my own quarters, whether alone or with company, I quite happily conduct my business.

{

In Tribute to My Republican Homeys

(Not that You Asked)

A lot of people have accused the Bush administration of failing to seek compromise with Democrats. They base this accusation on stuff like Bush planning the war in Iraq without "consulting" Congress, or allowing the nation's energy policy to be written by "industry lobbyists."

Well, I can assure all you lefty naysayers out there that the midterm elections (aka the Great Thumpin') have in fact heralded a much more inclusive Republican approach to governance.

I base this assertion on a wonderful phone call I received last week, which began with a recorded message from a young woman urging me to hold on for a second recorded message, this one from Representative Tom Reynolds (R-NY), the chairman of the National Republican Congressional Committee and a close personal friend—or rather, sorry, check that, *enemy*—of former congressperv Mark Foley.

Mr. Reynolds, it turns out, had a terrific offer. He wanted to recognize me as one of the small-business leaders in my state and to invite me to become an honorary chairman of something called the Business Advisory Council. I would be awarded a ceremonial gavel and allowed (potentially) to attend an economic summit/dinner with the President himself. I was then connected to an actual person, a young man named David Lucas, who explained that, for a mere $500 contribution, my name would join those of dozens of other business leaders in an ad scheduled to run in *The Wall Street Journal*.

I realize there are cynics out there who might be upset at such a phone call. They might accuse the Republicans of running a boiler room operation, of trying to scam money from gullible small-businessmen to feed their insatiable graft machine.

But I was heartened. No, more than heartened; I was *moved*. Here they were, these supposedly "evil" Republicans, reaching across the aisle to embrace little old me, an impoverished pinko writer who has publicly referred to George W. Bush as "an evangelical nutbag." If that's not inclusion, I don't know what is.

So, obviously, I wanted to help out. But five hundred bucks is a lot of money, particularly for an impoverished pinko writer, so I needed to ask my new Republican pal David a few questions first.

"What can you tell me about the gavel?" I said.

"The gavel?" David said. "We don't have too much on the gavel, sir. I know it does have a golden band, just like the one on the House floor."

I imagined Vice President Dick Cheney calling a joint session to order with just such a gavel and, as often happens when I think of Dick Cheney, I got a hard-on.

"What about the ad in *The Wall Street Journal*?" I said.

"It's a limited-time offer," David said. "This is something you'd need to do within the next day or two. We'd need you to pay."

"Right," I said. "What will it say, exactly?"

"Your name will be in the ad, listed as an honorary state chair of the Business Advisory Council."

"What is the Business Advisory Council?"

"It's a group that seeks to bring common business sense to Washington. It functions independently, with reporting lines to Tom Reynolds and party leaders. There are meetings, economic summits, and so forth."

"Okay," I said. "What would the ad say?"

"Just that you have shown a willingness to provide strong leadership in the business community."

"But how do you know that I've shown a willingness to provide strong leadership in the business community?"

"Because that's what the ad will say. That you're standing up for your state and ready to go to work in Washington in an economical way."

It certainly sounded legit to me.

"But tell me, David. The congressman mentioned a dinner with the President. Is that included in the five-hundred-dollar fee?"

"Well, there is a black-tie dinner in spring, but we don't have the date or time yet. And we're still recruiting business leaders for that. Of course, there's an additional cost associated."

"It sure would be great to have dinner with the President," I said.

"Yes, that is a great honor, sir."

"What sort of additional cost would that involve?" I was imagining ribs and slaw in Crawford, cold brewskis, cracking a few faggot jokes over horseshoes.

"I don't know for sure," David said. "I think last time it was twenty-five hundred for a seat. But that includes meetings before the official dinner."

I whistled. "That's something I'd have to think about."

"It's just five hundred for the ad," David said. "But we'd need to process your payment in the next day or two. This is a limited-time offer."

"Still," I said. "That's a lot of money for me. I'd have to check with my board of directors on this."

"That's the thing," David said. "Because of campaign reform, it's illegal to solicit corporate contributions, so this would have to be on a personal level."

I told him I understood, but needed more time to think about it.

David lowered his voice. "If cash flow is an issue, we could probably get your name in the ad for two or three hundred dollars."

"I thought it was five hundred," I said.

"Yeah, it is five hundred. But there is a minimum contribution of a hundred dollars."

This was almost *too much* generosity.

"If you have a credit card, we could take care of this right now."

I didn't want to have to break it to David, because I knew he regarded me as a pretty hard-core business leader at this point, but I wasn't sure my credit card was in good standing. "Let me call you back later," I said.

He was pretty disappointed.

I, on the other hand, felt buoyant. It was high time I stopped regarding the GOP as a bunch of greedy crooks devoted to enriching themselves at the expense of our national character. I needed to realize that they cared about the little guy. The party was filled with folks like Tom Reynolds and David Lucas, men who spent their days endeavoring to make sure that tiny voices like mine were heard in the great halls of power. I couldn't wait to tell my bitter pinko brethren about this brush with bipartisan phone solicitation. *Don't you guys get it?* I'd say. *This is how democracy is supposed to work.*

WHERE'D YOU HIDE THE BODY?

Because I don't own a TV, I'm often struck by the appearance of entire TV genres that have risen up in my absence. The other day I found myself in front of a TV (a wide-screen sucker at that), and in the space of two hours saw ads for the following series: *CSI, Without a Trace, Cold Case,* and *CSI: NY.*

The basic premise of all of these shows, from what I could discern, is pretty similar: There's a dead body and the investigators have to figure out how it got dead. So, in other words, we're talking about *Quincy, ME,* only with cooler gadgets and hotter actors. In most cases—and I think this is crucial—the bodies have been forgotten, overlooked, or otherwise misplaced. The best example I can cite is the promo for *CSI: NY,* which I had the pleasure of viewing seventeen times. It shows a woman on a bus nudging a fellow passenger, apparently a black youth dressed in baggy clothing, who is dozing. His baseball hat falls off and we discover that the kid is actually . . . *a skeleton.*

Now, I want to make clear that I have never seen any of these shows. I'm sure they're gripping and ingeniously written and expertly acted. But that's not why I find them interesting. I find them interesting because they (and their massive popularity) strike me as a deep expression of the current national neurosis.

By which I mean that we, as a nation, are suffering from an odd form of survivor guilt. We are being told, almost constantly, that we are at war. We are aware that killing is being done in the name of our protection. Like the President, we see the casualty reports on TV. But we are not seeing any of the bodies.

This is the single most conspicuous aspect of our so-called war coverage. No bloody footage allowed, nothing that would make the consequences of our military operations too apparent. The media isn't even allowed to photograph the caskets of the fallen. It's as if the bodies of the Americans (not to mention the foreign combatants, not to mention the foreign civilians) have disappeared . . . *without a trace.*

Not only are the bodies gone, they have been stripped of any concrete narrative. Why? Because if we saw all those bodies, and learned something about the life that animated each of them, their deaths would become too real. We might start to ask the appropriate moral questions that ought to accompany preemptive military action. Namely: Why did this person die? For what cause? Was that cause worth his death, and the anguish felt by his survivors?

In this sense, we can see the deluge of necro-investigative shows as a displaced psychic response, a kind of compensatory pantomime. While the military are engaged in an elaborate cover-up of all those bodies (with a friendly assist from our free press), our popular culture crafts shows in which intrepid techno-equipped heroes start with a body and uncover the truth about its death. These programs are not concerned with morality, though. They are intended to deliver the viewer a sense of closure, of a job well done. They inoculate us against the senselessness of death by rendering death as a mystery to be solved.

I'm not sure I can convey the strangeness of all this.

But just imagine if a person from an indigenous culture with no access to media tried to take stock of our current historical circumstance. She would find a culture completely insulated from the abundant by-products of actual killing and yet curiously obsessed with precise, artificial renderings of death.

Americans have always had a tremendous knack for self-delusion, of course. We were founded by self-deluders, and we have been happily sustained by the habit. But I do think the terrorist attacks of 9/11 raised our capacities to a new high. All we heard about in the days afterward was the scope of the tragedy. Initial estimates, if you'll recall, were up to forty thousand dead at the World Trade Center alone. And yet, oddly, we were shown very few images of human carnage. Instead, we saw an endless tape loop—the collision, the collapse, the rubble. The bodies simply disappeared.

A psychic vacuum was created, one we're still trying to fill. I don't mean to suggest that America's death fetish is premeditated, or even recognized. On the contrary, it's a powerful *subconscious* effort to explicate (and thereby tame) the horror of death.

One might locate the same paradoxical impulse in a Reality TV game show that subjects Americans to temporary states of starvation and disease when in fact these hardships define human existence in much of the world. Or a hit series such as *Dexter*, which stars a serial killer with a heart of gold whose elaborate torture methods are justified by the greater evil of his victims. (Don't get me started on the sado-fetishism of *24*.) Can it be any coincidence that Americans are offered such stylized visions of torture at the very moment our administration is arguing for its necessity against actual terrorist suspects?

Or consider the rash of recent films, such as *Turistas Go Home*, in which innocent Americans abroad—generally dressed in bikinis—are abducted by murderous foreigners. These movies arrive in the midst of a sustained campaign by this country's leaders to cast our citizens as victims facing a villainous immigrant mob ravenous to pour over our borders and steal our jobs. (And the really plum ones, too, such as cleaning toilets.)

I'm not suggesting that the Bush administration has a secret pipeline to Tinseltown. Notwithstanding the Disney/Cheney collaboration *The Path to 9/11*, they don't need one. These fables arise spontaneously, as a way of reinventing the world in a manner that absolves us of the violence carried out in our names. They are generated by the growing burden of our imperial guilt. America is talking to itself through these dramas, issuing frantic alibis that play more like twisted confessions.

It all comes down to dead bodies—the real ones, the fake ones, our profound national confusion over which is which. Do we even know anymore?

The figure that comes to mind when I consider this paradox is Lady Macbeth. As you'll recall, she isn't the one who does the killing. She sends her husband to do the dirty work. And yet she goes mad anyhow, rubbing and rubbing at a spot of blood that isn't there, but was, and will be.

DEMAGOGUE DAYS

OR, HOW THE RIGHT-WING HATEOCRACY
CHEWED ME UP AND SPAT ME OUT

*A Shameless Multimedia Extravaganza
Featuring Sean Hannity, Dante Alighieri,
Ann Coulter, and a special cameo by that
super-classy Secretary of State who never
met a war she didn't like . . . Condoleezza Rice!*

Canto I

This is the story of my descent into a modern inferno, so I'm going to start the way Dante did back in the day. As our saga opens, I'm pushing forty, about halfway through my life's journey. I'm not lost in a dark wood. I'm schlepping my suitcase through the Portland airport, where travelers are granted the foolish pleasure of free e-mail.

I open my account and find a message protesting Boston College's decision to have Secretary of State Condoleezza Rice speak at commencement. The Rice invitation has been public knowledge for several weeks, but it's news to me, because I'm just an adjunct professor at BC and because I'm on a book tour this term and because I'm in the midst of trying to buy my first home for my pregnant wife while on a book tour.

My initial reaction is your basic spasm of ick. How could my school do such a thing? This is a rhetorical question. I know exactly why Condi got the nod: It makes BC appear enlightened—*Look at us honoring a woman of color!*—while also generating the kind of prestige PR that helps pump dough out of the wealthy alumni. Before I can think better of it, I do something I have pledged never (*ever*) to do: I hit *reply all.*

Guys—

I'm astonished to hear BC has selected Rice as a commencement speaker. It is the sort of decision that leads me to reconsider whether I want to teach at the school.

Rice has been an integral part of a political machine whose values run contrary to virtually every humane tenet expressed in the New Testament and Catholic doctrine . . .

It's finally come home to BC. Are we going to respond?

Canto II

If I were another sort of person—a reasonable person, for example—I'd have stopped here. I'd rattled my saber. I'd done my best lefty kvetch. Now it was time for a soothing latte. But I am not a reasonable person.

The more I thought about the Rice invite, the less reasonable I became. I was having trouble *letting it go,* as the therapists say. I was having trouble letting it go because I had grown up in a family where a certain brand of cruelty had been tolerated, and I had never gotten over that injustice, and when the same cruelty played out in the political world, it afforded me the chance to return to the delicious misery of my childhood.

I had spent the months after the 2000 election, for instance, thinking (quite a lot, actually) about how best to murder James Baker. Then I remembered that shooting zombies never really kills them, it just makes them stronger. And now, six years, one stolen election, and two failed crusades later, Bush's office wife—a classically trained pianist and war criminal—had been invited to serve as a role model at my very own school. What was I supposed to do with that?

Canto III

In the *Inferno*, Virgil is the one who shows Dante the way into hell. I myself did not have the ghost of a dead, world-famous poet close at hand in Portland. (They are hard to track down on short notice.) But I did have a nondead, sort of famous poet named Julianna Baggott. Julianna and I were on a book tour together, because we had co-written a novel.

When I told Julianna about the Rice invite, that I was considering resigning in protest, her expression was not one of surprise or dismay. On the contrary, she knew me as someone deeply attached to my outrage. And so she was happy to give me a good hard nudge through the Gates of Hell. "If you're really that upset," she said, "why don't you send your letter of resignation to the *Boston Globe*?"

Canto IV

I didn't do this immediately, because I was in the midst of this long-distance house buying nightmare, one complicated by the fact that, unbeknownst to anyone but my wife and my lawyer, I had put offers down on two homes, which, as my attorney had sternly informed me earlier in the day, was *against the law*, but I was doing it anyway because the second home was an insane bargain and I myself had fallen so deeply into a temporary real estate psychosis that a little jail time didn't really faze me anymore, just so long as we got the house. I was making 173 phone calls per day, mostly on my obnoxious cell phone, mostly in transit, and thus kept misplacing my outrage about Rice.

Our hotel in Portland was one of the fancy downtown places that dress their doormen up like Beefeaters, in the errant belief that this is somehow not humiliating to everyone involved. I headed up-stairs, fully intending to draft a letter, but my lawyer called to re-mind me that I was in *legal jeopardy,* then one of the seven or so real estate agents now parasitically affixed to my life called, then Ju-lianna called and began speaking in the hysterical fashion that sig-nals a writer has located free food.

As it should happen, we had landed in Portland on the day our hotel threw its annual Client Appreciation Buffet. The spread was obscene: a raw bar featuring the entire edible population of Puget Sound, plus tuna sashimi, crab cakes, chicken skewers, a mountain of malodorous cheeses, petits fours, strawberries the size of small fists, and, shinily displayed in the *Lord of the Flies* banquet room, an entire snout-to-tail suckling pig. Julianna and I ate to excess, then continued eating. All around us, consultants and salesmen were devouring fish and fowl, belching ecstatically, dabbing at their greasy lips.

In the *Inferno,* before Dante enters hell proper, he sees a swarm of figures referred to as the opportunists. These are people who led morally unconsidered lives, who took no side between good and evil. And as silly as it might seem to say so, this is what I saw as I stood in that bloated lobby: my fellow Americans (and me) lapping at the trough, gulping down what we could, not for a moment ques-tioning our fortune, or whether such fortune lay on the side of good or evil.

That night, after our reading, I returned to my room and called my wife. I meant to give her a real estate update, but the first words out of my mouth were these: "BC is inviting Condi Rice to speak at graduation, and I'm fucking quitting."

Canto V

The next day, on a plane headed to Seattle, I wrote this letter to William Leahy, S.J., the president of Boston College:

Dear Father Leahy,

I am writing to resign my post as an adjunct professor of English at Boston College.

I am doing so—after five years at BC, and with tremendous regret—as a direct result of your decision to invite Secretary of State Condoleezza Rice to be the commencement speaker at this year's graduation.

As you well know, many members of the faculty and student body already have voiced their objection to the invitation, arguing—reasonably, in my view—that Rice's actions as Secretary of State are inconsistent with the broader humanistic values of the university, and the Catholic and Jesuit traditions from which those values derive.

But I am not writing this letter simply because of an objection to the war against Iraq. My concern is more fundamental.

Simply put: Ms. Rice is a liar.

She has lied to the American people knowingly, repeatedly, often extravagantly over the past five years, in an effort to justify a pathologically misguided foreign policy.

The public record of her deceits is extensive. During the ramp-up to the Iraq War, she made 29 false or misleading public statements concerning Iraq's weapons of mass destruction and links to Al-Qaeda, according to a congressional investigation by the House Committee on Government Reform. . . .

Like the President whom she serves so faithfully, she refuses to recognize her errors, or the tragic consequences of those errors to the young soldiers and civilians dying in Iraq. She is a diplomat whose central allegiance is not to the democratic cause of this nation, but absolute power. . . .

I am not questioning her intellectual gifts or academic accomplishments. Nor her potentially inspiring role as a powerful woman of color. But these, after all, are not the factors by which a commencement speaker should be judged. It is the content of one's character that matters here—the reverence for truth and knowledge that Boston College purports to champion.

Secretary Rice does not personify these values; she repudiates them. Whatever inspiring rhetoric she might present to the graduating class, her actions as a citizen and politician tell a different story.

Honestly, Father Leahy, what lessons do you expect her to impart to impressionable seniors? That hard work in the corporate sector might gain them a spot on the board of Chevron? That they, too, might someday have an oil tanker named after them? That it is acceptable to lie to the American people for political gain?

. . . I cannot, in good conscience, exhort my students to pursue truth and knowledge, then collect a paycheck from an institution that displays such flagrant disregard for both.

I would like to apologize to my students, and prospective students. I would also urge them to investigate the words and actions of Secretary Rice, and to exercise their own First Amendment rights at her speech.

> *Respectfully,*
> *Steve Almond*
> *Ex–Adjunct Professor*

Canto VI

To my mind, the letter showed considerable restraint. I did not mention, for instance, that Rice was working her AmEx at a Manhattan shoe boutique while thousands of poor people were trying to avoid drowning after Hurricane Katrina. I simply said my piece and zapped the letter off to some editor at the *Globe,* who I assumed would be too distracted to read the thing and/or too wimpy to run it.

I was more concerned with getting back to Boston so I could slap a down payment on the house we had decided to buy. But my flight, almost predictably, was canceled due to windstorms in Chicago, and I spent six hours trying to rebook. In the end (by which I mean there was some begging involved) I secured the last seat on a flight from Seattle to Charlotte to Hartford. At some point in the midst off all this, the *Globe* called to say they were going to run my letter. I believe my exact words were: "Fine."

Canto VII

I arrived in Boston at four in the morning and didn't bother to unpack my bags, because as soon as I handed over the down payment, I was flying to Toronto for another reading. The phone began ringing before 8 A.M. I assumed I had overslept (I had) and that my realtor was calling to wake me up. But it was someone named Brett, or perhaps Brent, calling from a local TV affiliate. He had read my letter in the *Globe* and wanted to know if I'd be willing to come on the air and talk about what he referred to, in that unctuous, caffeinated tone favored by TV producers the world over, as "my brave decision."

I told him I was heading out of town.

"Where to?" he said. "We might have an affiliate."

Now my cell phone began ringing. It showed a New York number I didn't recognize. I explained to Brent/Brett that I had to go. I answered the cell and a woman from CNN began speaking with great vehemence. I asked her to call back later and hung up. There was a moment of silence. Then, as if by some previous arrangement, both phones began ringing at the same time.

I was now—though I didn't quite realize it yet—in the midst of an official media feeding frenzy. It was a Friday morning in May, what the pros call a slow news day, and all over the nation, media underlings were scouring the major newspapers to figure out who and what constituted "news" and how to turn these people and events into telegenic brawls that might goose their own careers.

The *Boston Globe* had made me easy to find. Though I didn't know this either, the editors had run my letter at the top of the editorial page, under the thoughtful banner headline *Condoleezza Rice at Boston College? I Quit.*

My attack on Bush, Inc., was especially enticing to all those newsmakers because it seemed to reflect what pundits enjoy calling *the national mood*. Yes, it was finally dawning on Americans that their emperor had no clue. His approval ratings—90 percent when he stood atop the rubble, 75 percent when he declared mission accomplished, 60 percent when Saddam Hussein was captured—had just dipped below 30 percent.

A responsible Fourth Estate might take this as an invitation to investigate the integrity of his words and policies. But that was awfully complicated stuff. It was much easier, really, to focus on some wacky part-time prof who—*get this*—actually quit his job in an effort to question those words and policies.

Canto VIII

Dante wrote the *Inferno* as a warning. He was exhorting his countrymen not to drift into moral torpitude, to find salvation in the performance of righteous acts. But the poem is also a political allegory. Dante was bitter about his exile from Florence at the hands of the black Guelphs, so he wrote his enemies into hell and subjected them to various colorful degradations.

I would love to report that my resignation was a purely righteous act. Unfortunately, it also involved a revenge fantasy, one I've inflicted on friends and family with increasing vigor over the past few years: to become a *Demagogue of the Left*.

This would involve me getting a radio show, which would start local, but, owing to my astonishing eloquence, would quickly earn a national following and allow me to expose the sadistic hypocrisies of the Hateocracy, as well as the abject cowardice of their media enablers, and would culminate in a televised debate with Ann Coulter during which she would admit that she, like Adolf Hitler, has only one testicle.

I am suggesting, in other words, that I was not merely a noble liberal knight hoping to slay the dragons of the right, but a willing accomplice in the descent that followed.

Canto IX

The first interview I gave was to a local National Public Radio show. I was at the airport by now, about to fly off to Toronto. It was a perfectly reasonable conversation. No one shouted. Nonetheless, it marked the beginning of my formal descent into the inferno.

I know this will upset those of you who view NPR as a counterweight to the Hateocracy. But surely I can't be the only one to notice that NPR (in its own reasonable way) has no moral compass whatsoever. That it dependably dances to whatever tune Karl Rove calls out—immigration, gay marriage, flag burning, all the Goebbelsish spew invoked to distract citizens from more substantive and failed policies.

I can't remember the last time I heard an investigative report on NPR. Like about, say, the sitting president launching a war based on bogus intelligence, or the vice president inviting lobbyists to rewrite our environmental laws, or the Speaker of the House turning Capitol Hill into a gold brick factory. Instead, NPR waits until these scandals have become conventional wisdom, then calls in Terry Gross for mop-up.

I used to spend a lot of time at WBUR, the Boston NPR affiliate. The staffers I met there were intelligent and hardworking. They were also tragically demoralized. That's what happens when your job is to cover the most corrupt, incompetent administration in history, and every day you churn out timid drivel.

Canto X

So let's assign NPR to the first circle of hell, where virtuous pagans hang out and bitch about dental deductibles. And let's put John DePetro in the second circle.

Who is John DePetro?

DePetro is a short, weasel-faced man with a Rhode Island accent. In another era, he'd be the guy who hangs out with the reputed mobsters and laughs at all their jokes and occasionally gets punched in the face for trying to be clever. As it is, DePetro is the former morning guy on WRKO, Boston's official AM Hateocracy outlet. He bills himself as "The Independent Man," an independence he recently affirmed by calling a public official a fag on the air.

I'm not sure how many of you have been a guest on a right-wing talk radio program, but I can tell you exactly what it's like. It's like throwing a book at a monkey.

I spoke to DePetro for thirty minutes, during which his central rhetorical strategy was to read various portions of my letter in a sneering voice. I would then say something like, "That's very good, John. Your reading skills are excellent!" And he would screech like a monkey. A number of his listeners called in to screech, too. The consensus was that I was an elitist, which is a right-wing term for someone smarter than you. One guy was so incensed he yelled for five minutes straight while I said things like *That's right, let it out . . . It's good for you to let it out.* I was on the jetway by now and other passengers could hear him ranting through my earpiece. I'm pretty sure they thought I was a social worker.

DePetro asked me (sneeringly) what I thought of Cindy Sheehan.

I told him Sheehan was a grief-stricken mother whose son died in a war she didn't understand. I wanted to ask DePetro if he had any kids and how he might feel if one of *them* died in a war he didn't understand. Could he bring himself to that sort of humility? But I had just found my seat and the woman next to me was a nun, so I hung up.

"I'm sorry," I said. "I was on a radio program."

I felt a sudden urge to ask the nun if she could take confession from a Jew, if that was in any way allowed, because I had obviously sinned, I had conversed with men of unclean intentions, wantonly, on the public airwaves. But she was immersed in her magazine.

DePetro spent the rest of the week begging me to come back on the show. His appeals were deeply fraudulent and invariably tender. Listening to him plead filled me with reluctant pity. Is there nothing sadder than a wannabe demagogue, trapped in the outer circles of the inferno, dreaming of a way in?

(Fun fact: A few months after my appearance, DePetro referred to Massachusetts' Green Party gubernatorial candidate as a "fat lesbian" and got the shitcan.)

Canto XI

In Toronto, I turned off my cell phone and slept for six hours. Then I did that stupid thing I so often do: I checked my e-mail.

I had 359 new messages, among them these:

You are the enemy of my country just as much as bin Laden and Zarqawi. I see no difference. Good. Now fucking drop dead.

Fuck you pansy asshole

It is people like you who get our soldiers killed in Iraq.

I can tell you really don't like darkies, do you. . . .

I'm a Roman Catholic too and I suport Condoleca Rice as a brave and magnificent princess who is trying to save the world . . .

Your family should probably disown you.

I love to hear you liberals
Squeeeeeeeeeeeeeeeeeeeeeeeeeeeeeeeeeeeeelllllllllll like pigs.

Canto XII

Well.

How is everybody doing? Anybody need a drink?

I probably should have mentioned that the trip down was going to be a little rough in spots. Always is. There's any number of circles where we could put these fellas; the Seventh Circle, which houses the violent, makes the most sense. But there's also a certain touching purity to these notes. They are a distillate of the modern conservative movement, which, contrary to popular myth, is not a political philosophy at all but an emotional appeal to the primal negative feeling states of childhood: rage, grievance, fear.

And if you listen to the leading orators of the Hateocracy—guilty as charged—what you hear is not the articulation of coherent policy aims, but an almost poignant plea for someone to wash their mouths out with soap. In a mature democracy this would surely happen. But we are living in America, so *Time* magazine writes fawning cover stories about them.

If you step back for a moment, you will see what hard work these men and women must do! It is quite a remarkable psychological feat to experience a visceral sense of your own victimization while the party you support holds absolute power. It's that something special, frankly, that shoves representational democracy toward fascism.

So how do they do it?

They do it by tapping into their one inexhaustible resource: self-loathing. They take all the ugliness slithering around inside themselves and project it onto those least likely to fight back. I hope this helps explain why Bill O'Reilly (a sexual predator) goes after sexual predators, or why Rush Limbaugh (America's alpha demagogue) is forever accusing Democrats of demagoguery, or why Ann Coulter (a fame succubus) accuses the 9/11 widows of being publicity whores.

You are a racist. You kill our boys in Iraq. You should be disowned. You would be a lot of fun to rape. Where do these intimate notions come from is what I'm asking, if not from within the men who wrote them into the world? And what else do they reveal if not a map of their own unbearable fears about themselves?

Canto XIII

By Friday evening, I was receiving an e-mail every ninety seconds. Things had gone *viral*. Some of this was my own fault, in that I provide an e-mail address on my website. (In my defense, I am a writer of short stories. On a good day, I receive thirty e-mails, half of which inquire whether I would like a larger, more powerful penis.) Still, I couldn't quite figure out how so many people were finding my website.

Enter Michelle Malkin.

For those not familiar with her work, Malkin—an American of Filipino descent—recently wrote a book lauding the internment of Japanese-Americans during World War II. Her eerie, squidlike beauty and radiant self-hatred have won her an occasional spot in the Fox News rotation. Malkin is also a ringleader of some import within the cyber-Hateocracy. She was the first to post my letter on her blog, and to provide her readers a helpful link to my website.

The site Free Republic! went a step further, hosting a reader "forum" about my letter that included the following comment:

Steve Almond's email address sbalmond@earthlink.net

A little further down came this:

This guys [sic] really an idiot. His address and phone number are published.

This is a good start!!!!

Canto XIV

I am sorry to report that I was neither bound nor gagged by this cyber posse, though I did receive a few harassing phone calls. The most interesting came from a gentleman who identified himself as a newspaper reporter from Villanova University.

"Can I ask you a few questions?" he said.

"Okay," I said.

"You voted for John Kerry, didn't you?"

"Which newspaper are you calling from again?" I said.

"Actually, I work at Villanova."

"As a reporter?"

"As a professor."

"So you're not a reporter?" I said.

Suddenly, he began shouting. "You're so pathetic! You fucking pathetic liar!"

"Wait a second," I said quietly. "Why are you shouting at me?"

There was a brief silence.

"All right," he said. "Okay. I apologize. That wasn't cool."

It was a weirdly poignant moment. I could hear the struggle in this guy's voice. He was trying so hard to swallow the venom that had prompted his call, trying to assimilate the notion that I was an actual human being—really, I think it stunned him—and that dialing Information and finding my number and actually calling me up and cursing at me, that all this was really, maybe, in a sense . . . a kind of sickness?

"What's going on here?" I said.

He took a deep breath, as if to gather himself. Then he was roaring again. "Nobody listens to a word you say! That's why, okay. You know that, asshole? Nobody gives a shit!"

Canto XV

As it turned out, though, people did give a shit. People like John Gibson. Gibson has said many things in his career as a pundit. He has said that whites should have more babies, to prevent Hispanics from becoming a majority in this country. He has called Third World nations "little more than spots on the map." Perhaps the best way to capture the depth of Gibson's moral vision is to cite his 2005 book, *The War on Christmas: How the Liberal Plot to Ban the Sacred Christian Holiday Is Worse Than You Thought.*

Dante would have stashed the guy in the circle reserved for those who sow discord. I agreed to appear on his show for one simple reason: I had just murdered nineteen of Santa's elves in cold blood and I wanted to come clean.

Gibson began the interview by focusing on the figure he considers central to the entire Iraq War debacle: Bill Clinton. I pointed out that Clinton had actually left office six years earlier. Gibson seemed briefly disoriented. He shifted the discussion to an article in *Foreign*

Affairs Quarterly, which he claimed proved Saddam Hussein pos-
sessed weapons of mass destruction. When I insisted on returning
to the subject of Condoleezza Rice, Gibson broke into a lovely, full-
throated monkey screech:

> GIBSON: WELL, YOU HAVE CONVINCED YOURSELF THAT
> SHE'S A LIAR—
> ME: I haven't convinced myself. I've researched
> the facts, John. That's what you do when
> you're a rational adult. You research the facts,
> you—
> GIBSON: YOU DON'T SEEM TO WANT TO HEAR ANYTHING
> NEW. DO YOU WANT TO HEAR ABOUT THE WMD
> THAT SADDAM HUSSEIN HAD?

Duty compels me to note two things:

1. Gibson's mic was at least twice as loud as mine.
2. Gibson was lying his fucking head off.

I know this because I eventually read the article he was citing,
something he apparently didn't do. "Saddam," the authors note,
"found it impossible to abandon the *illusion* of having WMD, especially since it played so well in the Arab world." (Italics mine; implied screeching Gibson's.)

Eventually, Gibson returned to his default setting—attack Bill
Clinton—before proceeding to full meltdown.

> GIBSON: Did you think lying to a judge was a good
> thing?
> ME: Yeah, you know, that's what all of us . . . lefties
> advocate. And I'm so glad that you think bul-
> lying me, an adjunct professor, is going to dis-
> tract the American people from the fact that
> this administration is a disgrace and has con-
> ducted a foreign policy that is immoral. I'm

so glad you think the American public is that
stupid, John.

GIBSON: CAN I PRETTY MUCH COUNT ON IT THAT THIS IS
WHAT YOU WERE TEACHING YOUR STUDENTS
THERE AT BOSTON COLLEGE . . . THAT WHEN A KID
CAME INTO YOUR CLASS. IF HE DIDN'T REPEAT
THIS CRAP EXACTLY, YOU WERE GOING TO FAIL
THEM? DID YOU FAIL ANY OF THEM IN PARTICU-
LAR?

Yes, John. I failed the Caucasians.

Canto XVI

It will have occurred to you by now to wonder whether I was con-
tacted by any members of that liberal media about which we hear so
much. Yes. Exactly one. This resulted in an appearance on a radio
show based in Texas, which began unremarkably until a man called
in and began to tell me about the International Jesuit Conspiracy,
which began in 1371 and involved the covert collaboration of the
Vatican and something called, I believe, the Brotherhood of the Or-
thodox.

As a Jew, of course, I'm always comforted to hear about nefari-
ous conspiracies that implicate people who are not Jews. Still. Still
it was sad to realize that the Hateocracy had me all to themselves.
This probably qualifies me as a conspiracy nut, but I really had harbored the hope that some brave media outlet might use my resignation as a pretext to examine the veracity of my essential claim
(Condi = liar).

Not so much.

I did receive lots of kind notes from individuals. People wanted
to tell me what a brave guy I was, what a patriot, and so on. These
notes were all well-intentioned and thoroughly disheartening. I
hadn't done anything heroic. I had quit my part-time job. It was a
testament to the political lethargy of this country that such a pissant

gesture would excite adulation in the first place. In the end, these amens carried no political consequence. They were yet another example of liberals congratulating one another for their noble values rather than confronting the bullies.

Canto XVII

I should mention that my mood was also dampened over that long weekend by the circumstances surrounding my reading. I had come to Toronto to serve as the keynote speaker at something called the Sweets Expo. I assumed this would involve a small auditorium full of Canadian candyfreaks.

But the Expo was being held in a convention center filled with failing confectioners, children in a state of hyperglycemic frenzy, and suicidal parents. The man serving as MC for the Expo was named Jean-Paul. Jean-Paul was dressed in a blazer that resembled snakeskin. He wore many large rings and spoke in an amplified baritone, like Liberace reprogrammed as a boxing announcer.

"It's *faaaaabulous* to have you here," Jean-Paul boomed. "Now what do you do?"

"I'm an author."

"An author!" Jean-Paul offered me a smile whiter than I had thought chromatically possible. *"Terrifique!"*

"Where exactly is the reading venue?" I said.

We were standing beside a vast stage in the middle of the Expo, upon which children were sullenly devouring bowls of pudding in the hopes of winning more pudding. "What do you mean?" Jean-Paul said.

"Like, the actual place I'll be reading."

"All the acts are on the main stage!"

I gazed at the stage again. It was the size of a small soccer pitch.

"You're on at four P.M.!" Jean-Paul sang out. "Right after the fashion show!"

The fashion show featured an array of anorexic models dressed up to look like Tootsie Rolls and jelly beans, if you can picture such products endowed with cleavage. I had the pleasure of waiting around backstage with the models and eavesdropping on them as they discussed, in exuberant detail, the precise method by which they planned to murder their agents. Then the music stopped and Jean-Paul thanked the ladies and introduced me and I took the portable mic and made my long walk to the center of the stage with my book.

There is a moment in the life of every author when you realize with perfect clarity the depth of your irrelevance. Mine had arrived. Canadians of all ages surrounded me, staring up, waiting for me to do something, *anything,* that might be worth watching. I had been listed on the program as a *world-famous candyfreak,* and it now dawned on me that the crowd expected some significant anthropological event. Perhaps I could pass a Pixie Stick in one earhole and out the other. Or I could defecate in the precise shape of a Hershey's kiss. Instead, I stood under the bank of lights, absorbing disappointment. I tried to figure out how to hold my book with one hand, which led to my fumbling the mic. It hit the stage with a thunderous crack. A child started wailing, then another. I began to read. The crowd looked bewildered. People began to turn away. I pondered whether I might hire an agent, for the express purpose of murdering him. Left with no respectable exit strategy, I dropped the book and launched into this bizarre borscht belt routine that involved dragging children onstage and asking them candy trivia questions. Was it appropriate to call this a keynote speech? Probably not.

"*Fantastique!*" Jean-Paul said afterward. "They loved you!" Then he snatched the mic and summoned the salsa dancers to the stage.

Canto XVIII

I returned to Boston on Monday, May 15, exactly a week before Condoleezza Rice was scheduled to deliver her commencement speech. The phone was still ringing nonstop.

"Is this Steve Almond?" one young woman shouted. "The former BC professor guy?"

"Yes," I said. "Who is this?"

"Oh. This is Brandie Jefferson. Of the Associated Press."

Brandie was not of that traditional school of journalism that favors simply asking questions. No, her own thoughts were an important part of the interview. She asked me questions like "What's the point of quitting your job? I mean, isn't that a little *extreme*? When I was in college, kids were always protesting something or other and it never did any good."

I spent a long time on the phone with Brandie. I was fascinated by the idea that the Associated Press would hire someone so unprofessional. I also knew that most newspapers would be pulling her story off the wire. Our conversation thus took on an aspect of supplication. I felt like a mad courtier pleading my case to an idiot princess.

I'm not calling Brandie Jefferson an idiot. Really, she's just a typical American young person, happily cocooned within her own radical naïveté. The notion that her leaders might lie to her, that they might be making apocalyptic decisions on her behalf—that was all so . . . *sixties*. Politics was really just a second-rate Reality TV show to her, with ugly actors who never kiss. Her world, the one she actually lived in, was like that of my former students: a swirl of flashing screens and frantic buy messages, all of them vivid, smiling, and unbearably lonely.

For the record, Brandie's account ran in more than fifty newspapers. It contained a single quote from me, which had been carefully stripped of its context so as to neutralize any disturbing side effects: "I think Americans have lost touch with the idea of sacrifice."

Canto XIX

It was my conversation with Margery Egan that convinced me that I was at last drawing close to the heart of the Hateocracy.

Egan has built a nifty little career out of bland populist indignation. She has a column in the *Herald,* Boston's official tabloid of the
Angry White Male, and a radio show on the lesser of our two hate-
talk stations. In fact, Egan had badmouthed me on her show the
day my letter ran in the *Globe.* When she called me a few days later,
I figured she wanted to invite me to appear on her show. But no. Instead, she had a vital question for her next column. Are you ready
for her vital question?

"How much did you earn as an adjunct at Boston College?"

Egan had devoted her considerable investigative skills to this
question already. "I was told you were paid four thousand dollars
per class," she said gravely. "Can you confirm that?"

I am hoping that all of you will sleep just a little safer tonight in
the knowledge that there are intrepid journalists out there like
Margery Egan who stand prepared to defend your freedom by asking the tough questions, not just of this nation's rulers—in fact, not
of them at all—but of adjunct professors who quit their jobs without publicly disclosing their salaries. But being the insouciant
democracy wrecker I most assuredly am, I refused to confirm or
deny.

Not to worry. Egan had a second question ready: "How did your
letter of resignation wind up in the *Globe*?"

"It was an *open* letter," I said.

"Right," she said, trying her best to sound confused. "But it's addressed to Father Leahy."

I was so stunned by Egan's playing dumb that I could say nothing for a few moments. "Do you even know the sort of cowardly
hatemonger you are?" I said finally.

Egan was wounded. Why was I so angry at *her*? She was just
doing her job. And part of her job—a big part of it actually—resided
in pretending she was a journalist pursuing an actual story related
to the public good, rather than a purveyor of poorly manufactured
gotcha journalism.

Dante would have condemned Egan to wander the Eighth Circle

of hell, with its boiling lake and false prophets. But I found the transparency of her ploy oddly touching. It must have been quite painful for her to face the possibility that someone might perform a genuine act of conscience. So she did what false moralists always do when those feelings of self-loathing become unbearable—she projected her shamelessness onto me. The emotional logic never changes: *If my motives can't be good, yours must be bad.*

Canto XX

As it turned out—a late inning shocker, folks!—Egan got my salary wrong. I was being paid *five* thousand dollars per class at the time I quit BC, plus free Danish on Fridays. This should tell you a little something about the brutal economic shifts in higher education, which is now stocked to the gills with an academic underclass known as *us dumbass adjuncts.*

We do not, as a rule, teach for the money. (My pay stub, when divided by the number of hours I worked teaching a class, came out to less than the minimum wage.) We teach because we dig teaching, because we enjoy our students.

When I think of them now it is with the utmost tenderness: Beth Dunn, with her fearless prose and her embarrassed giggling. Donald Mahoney, with his redolent chicken fingers and bedhead. All of them juiced up on Dunkin' Donuts coffee and cigs, muffin crumbs caught in the cuffs of their sweaters. How unbearably young they looked! How hard they took everything! I couldn't help thinking, as I gazed at them these past few years, how cruel it was for any nation to send such soft humans into war, where their deepest needs—to be understood, to be forgiven—would be torn right out of them.

So it was more than enjoyment. I *loved* my students. I depended on them. They filled me with an irrational hope for the future, just by being so kind to one another, so brave in pursuit of the truth locked inside themselves. Every term, one of them would write a story of such reckless beauty that it would take me a few minutes to realize I had stopped breathing. That's what I had sacrificed by quitting my job: that feeling, the honor of that feeling.

Canto XXI

By the middle of the week, I had grown tired of the hate mail, the slimy reporters, my own self-righteous blather. Why then, did I consent to appear on *The Hannity & Colmes Show*? I suppose because, having come this far, I felt compelled to brave that ninth and final circle, which Dante reserved for political traitors. I knew I would never have another chance like this, and that if I didn't take this chance—to confront these traitors, to do so on national TV— I would be no different from the rest of the liberal collaborators in this country.

Also, Fox News offered to send a limo.

Hell, why not? This is the economic secret that helps keep the Hateocracy humming: It's such cheap entertainment! All you need is a few sociopaths, a studio, and a camera, and you're in business. None of this tedious news gathering stuff.

And Fox was offering me a piece of the action, too! "We would absolutely promote the book of your choice to our two million viewers nationwide," a producer informed me. Do you understand how completely psyched I was about this? I mean, the folks who watch *Hannity & Colmes,* those people are fucking *monsters* when it comes to reading modern short fiction. So now I was going to be a bestseller.

For those philistines who have not seen *H&C,* it features a conservative host (Sean Hannity) and a small punching bag (Alan Colmes). Hannity is the star of the program and, not incidentally, looks like a star: Reaganesque slab of hair, broad shoulders, oversized mandible. Hannity's reputation as an attack dog is matched only by his more recent role as press liaison for our vice president. When Big Dick rises from the coffin for some reason other than shooting aged lawyers in the face—say, for instance, to remind

Americans they should still live in fear—Hannity is his designated buttboy.

I hope it will not shock you to learn that Hannity has no journalism experience. In fact, he has no job experience whatsoever, outside of speaking into a microphone. He is untroubled by the moral complexities of the real world precisely because he has spent no time there.

Canto XXII

The deal was this: a ten-minute live interview on Monday night, pegged to Rice's commencement address. I spent the weekend pacing my apartment, rehearsing what I would say when Hannity accused me of being a satanic pornographer.

Monday finally rolled around. The reports from commencement were depressing. A small white plane did circle Alumni Stadium, towing a banner that read *Your War Brings Dishonor*. But no one was there to see it. Things were running late because of all the security measures, which included metal detectors, a bomb squad, and, comfortingly, a phalanx of sharpshooters positioned at high points around the stadium. The serious protesters who might have publicly challenged Rice were all kept at a safe distance.

And what did our secretary of state have to say after all this? Mostly, she dispensed the sort of tranquilizing bromides required of commencement speakers, which, in her case, came off as inadvertently chilling. Stuff like "All too often difference has been used to divide and to dehumanize." And "It's possible today to live in an echo chamber that serves only to reinforce your own high opinion of yourself and what you think." Contrary to initial press reports, Rice did not explode into oily shards of blarney at the conclusion of her speech. She received a standing ovation.

So now Hannity had himself another delicious opener: *I assume you saw the standing ovation Secretary Rice received this morning? Care to react?*

Canto XXIII

I spent my time in the green room doing breathing exercises and trying to think pleasant thoughts. I had come to an important realization over the past week: I needed, above all else, to *not take the bait*. Why? Because Hannity was a bar brawler. He won fights not based on skill, or facts, but because he operated more effectively in the zone of adrenaline. (This is why conservatives tend to stomp liberals on the TV playground—aggression is like Ritalin to them.)

The show opened with a lengthy report on the alleged rape of a black woman by white lacrosse players at Duke University. Hannity was interviewing two emaciated blond legal correspondents of the sort that Fox News apparently keeps stored in a warehouse somewhere in midtown Manhattan. The essence of their legal opinion can be summarized thus: *The black slut got what she deserved.*

As this segment wound down, I was ushered into a small back room and seated at a desk in front of a black screen, upon which an image of the Boston skyline was projected, so that it looked like I was high atop some skyscraper, rather than stuffed in a tiny, airless box in Watertown. The tech who led me in asked if I wanted to watch the live feed from the New York studio during my segment.

"Sure," I said.

"The only thing is you'll have a delay."

"Meaning what?"

"Everything you see will be, like, six seconds behind. Some people find it kind of disorienting."

"Better not," I said.

"Okay, just stare here." He pointed to a small black square mounted six feet away, beneath the camera. Then he demurely reached up my shirt, hooked a mic onto my collar, and gave me an earpiece. I stuck the bud in my ear and waited. After a few minutes, an excited voice said, "Professor Almond?"

"Yeah?"

"Great to have you! Thanks so much for joining us!" There was a lot of commotion in the background, voices, laughter. It was a regular hoedown. I stared at my black square miserably. "We've got footage from the speech, then we go to you, 'kay?"

There were two notable things about this footage. First, *H&C* provided by far the most thorough coverage of the event. Second, they managed to get the story entirely wrong. They made it look like Condi had been under siege by rabid liberal hordes, when in fact the protests had been smaller than anticipated. Such sensational treatment served the greater goal of convincing Fox viewers that a Communist invasion of the United States might still be imminent.

Suddenly, I heard one of those metallic whooshing sounds, which meant the segment was being thrown back to the studio. Then I heard Sean Hannity's voice blaring into my ear.

Canto XXIV

HANNITY: Joining us now, Steve Almond. He resigned his position as an adjunct professor of English at Boston College when Secretary Rice was invited to campus. Welcome aboard, sir. Thanks for being with us. Steve, I guess it's fairly obvious. You probably voted for John Kerry in the last election. So politics play any role in your position here?

ME: I think actually morality plays a role. I just feel public officials shouldn't lie to us, especially about matters that are as important as war.

HANNITY: I got that. But did you—but you are politically a Democrat. You're politically lefty. You voted for John Kerry, right?

ME: I believe that politicians shouldn't lie to the American people.

HANNITY: I didn't ask you that. Did you vote for John Kerry, sir?

ME: And I'm telling you that I don't believe that

> our public officials should lie, Democrat, Re-
> publican, or—

I should confess that this opening salvo caught me off guard, as did the speed with which the discussion had degenerated into an inquisition. Had I not been so acclimatized to the noxious atmosphere of the Hateocracy, I'm certain I would have lost my shit. As it was, I shook my head and chuckled sadly.

> ME: What is it that you want to say to me? Are
> you going to try to establish that I'm a lefty
> or Democrat? I believe that public officials
> shouldn't lie, and Condoleezza Rice has lied
> repeatedly.

Hannity, now incensed, began to yell.

> HANNITY: I already know you voted for John Kerry, but
> you won't admit it! Well, I'll quote John Kerry,
> the guy that I suspect you voted for. He says,
> "If you don't believe Saddam is a threat with
> nuclear weapons or WMDs, you shouldn't
> vote for me." Is the guy that you voted for a
> liar?
> ME: The Secretary of State, who has also been a
> part of prosecuting this war incredibly in-
> eptly—
> HANNITY: All right, you can't even answer a question. Is
> John Kerry a liar?

On this insinuating note, with Almond against the ropes and Hannity looking ready to devour a forty-ounce steak using just his eyeteeth, Colmes stepped in.

> COLMES: Steve, I don't care whether you voted for Kerry
> or not—

ME: Thank you. It's a matter of morality. Not everything is politics. Some of it is basic morality.

COLMES: Let me pursue a different line of questioning here. Why quit your job? Why not turn your back, or speak, or hold a protest rally, or hold an alternate ceremony to put forth your point of view?

ME: Well, there are plenty of ways. For me, you know, it was an act of conscience. I didn't want to collect a paycheck. It would be as if you worked at a TV station, for instance, and you were a strong advocate for women's rights, and one of your colleagues, a powerful colleague, sexually harassed his employees. And you didn't want to stand for that. You didn't feel the TV station had done enough to punish him, and you might, as a matter of conscience, resign because of that.

Now the silence was profound. It was interrupted only by a faint rustling, which may or may not have been the sound of a thousand Fox interns dropping their loofahs in astonishment. Yes, I had dropped the O'Reilly bomb. I had made reference to his sex harassment case, and I had done so during prime time, on his very own network. It was precisely at this point, I like to imagine, that an executive decision was made, which involved a senior producer yelling into his headset something like this:

Good Christ! Code red! We've got a live one on the air! Repeat: CODE RED! We're going to abort. Cue up the next ad block. Now! Go! Go-go-go!

But of course, it takes a while to cue up the next ad block, so they were stuck with me. Colmes looked at the camera, in that unbearably sexy quisling way of his.

COLMES: I might, or I might use my platform to speak out, or I might do things behind the scenes to speak out that have nothing to do with what I would do publicly, but you chose to quit.

ME: Well, I don't think I'm really the issue here. I think Condoleezza Rice and her campaign of deception and this administration's prosecution of an immoral war is the issue. There are no WMDs, unless you got them there at Fox News under your desk. And we've been hearing [these lies] for over three years and coming up on twenty thousand casualties, and the American people are getting sick of it—

HANNITY: You know what? If that's the case—and I suspect I'm right, and you voted for Kerry—you voted for a guy that made that exact same case as she did. What would that make you?

ME: I'm sorry, the administration in power is the one that has gotten us into this mess, okay? You're not going to blame it on Kerry—

HANNITY: John Kerry voted for it.

ME: You're not going to blame it on Clinton—

Suddenly, bizarrely, I lost the audio feed. I assumed this was a simple technical glitch, a mistake. But no, that wasn't it. They really and truly had pulled the plug on me. I ripped my earbud out and shouted, "You goddamn losers!"

Canto XXV

For a day or so, I felt exuberant, as if I had faced down the Hateocracy. The truth dawned on me only after I took a second look at the segment. My promised ten minutes of airtime had run 5:16, nearly half of which had been devoted to the footage from Boston College. By the time Hannity finished his initial cross-examination, less than two minutes remained. I had spoken for a grand total of twenty-five seconds. Something else I noticed: Several seconds after my veiled reference to O'Reilly, the background music that signals a cut to commercial had come on. The producers really had gone **Code Red** on my ass.

This, then, was my great victory—twenty-five seconds of free speech on Fox News.

Canto XXVI

Dante made his harrowing descent in the hopes he would find a path to paradise. And I do believe that I had some idea of paradise in mind when I resigned from BC and decided to throw my puny weight against the gnashing of the Hateocracy. Or maybe *paradise* is too grandiose a word.

What I had was more like a hunger for justice, one linked to a specific auditory memory of a newsreel I heard long ago, in which Joseph Welch, an elderly lawyer from Boston, implored Senator Joseph McCarthy to stop slandering one of the young lawyers on his staff. "Let us not assassinate this lad further," Welch says, in a tone of exhausted despair. "You have done enough. Have you no sense of decency sir, at long last? Have you left no sense of decency?"

It didn't happen quite this simply, but Welch's statement has always played as the beginning of the end for McCarthy, the moment in which his purported crusade to protect the homeland collapsed and Americans could see that he was merely trying to make himself a star by turning us against each other. That's what I was looking for—my Joseph Welch moment.

This no doubt has to do with my maternal grandparents, who were, as I've mentioned, the very people whose lives McCarthy ruined. They held fast to the outrageous notion that the bounty of the earth should be fairly divided among its citizens. They lived in fear for this belief, and my grandmother lost her job. So I take it personally when I see our democracy being hijacked by McCarthy's descendants, those who cling to power not by seeking to solve common crises of state, but by demonizing the weak and the just.

I'm sorry to report that my own family of origin suffered from the same essential tyranny. My brothers and I lived—as McCarthy did, as the extreme right wing would have us all live—in a shame culture. It was either humiliate or be humiliated. No retreat, no compromise, no apologies. We savaged one another in direct correlation to our self-loathing. And so my dream of Joseph Welch, which is the dream of every embattled child: that a good and caring father will step in and rescue us from our destructive urges, will demand to see *our* decency, at long last.

My father was a good man. He tried to rescue us. But we had him outnumbered and outflanked. We were children, after all, the first true demagogues, and we behaved as children often do, choosing to be cruel to one another when we might have chosen to be kind.

It is a choice, after all.

This is the main reason Welch's words have always haunted me, and the reason they once resonated so powerfully in our national psyche: not because he stood up to the bully of his era, but because he reminded us that McCarthy was, for all his monstrous actions, a human being capable of contrition.

You have done enough.

The precise tragedy of our present circumstance is not that conservatives in this country are incapable of compassion, but just the opposite: that they choose—as my brothers and I did—to ignore their best impulses day after day. There is no loving father, no Joseph Welch to stop them. And thus they turn to the glowering guardians of the Hateocracy, in the hope that the ecstasy of rage will cleanse their consciences.

As for the rest of us, we play our part. We worship the same false god of convenience, gulp the same burgers and happy pills, enjoy the same lives of plenty, slap bumper stickers on our slightly smaller cars, and thereby manage to convince ourselves we're the good guys.

In some sense, though, the left has come to depend on the Hate-ocracy as much as the right. They have become convenient scape-goats for our own moral laxity. Maybe this is why the great and decent people of this country continue to allow cruel children to lead them: because if we insisted on adult leaders, we would all have to grow the fuck up.

Canto XXVII

The day after my appearance on *H&C*, a young woman called to invite me on Sean Hannity's radio show. She promised Sean would let me speak this time. He wanted to engage in an honest debate. I told her I'd think about it—mostly, I suspect, for the sick pleasure of listening to her beg for the next few days. But I was done. I had spent two weeks absorbing the pathologies of these people, and felt utterly defeated by the experience. My career as a demagogue of the left was officially over.

This is what the Hateocracy does: They wear people down, into silence or cynicism. Yeats had it right: *The best lack all conviction and the worst are filled with passionate intensity.*

I do believe that Americans will look back upon this era some day and discern the seeds of their own ruin. History will regard the conservatism peddled by the Hateocracy as a contagion. But it gives me no joy to say any of this.

My daughter is an American.

Canto XXVIII

One final (bizarre) disclosure: My paternal grandfather, Gabriel Almond, was one of the political scientists who urged Condi Rice to join the faculty at Stanford, where she came to the attention of Bush the Elder. When my grandmother passed away five years ago, Rice—then the National Security Advisor—actually sent my grandfather a personal note of condolence.

Small world, right?

You have no idea.

A few weeks after the BC mishagoss, I flew to California to visit my family. We were all sitting around after dinner one night when my father said, more or less out of nowhere, "You know Condoleezza Rice was almost your aunt?"

"Bullshit," I said.

"It's true. Gramps tried to set her up on a blind date with your uncle Peter."

My cousin Karla said, "Wasn't she also supposed be my babysitter or something?"

"That's true," said Aunt Susyn. "Grandma asked her if she would look after you when you were a baby."

"It was very inappropriate," my mother added. "She was a young academic, not a babysitter."

"Wait a second," I said. "She actually dated you, Pete?"

He did not look pleased to have been reminded. "We had lunch."

"So it's true! I almost had an Aunt Condi!"

"It was one lunch," Pete snapped. "At the faculty club. Gabriel brokered the whole thing."

"No chemistry?" I said.

Pete shook his head. "She was dating an NFL player or something. I wasn't exactly her type."

Canto XXIX

I have only one more story to tell.

It does not take place in hell, though it does take place in Salem, Massachusetts, where, at this country's dawn, the Hateocracy enjoyed a brief and famous outburst. I had come to Salem to read in a small bookstore.

This was a few months after my resignation. I had slipped back into my normal life of private triumphs and miseries. My descent was coming to seem more and more like some strange fever dream.

After the reading, a young man named Tyler came to get his

book signed. He told me he thought maybe he wanted to be a writer. He didn't know exactly. But he felt certain things when he read books and he wanted *that,* to be able to feel those things, and maybe to make other people feel them, too.

I looked at this kid and I knew right away that he was one of those who, had I still been teaching, would have crushed my heart with hope. Other people were waiting behind him, so I signed his book and handed it back to him.

"Thanks, man." He paused for a second and looked down at his shoes. Hair fell into his eyes. "I was supposed to be in your class next year," he mumbled finally.

Canto XXX
I'm sorry, Tyler.

I'm sorry about the whole damn shooting match.

How I Became a Baby Daddy

(Not that You Asked)

YOU'RE WHAT?

THE BEWILDERING JOYS OF
THE HALF-PLANNED PREGNANCY

On an unseasonably warm Boston evening last January, I attended my weekly poker game, made what I often characterize as "a short-term charitable donation" to my opponents, and headed out to the car.

I had left my cell phone on the front seat and was surprised to find two messages from my fiancée, Erin, who was out in Southern California finishing up her MFA program. The first message said this: "Hey hon, it's me. It's nothing bad, but can you give me a call as soon as you get this message? Like, tonight. I'll be up." The second message said the same thing, at a slightly higher frequency.

Erin is a calm person. She is not prone to panicky phone calls, nor, somewhat regrettably, to drunk dialing. I figured maybe she had gotten a short story accepted in a magazine, or perhaps run into someone who hates me.

I looked forward to talking with her, as it would afford me the opportunity to complain about my brilliant play at the poker table, which had, for the 153rd straight week, been undermined by outrageous fortune. You know the deal.

I dialed.

"Hello?" she said.

"It's me. What's up?"

"I'm pregnant," she said.

She started laughing a little.

"Pregnant," she said.

I WILL NOW ATTEMPT to represent my shock. Let each blank line represent 160 volts applied to some tender region of my body, such as the armpit:

"Isn't that crazy?" Erin said.

"Honey?"

TO CLARIFY THE SITUATION, I had just returned from a visit to Erin. On the morning she drove me to the airport, she had an upset stomach and "spotting," which she took as a sign her period had arrived. I had not given any thought to pregnancy, mine or hers.

I was more preoccupied by the idea of being—after years of fairly disreputable male behavior—engaged. I should mention that, at the time of her phone call, we'd been engaged for a grand total of four days. I should also mention that we'd just spent the winter break together and that, yes, we'd had unprotected sex a few times.

Then again, Erin was over thirty. I was pushing forty and had smoked the equivalent of a large marijuana tree over the previous decade. Neither of us had ever been, to the best of our knowledge, involved in a conception scenario. We were both pretty sure we were going to have the opposite problem. That's why Erin had been checking fertility websites all week. In fact, she had gone to the pharmacy intending to purchase an ovulation kit. She had picked up the pregnancy test on a lark.

I DON'T MEAN to imply that I was anything less than tickled to hear her news. I was tickled to a deep, delighted red. I was especially thrilled to have knocked up Erin *before* we got married, because it seemed like such a bohemian arrangement. I was a writer. It was my *job* to scandalize polite society. I loved the idea of being, even briefly, a baby daddy.

Erin was delighted, too. The ensuing conversation was characterized by much giggling. We were so pleased, in fact, that we sort of forgot our original plan, which had been to hold off on the pregnancy until we were married and living on the same coast, presumably in the same house. Erin had also wanted a couple of years to work on her writing.

Instead, we had undergone a *radical paradigm shift*. In the space of a single conversation, we morphed from your-typical-self-absorbed-young-couple-eating-at-swank-restaurants-drinking-too-much-wine-and-fucking-to-the-best-of-our-abilities to parents-in-waiting.

The main thing that had to happen is that we had to make a bunch of decisions, pronto. That was fine with me. I'd spent long enough mucking about in that postadolescent haze known as the Indecisive Thirties. I had spent enough hours pondering paper or plastic, which facial cleanser to purchase, whether to splurge on dessert.

Marriage was the first thing. We had to get married. We had to get married because we didn't want our child to be a bastard (I am already a bastard) and because we needed family health insurance. Erin had insurance, but it would last only until she graduated. In true starving artist fashion, I did not have health insurance at all. There was also the matter of making sure we were in the same room during the ceremony, which, as I understood things, was standard operating procedure.

I now hatched a plan I felt was ingenious—this should have been the first red flag—we would elope! Yes, we would elope over Spring Break, during one of those beach parties where coeds pantomime performing oral sex on stage!

Or perhaps, more manageably, Erin would fly out to visit me in Somerville and we would get hitched at City Hall.

THERE WERE OTHER advantages to this plan, only one of which was that it would save me several thousand dollars, which I had no intention of handing over to the retail racketeering firm known collectively as the Wedding Industry.

Of even greater importance was keeping our relatives far, far away. One of the advantages of being, uh, the technical term is *old,* is that you have been witness to enough weddings to recognize that they are driven by familial guilt. You tell yourself at the outset that it will be a small ceremony, and before you know it you're pricing circus tents and crab cakes by the gross.

I was able to convince Erin to go along with this plan. In fact, I was able to convince her that we should keep both the elopement *and* the baby a secret. My reasoning ran something like this:

- There was a significant risk the pregnancy would not come to term.
- We could break the good news to our friends and family together.
- I was totally freaked out.

I'm not sure I was completely forthright about the last factor.

THE FIRST SIGN that Erin's pregnancy was not going to be easy had already occurred: She had puked.

In those early, heady days, we were almost pleased: This was morning sickness! It meant the hormones were kicking in, that she really and truly was knocked up. We joked! I took to calling her Pukey Pukestein. I suggested she start a band called Pukey Pukestein and the Puke Stains. Ha ha ha!

Over the next month, her morning sickness began a steady green creep across the hours. One evening Erin called me simply to moan into the phone. On another occasion, I would have greeted this turn of events as an erotic invitation. But this moaning was different: anguished, exhausted, not really all that sexy. "Awuahuh-hawawuhhh," she said.

"What's the matter?" I said.

IT DIDN'T REALLY SINK in until I saw her a month later, in Santa Fe.

I'd heard all these stories about how horny women get during pregnancy, so I naturally assumed this first rendezvous would be an even randier version of our usual visits, which were enthusiastically carnal in nature. Erin arrived at our very romantic bed-and-breakfast just before midnight. She looked terrifically sexy, her belly already swelling a little.

We hugged. I nestled into her.

"Baby baby baby," I said.

"Where's the bathroom?" she said.

"Are you okay?"

Erin smiled queerly and slipped into the bathroom.

"What's the matter?" I said, through the door. "You want me to come in?"

"No," she murmured.

I stood, listening to my future wife throw up. A late-night quickie seemed pretty much out of the question.

Erin emerged twenty minutes later, flushed and apologetic.

"Why are you sorry?" I said. "Don't be sorry."

"That was disgusting. Could you hear me?"

"I couldn't hear you."

"Yes, you could!"

I tried to cheer her up with a naked rendition of Pukey Pukestein's first and final hit single, "Save the Last Chunk for Me." This did not work.

Erin had made reservations for us the next day at this Japanese bathhouse place, where, I assumed, we would fuck in a totally hot Buddhist-porno manner. We certainly tried. We tried to fuck in a totally hot Buddhist-porno manner. But Erin still felt sick and we couldn't find a decent surface. So we settled for some light frottage and green tea instead. And it occurred to me later that evening, as I pressed my unrequited boner into Erin's slumbering hip region, that her body was no longer exclusively available for my pleasure. It was now engaged in the vigorously disruptive process of gestation.

THIS WAS COOL. I could deal with this. It was part of the broader paradigm shift. I needed to recognize that and not be one of those sexually demanding baby daddies constantly banging on the cervix door with the tip of my insatiable johnson.

Because the nausea was really just the beginning, a warning shot over the biological bow. I knew this because of my advanced age. I had lots of married dude friends. I had heard the stories about the long, anguished sex sabbaticals that awaited me. But now here's the weird thing, the thing I'm not even sure is a good thing: My own sex drive had been dampened by news of the pregnancy.

It's not that Erin was any less attractive. Pregnancy suited her, accentuated her shape, brought a pale glow to her cheeks. No, it was the idea that her body had more essential business to conduct than the dirty things I had in mind. She was growing an entire person inside her. All those years of hoping and groping and sweet-talking, and what was *I* after, actually? An ecstatic twinge. A bioemission. It felt kind of paltry.

THERE IS MORE to sex than bioemissions, of course. It is an entire language of intimacy, a central pursuit of human happiness. But a bit of psychosexual whiplash was to be expected.

For most of human history, bearing children wasn't a conscious decision. It was a biological consequence, and, a bit later, a matter of economic import. (It is still this way in most of the world.) Only in the superabundance of the current era has pregnancy become a discretionary matter. But as couples wait longer to get married, as breeding becomes a lifestyle decision rather than a cultural assumption, as women test the age boundaries of fertility, you wind up with more and more folks like us who figure, *What the hell, why not let biology decide?* Call it the half-planned pregnancy.

Erin and I were well aware of the alternative: months of scheduled intercourse, clinics, procedures, centrifuges, the anxious machinery of the modern babymaking business. If we'd failed to conceive for a few months, we would have been sucked right into that vortex. We knew we'd gotten lucky.

But somehow we didn't feel so lucky.

Erin didn't, anyway.

She was supposed to be finishing up grad school, working on her novel, teaching undergrads. But she was nauseous around the clock. She wanted her feet rubbed. Maybe even more than this, she wanted to talk about her pregnancy. It was something neither of us had realized: how entirely absorbed women get by their own pregnancies. How much they need to feel *supported* and *validated* and other verbs that men generally don't get.

The problem was that I was the only person she could talk to—owing to my brilliant notion about not telling anyone our good news until we eloped in March—and I was three thousand miles away.

A typical phone conversation ran something like this:

STEVE:	How're you doing, baby?
ERIN:	[Unintelligible]
STEVE:	Did you throw up today?
ERIN:	Uh-huh.
STEVE:	How do you feel now?
ERIN:	I want a McDonald's cheeseburger.
STEVE:	You're a vegetarian.
ERIN:	I don't care.
STEVE:	Okay. If that's what you want, you should get yourself one.
ERIN:	That's disgusting.
STEVE:	Did you try the ginger ale?

ERIN: I feel sick.

STEVE: Remember what Dave said about the ginger ale?

ERIN: Ginger ale makes me sick.

I DON'T MEAN to suggest that we didn't have our bright spots.

The sonograms, for instance.

Yes, we had pictures of our fetus! The big head, the delicate sepia bones, the fishy appendages. Our favorite showed the child in profile, nestled in a kind of intrauterine hammock, hands clasped behind its head, feet up. Stone cold chilling in the amniotic crib.

We took to calling the kid Peanut. Peanut Almond. It had a certain ring to it. Erin got to see Peanut in action, too, a live video feed from her tummy. Peanut did a lot of bopping around. Then Peanut fell asleep and Erin had to cough to try to wake the kid up. We also began taking weekly belly photos, so as to track the distension of Erin's abdomen. By week sixteen, the belly button ring was gone. (I imagined it popping across the room in her sleep.) A few weeks later, her belly button became, after years of pronounced inniedom, an outie. Also: the tits. Wowza. We knew the belly was going to grow; the tits were an added bonus. Two cup sizes in less than two months. After years of feeling flat-chested, Erin now had cleavage. Every now and again, I would catch her staring into the mirror, admiring the goods.

Somewhere in there Erin flew out and we eloped, which went swimmingly, if you don't count breaking the news to her parents. The next morning, we threw a brunch to tell all our pals. Much gasping. Much cheering. My parents, who had flown out from California for the weekend, had to be peeled off the ceiling for the occasion. Erin immediately began having long, intense conversations about lactation with the various mothers and mothers-to-be in our circle.

So this was good.

Erin (and her astonishing breasts!) returned to California happily married, still queasy but empowered to reveal the divine source of her quease. My mother commenced a long-delayed campaign to purchase every single Baby Gap outfit on earth.

ALL PROCEEDED CALMLY for the next three weeks. Then, in the middle of April, the ob-gyn called. Erin assumed the doctor was calling about the nausea, possibly with a cure more effective than ginger ale. Instead, she told Erin that the blood work had come back with abnormally high alpha-fetoprotein levels, which indicated a one in one hundred chance of trisomy.

Erin asked for a translation.

"Trisomy twenty-one corresponds to Down's syndrome."

I was not there for this conversation, of course. I can only imagine the dread that must have lurched through Erin, the sudden dimming of our sudden joy.

"Any time the test profiles indicate a probability greater than one in two hundred, we recommend an amniocentesis," the doctor said. "The best thing would be for you to talk to a genetic counselor." The doctor also informed Erin that any *action* she might want to take—to use her chilling, sanitized language—would have to occur by week twenty-four. We were at week eighteen.

ONCE AGAIN, WE needed to decide a bunch of stuff in a hurry.

The first thing was whether Erin would have an amnio. The procedure involved plunging a big needle into her belly. Erin was understandably reluctant to have a big needle plunged into her belly. There was also a small but nagging risk of damage to the fetus. Erin felt betrayed. She had thought pregnancy would be this beautiful, glowing experience. Instead, she had retched through her first four months, mostly alone, and now, just into the magical second trimester, the sickness had (perhaps) migrated to her unborn child. It sucked.

And it sucked in that particular way modern medicine sucks, wherein the huge, amazing advances in technology carry with them a corresponding increase in data, contingency, anxiety. As recently as a few decades ago, there were no alpha-fetoprotein triple screens, no sonograms, no genetic counselors. Most of the women of the world, in fact, still experience pregnancy as a process devoid of medical intervention.

I'm not so foolish as to advocate this approach. I know too many moms who have suffered preeclampsia or given birth prematurely, whose lives and babies have been saved by modern medicine. At the same time, the prenatal process has become so micromanaged. From the earliest stages of pregnancy, parents can see their baby and listen to its heartbeat, and all that is terrific fun. But they also spend more and more time fretting over its development and safety.

The modern fascination with the unborn child—a fascination skillfully exploited by the antiabortion movement—proceeds from a peculiarly modern fantasy: that with sufficient precaution we can keep our children safe from all harm.

THE FACT REMAINED: Amnio was the only way to know for sure if Peanut had a genetic problem. But did we even want to know? Wasn't there something unnatural, unseemly even, about preapproving the child's genes? What did it say about the limits of our love? That we wanted a child, just so long as he or she wasn't too much of a burden? Or worse, what if we got a bad result and disagreed about what to do? These were not discussions we wanted to be having while three thousand miles apart. We wanted to be able to touch each other, to shoulder this together.

At the same time—and I know this will sound pretty caddish, but it's true—being on opposite coasts probably helped us deal with the situation. It forced us to talk our way past the histrionics and self-pity to the real issues: our fear, our sense of indignation, our guilt, and ultimately our desires as parents. We spent a good week chewing on these issues via phone and e-mail. We were perfectly sweet and thoroughly terrified. I kept reminding Erin that the chances were still one in a hundred, that we shouldn't worry until there was cause. Then we would both spend another hour on the phone worrying.

There's a tendency, when a possibility like this gets raised, for the couple to feel that they've brought on (and secretly deserve) the worst-case scenario. Erin and I had gotten pregnant too easily! We didn't deserve such happiness! There had to be a catch! This brand of logic is total shite. But it's also oddly comforting. It grants you a measure of control over fate, which otherwise feels sadistically random.

THERE IS NO need to prolong the drama. Erin had the amnio. The procedure was painful, but it also revealed—after a few tense days—that Peanut was healthy. And that Peanut was . . . a Peanutta. This was our reward for the big scare. From the earliest days of the pregnancy, we had been rooting for a girl. Both of us had been terrorized by older brothers. So: Great relief. Great rejoicing. Which was important, because, as it turned out, my landlord was just about to give me the heave-ho, meaning we had to find a new place to live.

This is another consequence of having been such late bloomers: Everything happens all at once. In three months we: found a home, closed on a home, moved me across town, moved Erin across the country, visited fourteen states, and set perfectly ridiculous deadlines for our books. (I also quit my teaching job, but you already knew that.)

We live now amid a hundred boxes, stunned and sweaty with the onset of August. Erin is well into her final trimester. She has reached the *cumbersome* phase. Each morning, a bit mournfully, she weighs herself. She is fast approaching what we have come to think of as the "Jack Sprat Parallax," the point at which she weighs more than I do. We are deep into the particulars of the final trimester: weekly sessions with the ob-gyn, prenatal yoga, birthing classes. We have had several awkward discussions about perineal massage, which, if you didn't know, is intended to stretch the vaginal tissues so they won't tear during the child's expulsion.

Did I mention that these discussions were *awkward*?

Erin is also being bombarded with birth stories. The four-day labor, the magnesium-drip delirium labor, the emergency breech labor—she has heard them all. She is a good listener, polite to a fault. My sister-in-law recently related the story of her first birth, which involved a day-long home labor, no drugs, and hanging from a tree. Erin has no interest in such heroics. She has already announced her intention to call for Saint Epidural should the need arise.

Another friend showed us her birth video, which included a rather lengthy illustrated disquisition on the configuration and operation of the (bloody) placenta. And yet another friend has brought it to our attention that Erin will likely poop during the birthing process. I have promised to poop in solidarity.

DID I FORGET to mention the baby shower?

I did.

Here's why: because the baby shower strikes me as one of those events invented and largely nurtured by our fake friends on Madison Avenue. It is intended to supply the anxious parents with everything they need to make sure their baby doesn't die of cold or hunger or diaper rash or Sudden Infant Death Syndrome or boredom. But the general result of such gatherings is that the couple winds up with thirty-seven designer outfits from, yes, Baby Gap.

Now, look: I am just as susceptible as the next person to the sight of a little goo-face tricked out in designer togs. But I also happen to view food, shelter, and love as the only real requirements for the successful nurturance of an infant. The rest is just stuff. Some of this stuff is a matter of convenience: baby monitors, aerodynamic strollers, car seats. Most of it—the fancy-schmancy teething elements, the miniature Doc Martens—is retail masturbation. As a child of the gilded age, Peanut is going to get pelted with thousands of buy messages before she can even hold a penny. There's no reason to accelerate that process.

Thankfully, Erin and I agree on this point. We both believe that Americans would be a lot happier if they bought less and felt more, and we want to make sure we pass these values down to our daughter. At the same time, people want to buy us stuff. So we decided to throw an informal party that we billed as an effort to establish the Peanut Almond Library. Guests were instructed to bring a book, preferably used. Our final haul included forty-plus volumes, along with three adorable outfits, which certain guests insisted on buying for the child (in defiance of our direct orders) and which I plan to burn in a public Death to Capitalism rally when Peanut is old enough to appreciate the gesture.

AS I MAY have hinted above, we are both quietly terrified of the actual birth process. Erin worries about the troublesome physics of the thing. She worries that she will never get her old body back. She worries about handling such a small, fragile creature. My central concern, frankly, is that I will lose the undivided adoration of my wife.

And I will. It can't be avoided.

Sometimes, I walk into our bedroom and find Erin caressing her belly with a cupped palm. There is a look on her face of such contentment that I know I am intruding. Erin has begun the long process of falling in love with our daughter. I will go through a similar process, but let's be honest: There is nothing on earth to equal Mother Love. If there were, we would have ceased doing business as a species long ago.

I can feel myself getting displaced. And I can feel myself panicking. A few days ago, I picked a fight with Erin over her decision to give her cat some wet food as a treat. Hadn't we agreed to feed the cat only dry food? Was it really fair to our daughter to lavish such treats on an ungrateful animal? I was disgustingly manipulative and almost comically furious. It drove me crazy to imagine Erin spending any of her attention on the cat. You don't have to be a genius to figure out the math: I was redirecting my forbidden resentment of my daughter onto the animal. What can I tell you? I am resentful. And frightened. I'm frightened that I'm going to slip to number two in her book.

All fathers suffer this fear. And I've seen more than one marriage brought to ruin by it. My own parents nearly came apart under the pressure of their children. So this is what we've been dealing with as we wait for Peanut to make her debut. Can I adjust to a lesser role? Will Erin be able to embrace motherhood without feeling too much anxiety? Will we resist the temptation to bicker over who is working harder? Will our hearts expand as required?

Stay calm, stay happy, and the kid will be golden.

That's the mantra Erin and I keep chanting. We've got to bid adieu to our lives as nervous singles, to the flashy armor of our narcissism, to the notion that we will ever be able to control the course of our lives again. In other words, we're fucked. To feel such unprecedented love runs against the monstrous self-regard of the era. We can hardly wait.

10 WAYS I KILLED MY DAUGHTER WITHIN HER FIRST 72 HOURS OF LIFE

A HEARTWARMING SAGA OF LOVE, FATHERHOOD, AND SERIAL INFANTICIDE

Having your first baby is a joyous and unforgettable adventure, but one that can be compromised if you allow baby to die in your care. Unfortunately, the precipitous appearance of Baby tends to magnify the impression—at least among the inexperienced and un-medicated—that one has, rather by accident, killed him or her. This makes ensuing discussions with relatives awkward.

MOTHER-IN-LAW: How is my sweet little lovey-dovey dumpling?

YOU: Dead.

Good news!

Chances are, you have not killed Baby. Chances are, Baby is alive and well and merely plotting new ways to appear dead. I offer this reassurance from the perspective of a proud new papa who killed his daughter (Josephine Colette aka Peanut Almond aka Milkface McGee aka The Deceased) repeatedly in her first three days of life.

Death #1: Massive Exsanguination (Blood Loss)

Age of Deceased: 47 seconds

In an effort to prove my commitment to fatherhood, I insist on catching Baby. I do not catch Baby. No, Baby goes whistling right through my mitts in a fashion familiar to any Red Sox fan who has watched Bill Buckner attempt to play first base. This should be the initial cause of death (blunt trauma), but the ob-gyn, perhaps sensing my physical ineptitude, provides backup on the play.

Josephine Colette Almond, upon greeting the world, issues a single, stunned cry, then falls silent. She appears confused beyond terror.[1] The nurses swoop in to sponge the blood and mucus from her body, and she clasps her hands beneath her chin, like a tiny penitent. Her irises—the dull gray of solder—fix on mine for a moment, and my chest stings with the adoration.

The doctor reaches down to clamp the umbilical cord, which is dangling from her belly like a giant bluish strand of fusilli. "Do you want to make her belly button, Dad?" Before I can answer, she hands me a pair of scissors and gestures to a spot on the cord beyond the clamp. "Just cut here."

This should not be difficult. I know how to operate scissors. I am, if you will, *scissor literate.* The doctor nods, and my thumb and forefinger come together and the blade bites against the spongy cord. *Snip.* My daughter is officially off the amniotic dole, severed from my wife, who is lying back against the pillows, breathing deeply, her cheeks still marbled with exertion.

The problem is the blood. Yes, there's a trace of blood (which there shouldn't be, given the clamp), and I can see now that I've cut too far down. In effect, I've stabbed my newborn in the gut. I close my eyes and watch red seep down her legs and stain the bedsheets.

---

1. Who can blame her? One minute you're a fish, happily afloat in a warm dark sea, the next you're a shivering mammal, shoved into the bright cold beyond. Is it any wonder the Bible is so much about exile?

The small ration of blood inside Baby is gushing out now, and my daughter is draining to a chalky white.

"What have I done?" I whisper.

"You did a very good job, Mr. Almond," the doctor says calmly. "You may let go of the scissors now."

Death #2: Broken Vertebrae
Age of Deceased: 4 hours

In the maternity ward, the nurses tell us not to worry. They tell us to get some rest. We are both totally in awe of the nurses. If the nurses told us to bathe the baby in lye, our only question would be, *Should we heat the lye?* We hit the Help button every seventeen minutes.[2]

Erin limps to the bathroom, and, because I can think of no good reason to call for the on-duty nurse, I am for the first time alone with Baby, whom I was supposed to swaddle into a tight little burrito, though she looks more like a defective veggie wrap. As I set her down to sleep, she throws her arms up in the air and waves them like she just don't care. Later on, it will be explained to me that this is normal, something called the Moro Reflex. For now, I am briefly convinced baby has a future in hip-hop.

This maneuver, however, manages to tip her from her side onto her stomach, which we have been warned by countless paranoia-inducing baby books is the *Position of Death*. I reach down to flip her over—carefully, because (as I also know from the baby books) Baby doesn't have neck muscles yet. The thing connecting her torso to her head is just a band of fat with some tubes in the middle.

Baby reacts to this jostling by again waving her arms in the air like she just don't care and kicking the plastic rim of the bassinet. Gravity—that first cruel joke—sends her tumbling off my hands and onto her shoulder. Her muscleless neck twists at a grisly angle.

---

2. Point of clarification: *I* press the Help button every seventeen minutes.

"Baby," I whisper. "Baby!" I give baby a light shove. But Baby does not move.

"Baby," I plead. "Please don't be dead." Baby, curled like a brine shrimp, remains dead.

I poke her in the tummy, probably harder than is appropriate.

Baby spits up on my hand.

Death #3: Cancer
Age of Deceased: 9 *hours*

The nurses instruct us to change Baby's diaper every two hours. Erin has done the first three, so I'm up. I remove her diaper and marvel at her skinny little bowed legs and her abnormally long toes, which look disturbingly like fingers. Most of all, I make a determined effort to ignore my daughter's *gigantic red vulva*. Her diaper is empty, but I decide to wipe anyway. A practice wipe. I hoist her up by the ankles and proceed gently unto the breach.

Baby gets a curious look on her face. Her cheeks flush. Her eyes squinch up, as if she is bench-pressing another, much larger, baby. And then something very scary is happening: A thick, goopy substance is extruding from her tiny backside. My daughter is suddenly a tube of oil-based paint and she is being squeezed by the hand of some callous god. What comes out is a shimmery puce.

It is immediately evident what's happening: My daughter is shitting out a tumor. Yes, my daughter has cancer, cancer of the stomach and the intestines and the heart; her insides are not red and healthy, they are ravaged and feculent. And puce. This too is my fault. I have managed to transmit my malignant humours to the poor child, and now she is pooping out her poisoned life force.

Erin, risen from the bed, stands at my shoulder. For a moment, we watch baby shit tumor together. "Hey," she says. "It's meconium!"

Yes, I am seeing Baby's first bowel movement, a superconcentrated form of stool that includes mucus, bile, and (somehow—I refused to investigate the details) *hair*.

Death #4: Respiratory Failure
Age of Deceased: 19 hours

Baby has by now taken on a distinctly pugilistic aspect. Her face is red and puffed around the brows. She insists on holding her fists on either side of her chin and occasionally shoots out a left jab.

This is okay with me. I remind myself: Baby is alive. I have not yet killed Baby. Indeed, it has begun to dawn on me that Baby is not quite so fragile as she would have me believe. I have watched the nurses handle her, the brisk tossing of her body this way and that, and noticed that she remains alive.

Most of the time, Baby sleeps, and when she awakens she hits the local titty bar, which she attacks with such vigor that Erin yelps. I am the designated burper. I set Baby on my lap and pat her back. She tends to droop over and fall asleep without burping, then she throws up on herself. Baby is, in this sense, a bad drunk.

Chief Nurse Kelly (CNK) deems my burping technique insufficient to the gastric needs of Baby. "Put her ovah your shouldah and get her right heah," she explains, in cheerful Bostonese. She demonstrates. Baby looks as if she were operating a tiny jackhammer. She burps almost immediately. CNK hands Baby to me and leaves.

I do exactly what CNK did, but Baby senses she is being handled by an incompetent. Her fingers wiggle nervously. Then Baby begins making odd noises, little suspirating yelps. Her diaphragm heaves. In my eagerness to mimic CNK, I have crushed Baby's trachea. I hold Baby in my lap and watch her tiny death throes.

"How cute!" Erin cries from the bed. "She's got the hiccups!"

Death #5: Aneurysm
Age of Deceased: 27 hours

Baby has somehow acquired a stuffy nose. Her breathing calls to mind Peter Lorre. This is a problem, as she must also feed, and Baby is not yet coordinating the two very well. The nurses have left us with a bulb syringe, which I remember their inserting in Baby's nostrils just after birth to clear the mucus. I attempt the same thing. Because of a basic misunderstanding of physics,[3] and specifically the concept of suction, I fail to deflate the bulb before insertion. Instead, I blow air *up* Baby's nose.

The air travels up into the soft cup of her skull and pops the fragile balloon around her brainpan, which I am certain exists despite having no actual neurological expertise. The popping of this fragile "brain balloon" ruptures the frontal lobes, the synaptic nerve bundles, and every single micro-artery in Baby's head.

Death #6: Intestinal Detonation

Age of Deceased: 39 hours

Baby has what Micki, the lactation expert, calls an "improper latch." Mickey is a terrifyingly cheerful blond woman who has visited our room no fewer than seven times. Every time Baby needs to feed— which she signals by wailing in the manner of a deranged castrato—Micki bursts into our room and slams Baby's mouth against Erin's boob. She does this slamming at a number of angles, all the while saying encouraging things such as "She's almost got it now! Good girl! Oh, wait, is that blood? Nothing to worry about!"

I stand by the foot of the bed with my Supportive Dad smile while Erin and Baby weep inconsolably.

"Good news for Dad!" Micki says. "Dad gets to do some finger feeding!"

Contrary to my initial understanding, this does not mean that I will be serving Baby hors d'oeuvres. It means she will be fed through a tiny tube taped to my finger and attached to a syringe full of formula.

"What about, you know, a bottle?" I say.

---

3. My score on the 1984 Advanced Placement Physics Test (on a scale of 1 to 5): 1.

"Oh, no," Micki says. "That would cause nipple confusion!"

I want to tell Micki that the child is likely to inherit nipple confusion from me anyway, but the baby has gone Pavarotti on our asses now. My finger is quickly taped and syringed and Baby affixed thereto. Micki's beeper beeps and she rushes off. Erin, bone-tired, bloodied, falls into a deep sleep. Once again I am alone with Baby, who is sucking formula from my finger. Every few sucks she pauses to breathe and lets out a pleased sigh. The first syringe is gone in half a minute. Baby devours a second syringe, then a third. Midway through the fourth syringe, Baby's eyes droop shut. Formula rills down her chin. I am bursting with pride. I have fed Baby! Baby sleeps.

When I wake three hours later, Erin is hissing at me. "What did you do to her? She's all bloated! She's not breathing right!"

I stumble over to the bassinet.

Baby's tiny belly does appear distended. Her face is the shade of a winter plum. A memory comes to me, unbidden, of a film my parents forced me to watch when I was young. It was about Swedish immigrants, all of whom were—as is the habit of Swedish immigrants in depressing films—starving to death. Then this one little girl finds a giant cache of cereal and eats so much her stomach bloats up and eventually *explodes*.

"How much did you feed her?" Erin demands.

"A couple of syringes." I set my hand on her hand, in the cautious manner of a father who has yet again killed his infant. "She was *hungry*."

"Didn't you hear Micki? Her stomach is the size of a walnut!"

"It could be the hiccups," I say, and hit the Help button.

"She doesn't have fucking hiccups," Erin says.

Nurse Tina appears. "What's the problem?"

Baby closes her eyes and releases a bowel movement of volcanic magnitude, a shuddering liquid outburst of the sort that will soon come to be known in our household as the Hot Mustard Explosion.

Death #7: Asphyxiation
Age of Deceased: 43 hours

As a rule, the nurses have no patience for us dads. We are clumsy, luggish, good for nothing. We have purchased our proximity to the miracle of birth with a thimbleful of sperm, and the bargain strikes them, perhaps appropriately, as outrageous.

Mostly we stay out of the way. We gather in the common room and stuff our mouths with muffins and murmur things like "Scary shit, man" and "Way to go" and "Yeah, we did it." We do the stiff-armed man hug. We promenade our babies up and down the halls when they're cranky and nod to each other wearily, like we've just been through hell and back and boy aren't *our* vaginal canals sore!

The fact that I am finger feeding grants me a certain measure of maternity cred,[4] and I make it a point to flaunt my role. "Do you have any spare syringes?" I say loudly, whenever I pass by the nurses' station. "Yeah, I've got another *feeding* just now. I'm going with the index finger this time around. The pinkie made her a little gassy."

Following the Hot Mustard debacle, Micki has explained to me that I must keep the syringe lower than my finger, so as to force Baby to suck against gravity and prevent her from gorging. But I am already conducting my fourth feeding, which naturally means I know more about the process than anyone else on earth. And thus it should be taken as no problem at all when I lift the syringe quickly, in an effort to scratch my neck, and it comes to rest a foot or so above Baby's mouth, meaning that she is—with no actual warning—shotgunning formula.

Alas, Baby is not used to shotgunning. Baby has not even pledged a sorority. She signifies this by promptly sputtering, gagging, and reverting to her fallback asphyxiation shade (winter plum). Baby then vomits, which seems encouraging, except that I

4. No it doesn't.

have failed to turn Baby on her side, so the vomit funnels back down her throat.

I have Jimi Hendrixed my daughter to death.

Death #8: Poison
Age of Deceased: 51 hours

The nurses have begun openly to hate me. This has to do not just with my regular and tiresome fears of having killed my daughter, but the fact that I have begun stealing unreasonable quantities of hospital property: diapers, formula, syringes, blankets, waterproof bed pads, petroleum jelly, hospital gowns, socks, bagels.[5] The nurses watch from their station, flabbergasted, as I ferry the goods down to the parking lot in bulging plastic sacks. They are too embarrassed to stop me.

Why am I doing this? For one thing, the other dads have encouraged me. They have indicated that absconding with items is standard protocol. I have simply taken the practice to a new level, a level perhaps best described as grand larceny.

The truth is, having been relieved of finger feeding duty (see Death #7) I am bored. Thus I am trying to prove myself useful. I am—by a rather loose definition—hunting and gathering. It might also be conjectured that I am somewhat nervous about leaving the hospital with Baby and am therefore attempting to take a significant portion of the hospital home with me.

Nonetheless, after two days, a frightfully young pediatrician appears, examines Baby, and hands us our walking papers. Chief Nurse Kelly does not say, "We're sorry to see you go!" She does not say, "Do you need anything else?" She does not say, "What a cute baby!" She says, "I assume you'll have room in the cah for your daughtah."

---

5. At home, my wife will express awed disgust at the extent of my thievery. She will, for instance, remove a small pink plastic dish from my haul and hold it up for my consideration. "Did we really need a bedpan?"

We arrive home and place Baby in the fancy frilled bassinet Erin managed to secure from friends.[6] We stare at Baby for several minutes and wait—as do all parents in such circumstances—for a detailed instruction manual to float down from heaven and land in our hands.

Instead, we are left to fend for ourselves. Baby continues to latch improperly. I am placed back on finger feeding duty. The single item I failed to steal from the hospital now becomes apparent: the tape used to bind feeding tube to finger.

Is it wise for me to use duct tape instead? I suppose it is not. But when you are face-to-face with a hysterical newborn at three in the morning, your judgment clouds. And the duct tape works like a charm. Baby chows down, making her endearing Viking slurps and, toward the end of the feeding, producing a Mustard Explosion so prodigious it blows out the edges of her diaper.[7] Only later do I realize that Baby's power suckling has stripped away a portion of the duct tape from my finger and that Baby has thus ingested a good deal of the adhesive.

Baby appears to be sleeping peacefully, but I cannot shake the fear that this adhesive is toxic and that Baby will soon begin foam-

---

6. A loaner necessitated by the fact that Erin refused to see the sense in storing the child—at least for the first month or two—in one of the sturdy plastic bins that I occasionally remove from beneath public mailboxes, a bin that, as I've pointed out to her repeatedly, could easily be scrubbed and filled with clean blankets.

7. This circumstance will come to be known in our household as Code Brown. Curiously, shit no longer bothers us. Just the opposite. In these early days of child rearing, our interest in her feces borders on the fetishistic. We are overjoyed on the occasion of her first projectile defecation and brag about it to friends for weeks.

> Me: I'm telling you, this kid is a powerhouse. Two feet she shat!
> Erin: All the way to the laundry bag!
> Me: That's *over* the lip of the changing table.
> Friend: [Silence]
> Erin: So, when do you want to come see her?
> Friend: [More silence]

ing at the mouth. I tiptoe over and stare down at her in the dim light. Her breathing seems shallow and hurried. I scurry to my computer and Google "duct tape" and "toxic adhesive." There is a wealth of information about sealants and thermal insulation, but nothing on whether I've killed my daughter. I return to the bedroom and hover over Baby for the next twenty minutes.

"What's the matter?" Erin murmurs. "What did you do?"

"Nothing," I say. "How much do you know about duct tape?"

She rushes over to the bassinet and reaches for Baby, who jolts awake at her touch and throws a drowsy left jab.

Death #9: Heat Stroke
Age of Deceased: 59 hours

Issues have arisen as to heating. Erin would like the house at 70 degrees, so as to avoid freezing the child to death. I would prefer the low sixties, arguing that we can dress Baby in layers. After a brief discussion involving the possibility of separate dwellings, the thermostat is set at 70 degrees.

Owing to the general decrepitude of our home heating system—which appears to operate by means of a small British orphan shoveling coal into a burning sock—it is determined that 70 degrees is not warm enough. I drag my ancient portable heater into the bedroom. A few hours later I awaken, bathed in sweat. We are on the brink of dawn, the pink hour at which the room should be chilliest. It is a sauna. I have forgotten this crucial fact about the heater: It is an extremely badass piece of equipment. And now I realize, with sinking dread, that I have placed this monstrosity right next to Baby's crib and that (therefore) its supercharged heat quasars have been blasting Baby for the last four hours straight, a fact that explains her uncharacteristic silence.

I have boiled Baby's blood.

Unlike the many other forms of distress I've inflicted on my daughter thus far, heat is a silent killer. No coughing. No crying. Just a moist descent into coma, followed by the noiseless simmering of internal organs. I throw the blankets off, rip the heater's cord from the wall, and stagger to the foot of the bed. I burrow my thumb under Baby's onesie, searching for her tiny poached heart. When I feel the flicker, I drop to my knees.

Baby stares at me with her fuzzy gray eyes and yawns.

Death #10: Grief

Age of Deceased: 77 hours

Baby is crying. Baby will not stop crying. We have tried everything in our limited repertoire: food, a new diaper, rocking. We have run through all five of the measures recommended by the creepy doctor in our *Happiest Baby on the Block* video. We have even blasted the eerie amniotic horror music at the end of the DVD, a very bad decision for all involved.

Erin is becoming panicky, so I send her downstairs to do laundry.

Now it is just me and Baby. I walk her from room to room and whisper my secret vows of love, and Baby yells and weeps and chokes on her tears. Her face appears frozen in a gummy frown. Her ears are tiny red seashells. There is a hot momentum to her misery; she is speaking in tongues, an ecstatic.

It is her right as a citizen of earth, this aria of sorrow, this abject declaration. She puts everything she is, every ounce of her, into each shriek. Her breath is so sweet I want to climb inside her mouth. I kiss her cheek and she cries harder.

And as I watch her, as I listen to her crescendo, as I feel her muscles tense against my chest, I begin to recognize the source of my own terror. The world *will* kill this child, day by day, wish by wish. I can do little to protect her, almost nothing. The very love I inflict on her will only sharpen her disappointment in the end. She is a part of the great cosmic joke now, the daily lamentation of a species born into pain. Baby is only telling me the truth: *It hurts so much right now I could die.*

This is when it happens a final time. Baby seizes up. Her throat catches. Her body, with a culminating exhalation, falls limp against me.

Erin appears with a load of warm blankets. The house has gone still. It smells of garlic and burned sugar. A half moon hangs over us. The silence sounds now like the warm echo of the creature I am holding. Erin sets her hand on the small of my back. She rests her forehead against my chest. She stares at our baby with a love so dumb and fierce as to forgive everything.

"You got her to sleep," she says softly. "Nice work, Papa."

HAM FOR CHANUKAH

Every year, when Chanukah season rolled around, my brothers and I would make the suburban pilgrimage to the home of our grandparents, where we would ring in the holiday with a big, juicy Chanukah ham. We would then gather around the festively decorated Chanukah tree and tear open the brightly wrapped Chanukah gifts beneath, often while swilling syrupy Chanukah eggnog and munching Chanukah gingerbread cookies.[1]

It will be difficult to explain why, as full-blooded Jews, the spawn of actual rabbis, we took part in this deeply fucked-up ritual. But I am going to try to explain. Because that is what Jews do: We *try to explain*. I'll need to start with my great-grandfathers Morris Rosenthal and David Almond. Both were scholars of the old-school variety, both, according to the available evidence, completely out of their minds.

David was renowned in his family for his fanatic theories concerning diet, the most pronounced of which ascribed to fresh milk certain miraculous health benefits. Every Saturday, he took his children on a long constitutional through the farmland surrounding Chicago, the despised culmination of which was a visit to a local dairy farmer for a ration of the freshest milk available. (I do not mean to imply that David forced his children to suck milk directly

1. My parents—who read this essay for factual content and have reserved the right to take legal action—would like it noted that we never actually ate ham *during* Chanukah.

from the cow's teat, though I rather like the image.) In his later years, by now a veteran rabbi, David managed to invent a scientific discipline; *ontomology* was devoted to establishing God's existence using logical proofs. I have read his book on the subject, or tried to, and will offer no further comment at this time, as I do not believe in God or logic.

David Almond's counterpart on the maternal side, Morris Rosenthal, was a *yeshiva bocher* in White Russia, meaning that he was kicked out of his house at age six and forced to become an itinerant student of the Talmud. Later, he was conscripted into the czar's army, where he spent two years trading his sausage rations (not kosher) for potatoes and onions. As a young scholar fresh from the army, Morris attended a physics lecture at which the professor produced a rainbow by shining light through a misty veil of water. This demonstration was apparently enough to shake his faith in the Almighty. I suspect the privations of the clerical lifestyle played a role here as well. In any event, he emigrated to the Bronx and became, at age forty, a dentist of notorious methods. My mother still speaks shakily of her visits to Grandpa Morris's office; he did not believe in anesthesia. Morris remained a student of the Old Testament throughout his life, though in the oppositional sense. He devoted his later years to the writing of a book which set out to prove God *did not* exist.[2]

I mention this history by way of making a simple point: The family's proud rabbinical tradition was in fact marred by eccentricity, not to mention cranky despair. The children born to both men—can this come as a surprise?—turned away from formal modes of Judaism.

My paternal grandfather Gabriel endured a thorough Jewish education, then went off and became a famous political scientist. His basic attitude was that God had done some interesting work early on, but hadn't published much lately.

---

2. For those of you keeping score, that's one great-grandfather for God, one against, and no (thank God) they were never in the same room.

The most influential member of the family, in regard to our own peculiar Chanukah ritual, was Gabriel's wife, Dorothea. She was the only child of a wealthy German banker and a socialite, neither of whom was particularly observant. Dorothea and her parents escaped Germany before the worst of the atrocities, mostly because they were rich enough to get inside information about how bad it would get. (Other members of the family weren't so lucky.)

But I don't think Dorothea ever fully processed the experience. She remained intensely identified with German culture. Let me be more candid: She struck me as tacitly anti-Semitic, as if any acknowledgment of her Judaism would be an invitation to more upheaval. She was active in the Unitarian church. And it was she who insisted that the family gather at her home on Christmas Day, so that we could enact some good old consumerist gluttony in the name of the birth of Jesus Christ.

Do I sound bitter? I had hoped to avoid bitterness.

The obvious question is where my parents were in all this. They were where they always were during my childhood: in the land of Doing Their Best Under the Circumstances. They had three aggressively anxious boys to manage, after all, plus two complicated careers, and the aforementioned family ghosts.

My father was never permitted to experience his Judaism. The story that has always struck me as emblematic of his upbringing has him singing Christmas carols with a bunch of goyische buddies in Princeton, New Jersey. Among those serenaded was none other than Albert Einstein, who waved to them through his living room window. There is something almost unbearably tender and deluded to this image: my father (a Jew) singing "O Holy Night" to Einstein (another Jew); the benevolent, collaborating wave that passes between them. In my conjuring of this scene, I have put snow in the background, a golden nimbus of light all around, and, behind Einstein himself, a Christmas tree sparkling with ornaments.

I'm not saying I blame my dad. He was the eldest son of a spectacularly self-absorbed academic and a distant mother. He was shuttled around the country as a kid. He wanted to fit in.

My mother's situation was in some ways more extreme. Her parents were those crazy card-carrying Communists. Although culturally identified as Jews, they believed religion was the opiate of the masses. They were also scared stiff during the fifties. My mother never fully understood what all the anxiety was about as a child, which might have made matters worse.

As should be apparent, neither of my parents was given much grounding in the upside of Judaism. Or maybe it would be more accurate to say that the Jewish influence took shape exclusively in the secular realm. They were people of ideas, intellectual, ambitious, socially responsible. To the extent that two professionals could, they embraced the heady idealism of the counterculture movement. They were not naïve or self-hating about their Judaism; they were simply overrun by competing interests.

And so our religious inheritance was, to put it Yiddishly, *moyshe kapoyer.* Consider our names: David Emmanuel, Michael Isaac, Steven Benjamin.[3] Or consider our education. We were sent off to Sunday school for a few years, but I remember almost nothing of the experience: being forced to eat prune cookies at Purim, the acrid waft of a sun-softened blacktop. For the most part, we were public school kids, trying our best not to get our asses beaten by the toughs.

The apotheosis of our quasi-Jewish upbringing was the bar mitzvah ritual. I have implied on previous occasions that my bar mitzvah took place in our hot tub. This is not actually true. But it was a D.I.Y. home bar mitzvah, overseen by my father (as opposed to a rabbi). And it did feature a somewhat exclusive hot tub after-party. First, of course, came the traditional prayers, speech, and buffet, which took place in our living room/dining room, into which we crammed 150 folding chairs and a metric ton of cold cuts. My father, blessed be his mishagoss, helped us compose our

3. As for Almond—a name that doesn't exactly scream Jewish—it was a naked bid at assimilation on the part of rabbi David after his emigration to London. Our name had been Pruzhinski.

speeches[4] and prepared cheat sheets with the required Hebrew prayers spelled out phonetically (*baw-rooch ah-taw ad-doh-noi* . . .). I am hazy on the other details, mercifully so. I remember the itch of my blazer, a certain disembodied anxiety. I wanted very badly not to screw up and embarrass my pop. The comment that perhaps best sums up the liturgical experience came from my grandfather Irving, a man renowned more for candor than tact. "Was that supposed to be Hebrew?" he said to me, while forking sliced tongue onto his paper plate. "It sounded like you were speaking Spanish."

Yes, well, *yo no hablo Hebrew.*

And why didn't we join a temple? Good question. My parents have expressed considerable regret over this in the past few years. They feel—and I tend to agree—that we could have found a larger community in this way, and relieved some of the pressures that beset the family. We were living in Palo Alto, after all, a suburb with no shortage of congregations. But the possibility never came up for discussion. And so the only time that religion impinged on our lives at all was during the holiday season.

Which brings us back to why, year after year, we schlepped over to the ancestral home on Old Trace Road and took part in our bizarre Chrisnukah ritual.

This, like most everything else in life, boils down to family politics. Dorothea was the one pushing the Christmas agenda, and she

---

4. My father recently presented me with a copy of my bar mitzvah speech, a document I presumed to have died of shame sometime in the early 1990s. The document, which is allegedly about the Covenant with Abraham, reveals a predictable fascination with genital mutilation:

> In another story God asks Abraham to have all of his men circumcised. Here we find out that God wants to distinguish his people from all others by permanently altering a semi-noticeable [*!!!*] part of the body. This is a very strong commitment because it can never be changed. This is not found in most other religions. Circumcision is metaphoric of the all-out commitment that began with the covenant.

You're welcome.

was a control freak of the first order. My mother was a control freak too. But she discerned pretty quickly that fighting Dorothea on the Christmas thing was wasted energy. Dorothea had the conviction— however misbegotten—and the material advantage. Because let's face it: When you're a kid, your allegiance to holidays boils down to loot. From this perspective, Chanukah has never stood a chance against Christmas, with its mighty, sleigh-riding, toy-pimping saint.

My parents did remind us that, despite the *schweinfest* at Grandma and Grandpa's, we were Jews. Most years, we conducted an informal Chanukah ceremony, which meant gathering around the kitchen table to light the candles after dinner. What I remember of this ritual was the moment, just as my mother reached to light the candles on our battered menorah, when my father would turn to us and begin to sing the blessing in his soft baritone. The expression in his eyes was one of excruciating yearning. He wanted to know which of his sons would join him. Most of the time, we left him high and dry. Who were we to act all Jewy? It felt like a put-on. It made us squirm.

More occasionally, my mother would prepare a Chanukah feast: latkes with sour cream and applesauce, which meant for me (picky little shitheel that I was) a quart of applesauce for dinner. Of the gifts, I recall only the chocolate coins in gold foil. The first time I saw a dreidl, I thought it was a piece of candy and popped it in my mouth.

No, the big day was always Christmas, because this was when the serious giftage came out and you had to dress up and behave with a modicum of respect in order to get at the goods. My grandmother presided over these gatherings in a state of nervous exaltation. We were not to climb the furniture or lick unapproved surfaces. Her house was filled with strange artifacts—vases and delicate clay figurines—kept in museum-style cabinets. She could be ferociously tidy, though she tended to leave perishable foods such as butter out on her kitchen counter for hours at a time. When it came time to open gifts, we would bumrush the tannenbaum, while she admonished us in her sibilant German accent not tear the wrapping paper. The family albums are filled with pictures of her grandsons joyously shredding all available wrapping paper.

The strangest thing, of course, is that none of this seemed strange at the time. And it *should* have been strange, because the bottom line is that Christ—as conjured by the zealots of the Church—has meant nothing but misery for the Jews.

I could argue that the actual event (the gathering, the food, the presents) was so watered down as to qualify as theologically neutral. And I could further argue that Chanukah isn't much of a holiday at all. The episode from which it derives plays no significant role in the Old Testament, and the miracle at the center of the ritual boils down to a maintenance issue. It's more like a late-inning retail counterstrike.

But these feel, finally, like rationalizations. We were purebred Jews acting like purebred Christians.

Honestly, it makes me sad. It makes me sad to think of our family, so unmoored from its own history, spinning in our private orbits of obligation and grievance. It makes me sad to think of my grandmother embracing the culture that sought to annihilate her.

I don't mean to suggest that celebrating Chanukah, or affiliating ourselves more broadly with the traditions of Judaism, would have solved things. I mean only that our inability to unite as a family under the umbrella of our heritage suggested a glaring crisis of identity. We lacked the willingness to fold ourselves into some larger human brotherhood, which is the central and enduring appeal of religion.

"We weren't joiners," my father has often explained.

But I think our dilemma was more fundamental.

What we actually lacked was belief. I don't mean belief in a higher being, but something closer to an emotional capacity for hope. Our house was too full of insecure machismo to allow for much hope. We were too embarrassed to express such feelings, which implied weakness and dependence and left one vulnerable to mockery. We all felt the jones for connection—to each other, to our history. It simply went unrequited, as it so often does in troubled families.

It's no coincidence that I decided to spend half my sophomore year studying in Jerusalem. I kept hoping, as I wandered the old yellow stone of that city, that some mystical, transformative spirit would seize me. It didn't happen.[5] No, I was an atheist through and through. God was, to me, a lovely dream, a brave make-believe daddy who provided comforting answers to those who couldn't bear the prevailing evidence.

My appreciation of Judaism had more to do with pride. I viewed my people as the pound-for-pound champions of consciousness—Christ, Marx, Freud, Einstein—stars of the longest-running ethnic drama on earth, and, what's more, authors of our single greatest work of literature! (Hint: Every hotel room has one.)

It was also true that I simply liked Jews more than other people. They were, as a rule, funnier, more curious and self-reflective, than goys. They loved food. And they knew how to talk. They were talkers. My mother's people represent the purest example of this verbal bent. Not coincidentally, they are the side of the family that grew up speaking Yiddish. I cannot begin to express my adoration for Yiddish, the official language of the shtetl Jews and the most emotionally precise vernacular ever devised. More than any holiday ritual, Yiddish is the legacy my mother passed on to me. I once actually wrote an entire cycle of poems (awful, all of them) devoted to the Yiddish word *schmaltz*.

My wife is, in her own words, a "recovering Catholic."[6] I am happy to report, however, that she shares my affection for Jews. Early in our engagement, she surprised me by announcing that she wanted to convert to Judaism. I was flattered, flustered, quite close

---

5. I did briefly consider moving to Israel, but I'm afraid that had more to do with the native female population, lady soldiers with big hips and thick hair and rifles. Yum.

6. As a good Catholic girl, she had a crucifix on her bedroom wall. "Not just the cross," she notes. "The body was on it, too." This, I believe, helps explain her attraction to me: She grew up worshipping a half-naked Jewish man.

to asking if she was nuts. She explained (calmly) that she'd always admired the religion's emphasis on ethics and learning, and that she liked the idea of raising children in one faith.

And now that we have a daughter (one who arrived just in time for Chanukah), I'm seeing the advantages of this arrangement. My wife, after all, will have to undergo an education to convert formally, and this should mean that at least one of us will know the blessing spoken over the candles, which I forgot long ago.

As for the rest of my family, they have all shown a greater interest in Judaism as they have grown older, my father in particular. He became a member of the chorus at a local synagogue and spent several months studying Hebrew. A few years ago, he visited Israel for the first time in many years. He sent me a postcard in which he confessed, somewhat joyfully, that he had burst into tears as he stood before the Wailing Wall.

And I believe, in fact, that he was weeping for what he had never experienced, the faith his parents had deprived him of, the faith he failed to instill in his sons, the possibility of some great spiritual bosom into which he might nestle and rest his weary bones. I am speculating, of course, based on my own mawkish proclivities.

I know this much: that my daughter will be raised as a Jew, that she will be afforded the chance to believe in the miracle of Chanukah, and all the other silly miracles, as suits her fancy, that she will learn the blessing (perhaps we will learn it together), and that she will make up her own mind about whether there is a God in heaven, or whether God exists between us creatures on earth.

She will know where and who she came from. She will be loved unreasonably. The rest is hers to determine.

Acknowledgments

Thanks to Kurt Vonnegut right off the bat, for imparting the perfectly foolish notion that writing is an elegant and hilarious manner of rescue. This book was supposed to be about Vonnegut actually, a sort of *Behind the Music* biopic. That's the pitch I sent the folks at Random House last spring. They wanted a book of essays instead. So it goes.

To those who read early drafts and managed to deliver the bad news with kindness—Erin, Barbara, and Richard Almond, and Keith Morris, Billy Giraldi, Dave Blair, Pat Flood, Peter Keating, Karl Iagnemma, and Holden Lewis—I offer the hallowed words of gratitude employed by my nephew Lorenzo: *Spank you very much!*

This spanking should and does extend to the following citizens: any editors who published this work originally, musicians who continue to make sexy music against the odds, those writers who love their characters without restraint, and the friends who continue to tolerate my panicky affections. I am especially indebted to Julia Cheiffetz and Daniel Menaker for their careful consideration of the manuscript, and irrational support.

This brings me (thank God) to my wife and daughter, without whom I would be as lonely and angry and lost as this book often suggests.

Finally, I would be remiss at this particular juncture if I failed to thank those humans who are striving, through words *and* deeds, to awaken this country from its false dreams of conquest and convenience. It is possible that Americans will again wage war on poverty rather than people, will choose mercy over grievance, and will adopt as their final great cause an end to the suffering we know to exist on this planet.

Or, as our pal Ann Coulter might put it, "Steve Almond is a faggot."

Awesome.

STEVE ALMOND is the author of the story collections *My Life in Heavy Metal* and *The Evil B.B. Chow*, the nonfiction book *Candyfreak*, and the novel *Which Brings Me to You*, co-written with Julianna Baggott. He lives outside Boston with his wife, Erin, and daughter, Josephine, whom he cannot stop kissing.

Printed in the United States
by Baker & Taylor Publisher Services